The Coherence of the Russian Classics

This book is part of the Peter Lang Humanities list.
Every volume is peer reviewed and meets
the highest quality standards for content and production.

PETER LANG
New York • Berlin • Brussels • Lausanne • Oxford

Jim Curtis

The Coherence of the Russian Classics

Essays on the Dynamics of Creativity

PETER LANG
New York • Berlin • Brussels • Lausanne • Oxford

Library of Congress Cataloging-in-Publication Data

Names: Curtis, James M., author.
Title: The coherence of the Russian classics: essays on the dynamics of creativity / Jim Curtis.
Description: New York: Peter Lang, 2022 | Includes bibliographical references and index.
Identifiers: LCCN 2022014986 (print) | LCCN 2022014987 (ebook) |
ISBN 978-1-4331-9394-1 (paperback) | ISBN 978-1-4331-9395-8 (ebook) |
ISBN 978-1-4331-9396-5 (epub)
Subjects: LCSH: Russian literature—19th century—History and criticism. | LCGFT: Literary
criticism. | Essays.
Classification: LCC PG3012. C87 2022 (print) | LCC PG3012 (ebook) | DDC 891.709/003—
dc23/eng/20220518
LC record available at https://lccn.loc.gov/2022014986
LC ebook record available at https://lccn.loc.gov/2022014987
DOI 10.3726/b19193

Bibliographic information published by **Die Deutsche Nationalbibliothek**.
Die Deutsche Nationalbibliothek lists this publication in the "Deutsche
Nationalbibliografie"; detailed bibliographic data are available
on the Internet at http://dnb.d-nb.de/.

Peter Lang Publishing, Inc., New York
80 Broad Street, 5th floor, New York, NY 10004
www.peterlang.com

Contents

Preface

The essays collected in *The Coherence of the Russian Classics* represent the results of my engagement with Russian literature for over 50 years with particular attention to Tolstoy and Dostoyevsky. My research on these two great writers resulted in an article, "Metaphor is to Dostoyevsky as Metonymy is to Tolstoy," which was printed in *Slavic Review*. That journal has graciously given me permission to publish a revised version in this book. Pondering the relevance of metaphor and metonymy for these two great writers led me to formulate what I call a creative matrix that operates for at least some artists. As I understand it, a creative matrix defines and thus limits how an artist creates. Obviously, in the case of great artists like Tolstoy and Dostoyevsky, these limits are very large, but they do exist.

More generally, my work is relevant in a minor way to a large historical change in Russia. In particular, one little-noticed effect of the Bolshevik Revolution was a radical shift in Russia's cultural orientation. If before 1917, it had been France whose culture preoccupied Russia's brightest creative spirits, after 1917, it was America. While contemplating American influence in Russian culture, which became more pronounced after 1991, I began to think about the relevance of American scholarship to Russia, and innovative insights that it might produce.

The issue of the relevance of American scholarship to Russia and to Russian literature has numerous implications. To state the obvious, it is not possible for any one individual to read a substantial percentage of the scholarship on the Russian classics whom I discuss in this book. Therefore, one must pick and choose which scholars to cite, and which ones not to cite.

I have two criteria for the scholars cited in this book. First, my preference is for critics such as Harold Bloom and Roman Jakobson, critics whose work makes it possible to re-conceptualize major works and think about them in a new way. I know of no one who has seriously argued that there is an expiration date on stimulating ideas, and that simply because critical ideas were published in the previous century, they are not, and cannot be, relevant today.

In this book I use the work of Jakobson, Bloom, and others of their ilk because I believe that their ideas were stimulating when they first published them, and they remain stimulating today. There is a word for the belief that whatever is current is better than what was in the past, and that word is presentism. Presentism affects scholarly inquiry just as much as it affects other human activities.

Perhaps in reaction to Soviet critics, who tended to reduce great works of literature to what they called "the evil of the day," scholarship on Russian literature, both in Russia and in the West, tends to shun the social sciences. Since the 1960s, a substantial social science literature consisting of contributions relating to creativity by psychologists and sociologists has appeared. This literature has great potential to address issues that have generally gone unaddressed in the extant scholarship on Russian literature. These are issues such as the relevance of such family issues as birth order and relationships with the father that have been shown to affect creativity in the careers of Western artists. I consider it a valid scholarly enterprise to show how these issues affected Russian writers as well.

Generally speaking, Russian scholars write dense expository prose, which sometimes has metaphysical implications. One notices, for example, the use of a phrase such as "his fate," which they use where American scholars would simply say "his life." Thus, the belief in fate helps to explain why Russian scholars very rarely ground the artists that they discuss in their family circumstances and do not generally draw on the rich literature on creativity that has accumulated in the West. Essay III, "The Biographical and Literary Contexts of the Russian Classic Writers" and Essay VII, "A Proposed Periodization of Russian Literature, 1825-1918," show the results of applying American scholarship to the lives and works of the Russian classic authors.

It remains to thank my wife Donna for her tireless editorial work on this book. Every page of *The Coherence of the Russian Classics* has benefitted from her expertise and patience. Despite her best efforts, there are surely errors that remain, and they are my responsibility.

I.

The Critical Legacy of the Twentieth Century and Russian Studies Today

"Russian literature is compact, intensely self-reflexive, and always about to forget that it is merely made up of words. Imagined characters walk out of fiction into real life, while real-life writers are raised to the status of myth."[1] This pithy statement by Caryl Emerson defines some essential features of Russian literature in its social context. Widespread literacy came late to Russia, and, as a result, writers like Pushkin and Tolstoy who produced the compact corpus of the Russian classics are raised to the status of myth. The special status of writers in Russia to which Emerson refers has numerous implications. Among other things, it brought them to the attention of authoritarian leaders, who immediately sensed their potential for use as instruments of state policy. For his part, Joseph Stalin raised—if that is the proper word—writers, not to the status of saints, but to the status of "engineers of human souls." It is also true that the special status of writers made some of them vulnerable to persecution, exile, and execution in the Soviet era.

The point is that the special status that is, and has been, attributed to Russian writers has appeared because of specific, identifiable historical circumstances. However, not everyone who loves Russian literature lives in Russia or possesses the Russian mindset. What are such outsiders to make of Russian literature? This book gives one answer to that question.

Russian critic Mikhail Bakhtin said that difference is the essence of dialog. When two people are engaged in dialog, he argued, the difference between them makes for a creative interchange. The same also applies to people from different countries. As an American, I perceive Russian literature differently from Russians do, and I offer this book as an American scholar's perception of Russian literature.

To begin with one obvious difference between Russia and America, I do not share the Russians' belief in fate (*sud'ba*). It is very difficult for Russians to talk about the sufferings of writers without having recourse to the concept of fate. For my part, I do not believe that fate had anything to do with Futurist poet Benedikt Lifschitz's death in 1938, for example. He was shot when and where he was shot because of specific decisions by specific individuals, who bear moral responsibility for their actions. Fate had nothing to do with it.

As an heir to the tradition of American pragmatism, I avoid the concept of fate because doing so derives from my larger project of stripping the metaphysics from Russian literary history. I thus propose to remove the special status of Russian writers to which Emerson refers and unite them with the rest of the human race. I treat the writers whom I discuss in this book as men who were born into particular circumstances at a particular time. (All of these writers were men with the exception of the women writers mentioned in passing in Essay VII, on the periodization of Rusian literature.) They lived in a particular era—the nineteenth century—which had its own dynamics. Their work constituted a response to the dynamics of the nineteenth century, although its larger meaning transcended that era, as the work of all great artists always transcends its era. In fact, that is one of the definitions of greatness.

It is not just Russian literature that is "intensely self-reflexive," to use Emerson's phrase. This also applies to scholarship about Russian literature. Take a venerable classic such as Ronald Hingley's *Russian Writers and Society, 1825-1904*, for example, which cites no general studies of modernization and industrialization in the bibliography, although these processes determined a great deal about the life and work of writers in this time period.[2]

Since the Russian writers lived in a particular time and place, it is helpful to state such facts as specifically as possible. That is why I have compiled an abundance of data about their births, deaths, and family circumstances.

If—despite what some Russians often imply—the Russian classics do belong to the human race, it is possible to analyze their commonalities with other gifted high achievers in the arts who lived in other times and in other places. For example, we know from the very rich scholarly literature on creativity that has appeared in the West that certain biographical patterns appear again and again in the lives of artists. These patterns, which psychologists and sociologists have identified, include birth order and the relationship with the father, among other factors. So far as I can determine, no one has ever applied these findings to the Russian classics, as I do in this book, possibly because the belief in their alleged special status made it inappropriate.

More generally, there have appeared numerous works on the meaning of generations in history, and this literature has numerous applications to the concept of literary generations. These works have rarely, if ever, been cited by Russian scholars. Obviously, one's concept of literary generations determines one's concept of literary history, as I show in the chapter on the periodization of Russian literature.

But of course the literary process does not consist only of writers. It consists of readers as well as writers, and these readers are conditioned by historical circumstances, just as writers are. This generalization especially applies to those readers who call themselves literary critics. Just as literature has a history, literary criticism also has a history. Literary history cannot come into being without critical concepts that engage with literature and make sense of it. To put it another way, literary history is the application of critical concepts to specific works and writers. These critical concepts often remain unstated, and those who use them often do so unconsciously. In the belief that using critical principles consciously produces better, better-informed, and more rigorous literary history, the following remarks introduce some critics whose work I propose to apply in the subsequent essays.

Discussions of such classic texts as *War and Peace* and *The Brothers Karamazov* will use a method that derives largely from the work of Russian critics of the 1920s, such as Boris Eichenbaum and Yury Tynyanov and Mikhail Bakhtin. I will also draw on the work of such English-language critics as Northrop Frye, Harold Bloom, and T.S. Eliot with references to contemporary scholarship as needed.

Readers with a scholarly background will notice that all of these critics published their key works in the twentieth century. I draw on their work both as an *hommage* to the very great achievements of the previous century in criticism and also as an affirmation of my belief that there is no expiration date for ideas. Literary criticism is not journalism, which rapidly becomes dated. The question that responsible readers ask about literary criticism is not "How long ago was it written?" but "Have these ideas been so thoroughly applied to the literary classics that we can no longer gain any new insights from them?" With regard to the works that I cite here, I can answer "No!" emphatically to that question.

So far as I can tell, no one except me has ever applied the work of Harold Bloom to the Russian classics. Moreover, using Bloom's ideas as I do is not merely an intellectual exercise. I argue here that an understanding of the interplay between what he calls ephebes and precursors results in a fundamental reorganization of Russian literary history.

If Russian literature is self-reflexive, to cite Emerson's term again, then one implication is that it features recurring patterns, and the identification of such patterns is a major task of this book. As Northrop Frye once commented, "… The critic should see literature as a coherent structure, historically conditioned but shaping its own history, responding to but not determined in its form by an external historical process."[3] This principle seems eminently sensible and has immediate relevance to these discussions. Bloom states the same principle a little differently: "There are no texts; there are only relationships between texts."[4] If only relationships between texts exist, then these relationships are formed by the coherence of texts with one another. These relationships between and among texts cohere in such a way as to form the literary history of Russian literature, which has its own structure, a structure that evolved as one new classic after another appeared in the nineteenth and twentieth centuries, and that continues to evolve in the twenty-first century.

These ideas, of course, merely paraphrase another source from the 1920s, T.S. Eliot's concept of the dynamics of literary history as stated in his essay "Tradition and the Individual Talent":

> The existing monuments form an ideal order among themselves, which is modified by the introduction of the new (the really new) work of art among them. The existing order is complete before the new work arrives; for order to persist after the supervention of novelty, the *whole* existing order must be, if ever so slightly altered; and so the relations, proportions, values of each work of art toward the whole are readjusted; and this is conformity between the old and the new.[5] (Eliot's emphasis)

In a sense, then, this book is an exercise in Eliotesque criticism, which is why its subtitle includes the phrase "the dynamics of creativity."

However, as Eliot himself well knew, writers who create new—"really new"— works often do so in response to new historical circumstances. Critics, especially those who write about Russia, often relate new works to new historical circumstances, such as the 1917 revolution, and allow those circumstances to determine their meaning. However, I will offer historicist readings of what Eliot would recognize as new works. These are works whose innovations derive from the difficult work of synthesizing changed historical circumstances with literary tradition in such a way as to create a new perception of tradition. That is what Eliot did, and that is what some of Russia's greatest writers did. For example, an understanding of the way Dostoyevsky worked through his anxiety of influence from Gogol, for example, results in a changed understanding of both Dostoyevsky and Gogol.

Eliot himself was greatly influenced by French Symbolist poets such as Stéphane Mallarmé, who in a conversation with the painter Edgar Dégas made a comment that lies at the heart of Eliot's criticism. Mallarmé asserted, "You can't make a poem with ideas…You make it with words."[6] A variant translation might be, "There are no ideas in a poem; there are only words."

I cite Mallarmé's comment here because it has exciting, but deeply subversive implications for the study of Russian literature, which has often been read for its ideas as abstracted from their context. In proceeding in this way, I am taking into account the practice of Bakhtin, who writes, "In our analysis we will move away from the content side of the ideas introduced by Dostoyevsky—their artistic function in the work is important to us."[7] For Bakhtin, then, it is inappropriate to abstract ideas from individual statements by Dostoevsky's characters because the work, the characters, and their personalities all have their own autonomy from their social context. Bakhtin says, "The truth about the world, according to Dostoyevsky, is inseparable from the truth of the personality."[8]

Despite Bakhtin's best efforts, separating the statements about the world from the representation of the characters served the purposes of Soviet critics and scholars, and Western scholars of Russian literature adopted it as a standard way of making a connection between literature and society. In the tradition of Mallarmé and Eliot, however, I do not believe that there are any ideas in imaginative literature, and I do not find that the word "ideology" serves any useful purpose in discussions of literature. I also choose not to use the word "realism." It is perfectly possible to discuss the Russian classics without using the words "idea," "ideology," or "realism." I will proceed in this way not because of personal whims, but as an application of a particular philosophy that has particular relevance for criticism.

If writing literary history is ultimately a logical exercise, and I believe that it is, then it behooves critics to make their assumptions as explicit as possible. To that end, I wish to cite here a passage from *Language, Truth, and Logic*, written in 1936 by the British philosopher A.J. Ayer.

> It happens to be the case that we cannot, in our language, refer to the sensible properties of a thing without introducing a word or phrase which appears to stand

for the thing itself as opposed to anything that can be said about it. And, as a result of this, those who are infected by the primitive superstition that to every name a single real entity must correspond assume that it is necessary to distinguish logically between the thing itself and any, or all, of its sensible properties.[9]

In his polemical way, Ayer goes on to assert that it is a fallacy to believe that "to every word or phrase that can be the subject of a sentence, there must be a real entity corresponding."[10] Logically, then, Ayer insists on verification as a key to the meaning of propositions. That is to say, if a word such as "realism" or "ideology" cannot be shown to refer to something in the real world, then that word or phrase is meaningless.

Thus, if poet Fyodor Tyutchev's famous statement "One can only believe in Russia" is accepted, then Russia must be an unverifiable idea. The belief that writers such as Dostoyevsky are "writers of ideas" is also unverifiable. However, Russians are so committed to metaphysical literary history that even so thoughtful a critic as Vladimir Linkov can find metaphysics even in realism: "The beauty of the ordinary in realism is the recognition of the unknowable infinite essence of man."[11] In the spirit of Ayer's rigorous logic, I believe that the belief in "ideas," whether Linkov's or Lenin's or anyone else's, has had disastrous consequences in Russia, and that therefore the use of the words "idea" and "ideology" creates logical dysfunction.

I also take issue with the attitude that Solomon Volkov formulated in the first sentence of his book *The Magical Chorus. A History of Russian Culture from Tolstoy to Solzhenitsyn*: "Culture and politics have always been indivisible, and to maintain the contrary is also making a political statement."[12] Volkov is a Russian who vividly remembers the announcement of Stalin's death in 1953, so he understandably believes in the indivisibility of culture and politics, and feels empowered to make such a dogmatic statement of principle. However, a critic's historical experiences, no matter how vivid and memorable, do not and cannot constitute intellectual argumentation.

Volkov's statement also lends itself to analysis in terms of symbolic logic. In logical terms, the proposition that culture and politics (or any other two entities) are indivisible is an identity, represented as $A=A$. As a logical statement, $A=A$ is possible only as an expression of monism, which assumes that the world consists of a single entity, all parts of which are the same. In this book, I align myself with the pluralism of the Russian Formalists.[13] Volkov grew up in a dogmatic era, so one can understand why he feels empowered to make dogmatic statements of his own.

The logic of pluralism is consistent with a key distinction that the world has received as part of Noam Chomsky's revolution in linguistics—the distinction between surface structure and deep structure. The statements that the representatives of any given culture make about their own culture—no matter how sincerely or forcefully made—almost always belong to surface structure, not deep structure. This book concerns itself primarily with deep structure.

More specifically, I would reply to Volkov and others of his ilk with a negation of a negation. While I do not believe that culture and politics are indivisible, I also do not believe that they are unrelated. In certain circumstances, culture and politics may be related, but not always, and hardly ever in straightforward and obvious ways.

This statement has roots in the 1920s. It is a paraphrase of Tynyanov's interpretation of the world as a pluralistic system consisting of what he called *ryady*, which may be translated at "series" or "rows." At the end of his key programmatic essay "On Literary Evolution," he writes:

> I summarize: The study of the evolution of literature is possible only in relation to literature as a row, a system, coordinated with other rows, systems that are conditioned by them. ...Evolutionary study must proceed from the literary row to the immediate coordinated row, not to the distant ones, but to the main ones. The dominating significance of the main social factors is not only not negated by this, but must be clarified in its full volume, precisely in the question of the *evolution* of literature...[14] (Tynyanov's emphasis)

Tynyanov's pluralism, the belief in multiplicity as an essential inherent, irreducible feature of the world, and the implications for literary study that he derives from that belief, contrast with the attitude of many Russians such as Volkov. Following Tynyanov, however, I propose to distinguish between culture and politics, and between society and government, all the while keeping in mind that these entities are not entirely separate.

In addition to the literary history of literature, which Eliot espoused and which Bloom practiced, I believe that one can also formulate a social history of literature. In making this statement, I disagree with Eliot and Bloom, who do not take social factors into account, as much as I also disagree with Volkov, in whose monistic universe culture and politics are inseparable.

Both in Russia and in the West, many critics have conflated the literary history of literature and the social history of literature. They practiced, and some continue to practice, what they called "reflection" theory, which has two different versions. Western critics practiced the personal version of "reflection" theory, according to which a given work of literature "reflected" writers' personal experiences and/or the society of their time. During the Soviet period, official critics practiced the social version of "reflection" theory, according to which a given work of literature "reflected" the "evil of the day," as a much-used phrase had it.[15]

While this book respects both the literary history of Russian literature and the social history of Russian literature and acknowledges that they interact, it understands them as separate rows, to use the term that Tynyanov proposed. I offer epistemological pluralism as an answer to the question that Bloom poses in his book *The Anatomy of Influence*: "The question is, Why is poetry *poetry* and not something else, be it history, ideology, politics, or psychology?"[16] (Bloom's emphasis) The Formalists' term for the practice of treating poetry, or literature in general, as what Bloom calls "something else" was reductionism.

However, in the pluralistic universe that Chomsky's distinction between surface structure and deep structure pre-supposes, it is possible to make the following distinction. Although writers (and other artists as well) respond to social evolution, often in insightful ways, they do not do so consciously or directly. As a result, the works that they write cannot be said to "reflect" their consciously held opinions. It further assumes that creativity usually occurs as an unconscious process that artists do not and cannot fully understand or control. To refer to Chomsky again, this interpretation derives from my belief that creativity occurs in the deep structure of the creative unconscious, and is therefore not available for conscious examination.

To be sure, extra-literary factors affect the literary history of literature as it evolves and creates distinct periods. In Russia, these periods are usually created by political upheaval, the deaths of key individuals, or both. Note, however, that deaths also cohere into patterns. Thus, the death of Dostoyevsky in 1881, for example, matters because it fits into the larger pattern of deaths of other major artists in the 1880s. Similarly, the death of Tolstoy in 1910 fits into the larger pattern of other deaths of leading figures in the arts in or around 1910.

Although extra-literary factors do affect the literary history of literature, the literary history of literature consists only of literature. Although circumstances prevented Tynyanov from developing his concept of society as consisting of "rows," one can readily imagine that Tynyanov's social rows would consist of both personal and social elements, and that both of them affect literature. Let us begin with personal, i.e., demographic elements.

The task of identifying the coherence of the Russian classics is simplified by the demographics of the writers. To state the obvious again, the nineteenth-century classics were all men, and with the exceptions of Goncharov, Leskov, and

Chekhov, they were all born into aristocratic families. Thus, the way in which gender roles for aristocratic men were constructed at the time is a matter of great importance for this study.

In discussing writers and writing I will apply some suggestions from *Creativity*, a book by Mihaly Csikszentmihalyi, who is a prolific scholar and whose magisterial pronouncements I will have several occasions to cite and comment on. Csikszenkmihalyi offers the following useful definition of the dynamics of creativity: "Creativity is jointly constituted by the interaction among domain, field, and person."[17] A great advantage of this generalization is that it applies equally well to Renaissance Italy as to nineteenth-century Russia, and thus poses the familiar question of Russian exceptionalism. Take, for example, the statement "Russia is different." What matters in the present context is the semantic field in which one makes this statement. One may ask, "Does the statement 'Russia is different' mark the beginning of a discussion, or the end of one?" Russia's ever-present nationalists tend to believe the latter. I believe the former.

Although it is true that each country, like each person, is unique, this trivial truth does not promote our understanding either of a country or a person. What does promote our understanding is the awareness that a full understanding of anything involves the interaction—to use a key word in Csikszentmihalyi's just quoted statement—between what is unique, and what is shared. (Interactions are to Csikszentmihalyi what relationships are to Bloom.) In this book I discuss both what is shared and what is unique. In Essay IV, I will discuss what I believe to be the genuinely unique features of the work of the Russian classics, yet in Essay I I will show the numerous aspects of their lives and careers that they share with other creative men.

It is generally agreed that Tolstoy and Dostoyevsky were connected to Russia in some deep ways that they did not—and could not—understand. Csikszentmihalyi makes a preliminary statement about this connection:

> If Dostoevsky and Tolstoy showed more than their share of pathology it was due less to the requirements of their creative work than to the personal sufferings caused by the unhealthful conditions of a Russian society nearing collapse.[18]

Csikszentmihalyi suggests here a specific instance of a general thesis of this book, which is that the careers of the Russian classic writers developed as part of, and in response to, the ongoing evolution of nineteenth-century Russia. However, stating the matter in this way immediately poses the issue of the problematic relationships among individuals, their families, and their society. While these relationships are surely complex, that does not mean that they cannot be usefully discussed. As a matter of fact, it is precisely because of the complexity of these relationships that they have attracted the attention of some gifted investigators over the course of the last hundred years or so. Their work has identified some key patterns in their relationships.

However, it serves no useful purpose to accept such a vague statement and let it go at that. Rather, we can borrow a phrase from anthropologist Clifford Geertz, and enlarge the universe of human discourse not to remain content to ask "Why is Russia different?" One can ask, more generally and more rigorously, "What historical factors have created the differences between Russia and the West?" Like the relationships between Russian writers and their society, this is a complex matter, but once again complexity does not preclude the possibility of analysis.

A useful way of defining the terms for such an analysis may begin with the Protestant Reformation. We now have some understanding of the full scope of the Protestant Reformation and its interrelated features.[19] Beginning in the sixteenth century, and continuing in the seventeenth century, it transformed northern Europe, primarily Germany, Holland, and England, and to a considerable extent defined the civilization that would appear in North America. Martin Luther and Johannes Gutenberg, two of the instigators of the Protestant Reformation, combined to produce inexpensive copies of the Bible in German. The accessibility of the Bible in German promoted literacy and a sense of individualism. The possibility that people could read the Bible for themselves undermined the authority of the Catholic Church, whose priests had previously had exclusive access to the Bible when it was available only in Latin. A major long-term effect of the Protestant Reformation was to legitimize the worldly activities of commerce and industrialization. My point in recounting these well-known features of the Protestant Reformation is to make explicit the fact that none of this happened in Russia. Thus, a succinct way of explaining why Russia is different is to say that the Protestant Reformation did not occur there.

If the absence of the Protestant Reformation has such importance in Russia, then it becomes possible to carry out an adaptation of the linguistic exercise known as in Chomskian linguistics as rewriting. Rewriting states the smaller constituents of a given entirety. Thus, it is useful and clarifying not to treat the opposition "Russia and the West" as a discrete historical entity, but to rewrite it so as to acknowledge the religious sensibilities of the respective areas. It is therefore possible to rewrite the opposition "Russia and the West," as "An Orthodox Country and a Protestant Region." For the sake of even greater analytical utility, one can also rewrite it in such a way as to combine religion and economics: "A

Rural Orthodox Country and an Industrialized Protestant Region." Since Orthodoxy is primarily a monastic religion that puts great emphasis on ritual, while Protestantism justifies worldly activities, possibilities for misunderstandings abound on both sides.

Although it is exceptionally important to understand that the Protestant Reformation did not occur in Russia, it is equally important to understand that Russia's leaders have nevertheless felt the attraction of the Protestant Reformation. When Peter the Great decided to go to Europe in 1697, he went, not to Paris, as one might expect, but to Amsterdam, the most Protestant city in Europe, and the site of the world's first stock exchange. His choice of Amsterdam highlights a major ongoing contradiction in Russian history, which is that Russia's leaders have wanted their subjects to show the efficiency of the Protestant work ethic, while they themselves retained the absolute power that the Protestant work ethic undercut in the West.

Let it be noted, by the way, that this generalization applies as much to Vladimir Lenin as to Peter the Great. As historical figures, these two men created similar legacies. These leaders carried out social revolutions that remained incomplete because they proved to be better at assessing social needs than at creating social structures that could create long-term stability in Russian society.

When we examine religion in its social context, as I propose to do in this book, it is convenient to use the word "churchiness." If this word seems odd in English that is because it is my translation of the Russian word *tserkovnost'*. The advantage of using this unusual word in religious discussions is that it reminds us that the social meaning of any religion is not, and cannot ever be, restricted to the personal beliefs of individuals. Rather, churchiness refers to the set of social practices that derive from religion, although they themselves are not explicitly religious. One might say, for example, that Max Weber's influential book *The Protestant Ethic and the Spirit of Capitalism* is a study of Protestant churchiness. To take two exceptionally important cases of churchiness in Russia, Dostoyevsky was a devout believer, while Tolstoy was excommunicated from the church. However, both Tolstoy and Dostoyevsky show evidence of Orthodox churchiness in their lives and work. Any discussion of their lives and work that does not take Orthodox churchiness into account is inadequate.

Important though Orthodoxy is, and has been, in Russia, religion is not the only factor that has relevance for a full understanding of the Russian classics. To achieve an adequate understanding of the context in which the careers of the Russian classics unfolded, we must add social class. Although Tolstoy was the only Count among them, most of them were aristocrats. Thus, the interaction of Russia and the West in literature means that they were Orthodox aristocratic writers who were responding to the work of Protestant middle-class writers.

This reading of the Russian classics, which involves a rewriting of their historical situation, is by no means generally accepted. So important a scholar as Gary Saul Morson, for example, says in *Hidden in Plain View*, his book on *War and Peace*, that "Tolstoy intended *War and Peace* as a challenge to the genre of the novel, and indeed, as a challenge to all narrative, both fictional and non-fictional."[20] Surely it is remarkable to think of Tolstoy the obsessive story teller as someone who "challenges" all narrative. This statement cries out for further explanation. However, Morson treats "the novel" as though it were a genre with generally accepted features that were shared both in Russia and in the West. He also treats Tolstoy as an unmoved mover, whose (supposed) intentions must determine our interpretations of his work. If however, we understand "the novel" as "the European Protestant novel," then it becomes perfectly understandable that Tolstoy would want to—need to—challenge it. A later chapter will show that Morson's assumption that Tolstoy functioned as a discrete entity standing outside the novel has implications for his treatment of Tolstoy's characters.

Stating the matter in this way introduces the topic of the formal changes that Russian writers such as Tolstoy created by challenging Protestant literature. Such a discussion must begin with the acknowledgment that the novel had generally accepted features, as Morson implies. A historicist understanding of the novel, as it was practiced by, say, Jane Austen, says that it was not a historically neutral form. By the time Austen published *Sense and Sensibility* in 1811, the British novel had a long history as an expression of Protestant mores and even of Protestant domestic architecture, as Ian Watt showed in his pioneering study *The Rise of the Novel*.[21] If the novel as the Russian classic writers received it in the nineteenth century was formed by, and expressed, a Protestant middle-class sensibility, then it is not surprising that their aristocratic Orthodox sensibility found it unsatisfying. This dissatisfaction produced a creative tension that resulted in significant formal innovations.

In his important, much-discussed book *Tolstoy or Dostoevsky. An Essay in Contrast*, George Steiner also notes this feature of the Russian class structure and notes, "In neither Russia nor America had there taken place the full evolution of a middle class 'in the European sense of the word.'"[22] What logically follows from the fact that Russia and America both lacked some distinctive features of contemporary France and England is that the literature that these countries produced had some similarities. American novelists did not write like Flaubert any more than Russian novelists did.

Given the predominance of the Western (i.e., Protestant) concepts of the novel at the time, some Russians declared that they were not writing novels at all, at least not in the sense in which that term was being used in the West at the time. In Russia it wasn't just Tolstoy who wanted to challenge the novel. To take the most obvious example, when Pushkin wrote his longest and best-known work, *Yevgeny Onegin*, he called it not a novel but "a novel in verse." Gogol called *Dead Souls* a "poem." As for Tolstoy, he insisted to his publisher Mikhail Katkov and to anybody else who would listen that *War and Peace* was not a novel. In a letter to Katkov dated 3 January 1865, Tolstoy wrote:

> No matter how I tried, I couldn't write a preface [for *War and Peace*] the way I wanted to. The essence of what I wanted to say was that the composition is not a novel and not a short story and does not have a premise such that all the interest is annihilated with the ending. I am writing this to you in order to request that in the heading and perhaps in the announcement you *not call my composition a novel*. This is very important for me and I therefore ask you urgently about this. (17, 284)[23] (Tolstoy's emphasis.)

This is a key statement about a key work of Russian literature, and one to which I will return in a later chapter, because critics have not worked through its implications for literary history.

Thus, the nineteenth-century novel, as practiced in the West by Jane Austen and other British and French writers, was informed by social factors deriving from the Protestant Reformation and the French Revolution, and these factors produced a form that Tolstoy found unacceptable for his work.

There was a great deal about the world that Tolstoy found unacceptable, because he wrote his great works after the emancipation of the serfs—his serfs—in 1861. In fact, the emancipation of the serfs was the repressed other in Tolstoy's life, a decisive factor that explains much of Tolstoy's fixation on the peasants. Much of his writing about the supposed wisdom of the peasants, in the character of Platon Karatayev in *War and Peace* and in his later writings, smacks of overcompensation and possible guilt. In various ways Tolstoy lashed out at the world created by the emancipation, which had provided him with the authority that he had grown up with.

A historicist reading of *War and Peace* takes into consideration the fact that Tolstoy was writing in the immediate aftermath of the emancipation of the serfs, a huge change that called into question his own status, his finances, and the standing that his family had enjoyed for several centuries. It makes perfect sense that Tolstoy the writer would assert his authority over his fictional world, as

Morson says that he does, as literary compensation for the social authority that he and others of his class had lost. Tolstoy's challenge to fictional authority can be read as a response to his diminished social status. Fortunately, we do not have to rely on speculation about the effect of the emancipation of the serfs on aristocrats like Tolstoy.

Terence Emmons says in his book *The Russian Landed Gentry and the Peasant Emancipation of 1861,* "The emancipation dealt the gentry class an economic blow from which it never recovered."[24] He adds, "On the whole, conservative fears that the emancipation would bring the gentry to economic ruin were profoundly justified."[25] Emmons' research suggests yet another element to be incorporated into the rewriting of the opposition of Russia and the West as it affects Russian literature. It is not just that Russian writers were Orthodox men confronting a Protestant West; after 1861 they were Orthodox men who came from a damaged class and who were confronting a prosperous Protestant West.

As stated above, this analysis, which works through to the deep global structure of the relationship between art and social structure in the nineteenth century, derives from the premises of Chomskian linguistics. For the sake of completeness it should be noted that this method is the exception, not the rule, in Russian studies. Russian scholars usually prefer the methods analogous to those of descriptive linguistics, which involve the meticulous explication of the words on the page.

For example, Anna A. Berman's article "Lateral Plots: Brothers and the Nineteenth-Century Russian Novel," contrasts the treatment of brother relationships in the British and Russian nineteenth-century novel. Thus, Berman writes, "The master family plot at the heart of the nineteenth-century Russian tradition does not follow the line of the English novel and was already more focused on adjacent 'fraternal plots'."[26] As one would expect from a scholar of Berman's stature, this is an accurate and important observation. Although Berman makes a passing reference to the role of the different legal systems in Russia and England, she does not address the differences in social structure between the two countries. In this book I will have occasion to refer to the work of other scholars who have in effect adopted the methods of descriptive linguistics. Or, to put the matter another way, her procedure has close analogies to the study of poetry in Russian. It more or less conforms to Mikhail Gasparov's description of immanent analysis, "which does not go beyond the limits of what is directly said in the text."[27]

It is appropriate to conclude this essay with a general comment. If one assumes, as I do, that Russia, and Russian writers belong to the world at large, then it is possible to rewrite the opposition "Russia and the West" in another way. If one assumes that the historical dynamics of nineteenth-century Russia were not unique to Russia, then one can assimilate them into a global arena. S.S. Friedman has provided a useful, stimulating rubric for doing so. He describes a key dynamic in world literature as one between what he calls "European agency and colonial derivativeness."[28] This phrase is a very helpful, and much-needed reminder that the agitation that nineteenth-century Russians experienced was by no means unique to Russia; it had close analogies in Asia and Africa, for example.

Notes

1 Caryl Emerson, *The Cambridge Introduction to Russian Literature* (Cambridge: Cambridge U. Press, 2008), 1.

2 See Ronald Hingley, *Russian Writers and Society, 1825-1904* (New York/ Toronto: McGraw-Hill, 1967).

3 Northrop Frye, *The Critical Path and Other Writings on Critical Theory, 1963-1975*, Jean O'Grady and Eva Kushner, eds. (Toronto: U. of Toronto Press, 2009), 15.

4 Harold Bloom, *A Map of Misreading* (New York: Oxford U. Press, 1975), 3.

5 T.S. Eliot, *The Sacred Wood and Major Early Essays* (Mineola, NY: Dover Publications, Inc., 1998), 28.

6 See http://jorymickelson.com/category/mallarme.

7 Mikhail Bakhtin, *Problemy poetiki Dostoyevskogo*, 3rd ed. (Moscow: Khudozhestvennaya literatura, 1972), 130.

8 *Ibid.*, 130-1.

9 A.J. Ayer, *Language, Truth and Logic* (New York: Dover Publications, 1952), 42.

10 *Ibid.*, 43.

11 V. Ya. Linkov, *Istoriya russkoy literatury (Vtoraya polovina XIX veka)* (Moscow: Izdatel'stvo moskovskogo universiteta, 2010), 23.

12 Solomon Volkov, *The Magic Chorus. A History of Russian Culture from Tolstoy to Solzhenitsyn* (New York: Alfred A. Knopf, 2008), vii.

13 On the origins of the Formalists' belief in epistemological pluralism in the writings of Henri Bergson and Semyon Frank, and the way pluralism informed their critical practice, see "Znakomstvo Eykhenbauma s knigoy Semyona Frank 'Predmet znaniya," in Dzh. Kertis, *Boris Ejkhenbaum: Yego sem'ya, strana i russkaya literatura* (St. Petersburg: Akademicheskii proyekt, 2004), 87-123.

14 Yury Tynyanov, "O literaturnoy evolyutsii," in *Arkhaisty i novatory* (Leningrad: Priboy, 1927), 47.

15 On "reflection" theory in the Stalinist era, see "'Reflection' Theory, Monism, and the Literary Jeremiad in Russia," in Jim Curtis, *Stalin's Soviet Monastery. A New Interpretation of Russian Politics* (New York: Peter Lang, 2020), 181-208.

16 Harold Bloom, *The Anatomy of Influence. Literature as a Way of Life* (New Haven and London: Yale U. Press, 2011), 12.

17 Mihaly Csikszentmihalyi, *Creativity. Flow and the Psychology of Discovery and Invention* (New York: HarperCollins, 1996), 29.

18 *Ibid.*, 19.

19 See Alec Ryrie, *Protestantism. The Faith That Made the Modern World* (New York: Viking, 2017).

20 Gary Saul Morson, *Hidden in Plain View. Narrative and Creative Potentials in "War and Peace"* (Stanford: Stanford U. Press, 1987), 18.

21 See Watt, *The Rise of the Novel: Studies in Defoe, Richardson, and Fielding* (Berkeley and Los Angeles: U. of California Press, 2001).

22 George Steiner, *Tolstoy or Dostoevsky. An Essay in Contrast* (London/Boston: Faber and Faber, 1959), 37.

23 Volume and page numbers after quotations from Tolstoy refer to the following edition: Lev Tolstoy, *Sobraniye sochinenii v dvadtsati tomakh* (Moscow: Gosudarstvennoye izdatel'stvo khudozhestvennoy literatury, 1960-3).

24 Terence Emmons, *The Russian Landed Gentry and the Peasant Emancipation of 1861.* (Cambridge: Cambridge U. Press, 1968), 421.

25 *Ibid.*, 422.

26 Anna M. Berman, "Lateral Plots: Brothers and the Nineteenth-Century Russian Novel." *The Slavic and East European Journal,* Vol. 61, No. 1 (Spring, 2017), 4.

27 Mikhail Gasparov, *O stikhakh* (Moscow: FTM, 2017), 1.

28 See S.S. Friedman, "World Modernism, World Literature, and Comparativity," in *The Oxford Handbook of Global Modernisms*, Mark Wollaeger with Matt Eatough, eds. (New York: Oxford U. Press, 2012), 499-525.

II.

Russia and Russian Literature in the Nineteenth Century: Some General Remarks

The general considerations of the previous essay provide an introduction to the more specific features of the historical dynamics that determined a great deal about the careers of the Russian classics. To get a sense of the historical dynamics in question, we can cite the title of Nikolay Chernyshevsky's zeitgeist novel, which was published in the immediate aftermath of the emancipation of the serfs, in 1863: *What is to be Done?*

This question struck a nerve in Russian society at the time, and to understand why living in the world proved so problematic for Russians, we must begin with the monastery, whose principles took on general significance. Their ubiquity created unconscious thought patterns even among militant atheists. Since Orthodoxy was a monastic religion that placed great emphasis on ritual to the detriment of theology, it offered very little guidance for people who wished to live outside the walls of the monastery. Some of the key texts of Orthodoxy are the *zhitiya*, or lives of saints, which recount pious acts (*podvigi*) requiring withdrawal from the world into the monastery and adherence to ascetic practices. There is nothing in Orthodox literature comparable to John Bunyan's *Pilgrim's Progress*, which deals precisely with spiritual life outside the monastery walls.

These considerations help to define the fateful dilemma that Peter the Great posed for Russia, a dilemma that in some respects remains unresolved even in the twenty-first century. On one hand, Peter carried out a series of well-known reforms whose ultimate impact was to create a secularized society. On the other hand, the absence of a widely accepted, generally accessible theology that would guide lay people living in a secularized society left them confused and disoriented. We find evidence for these attitudes in the period of great creativity that begins with Pushkin and Gogol. In Pushkin's "The Bronze Horseman," and Gogol's "The Overcoat" and *Dead Souls* we find passages familiar to every Russian intellectual that have the intense, surreal quality of dream images.

All three of these works relate to what the Russians call "cursed questions," which were formulated in various ways in the nineteenth century. However, one useful formulation is this one: "How can ordinary Russians live their lives when the secularized society created by the reforms of Peter the Great has estranged them from monastic principles?" In Russian discussions, "The Bronze Horseman" and "The Overcoat" are said to raise the "theme of the little man," and indeed they do.

It is, however, more helpful for understanding the dynamics of Russian society to pose the issue not as one of character types, as Russians are wont to do, but as one of space. Ian Watt showed that in England the Protestant Reformation, with its emphasis on reading, legitimized private space for the middle classes. Nothing comparable occurred in Russia, however, and in the character of Yevgeny, Pushkin shows the conflict between his character's need to conform to the mores of the West on one hand and on the demands of imperial power on the other.

Thus, Yevgeny fantasizes about doing precisely this. When he gets home from work, he throws off his overcoat (this may be the detail that gave Gogol the idea for his story), and begins to fantasize, "Get married? Me? Why not?" He imagines that he will create "A modest simple refuge/And in it I will comfort Parasha."[1] Yevgeny contemplates a long, serene life of private happiness with her: "We will walk hand in hand to the grave/And our grandchildren will bury us."[2]

But, alas, the absence of the Protestant Reformation in Russia dooms Yevgeny's fantasy of a typical middle-class life in private space. He wonders, "Is all our/Life nothing, like an empty dream?"[3] Indeed it is. This is Russia, and Russia's literary geniuses understood that they could not present private space as legitimate and normal. As a result, Yevgeny is the first but by no means the last Russian literary character to be displaced from private space.

Pushkin creates this displacement by drawing on Petersburgers' experiences from 1824, when the Neva flooded Peter's city. He uses the animation of nature to present the river as a gang of bandits. As the water recedes leaving debris in its wake, "The bandits rush home, dropping their prey along the way."[4] Crucially, the flood leaves Yevgeny homeless, and he becomes deranged. In his fevered state he imagines that the statue of Peter the Great, the Bronze Horseman himself, leaves his pedestal and pursues him across—a telling detail here—"an empty square." The exercise of power, presented here as an allegory, means ejecting people from private space, which is at best only a temporary refuge, and leaving them stranded and defenseless in empty public space.

Of course, this is exactly what happens to Akaky Akakiyevich, the main character of Gogol's 1843 short story "The Overcoat." After getting a new overcoat, an action accompanied by much symbolic angst, Akaky is robbed. In effect, what Gogol did was to take up Yevgeny's overcoat and what happened to him—Russians would call it his "fate"—and treat these elements in his own distinctively Gogolian way.

When Akaky Akakiyevich is walking around St. Petersburg one wintry night in his new overcoat, he encounters a symbolic space for which Gogol uses a key adjective, "He approached that place where the street was intersected by an *infinite* square with barely visible buildings on the other side, which seemed like a frightful desert."[5] (My emphasis) With its straight streets and rectilinear squares, the infinite Euclidean space of St. Petersburg denies its inhabitants the comforting enclosure of the monastery. It is as though Peter the Great had ripped this Russian Everyman from the womb of the monastery and deposited him in a space that is "without form and void," as the world is described in Genesis.

Instead of Pushkin's animation of nature, in which the Neva is presented as a gang of bandits, Gogol creates two human bandits, and they accost Akaky. "Akaky Akakiyevich felt only that his overcoat was taken from him, he was kicked, and fell face down in the snow, and did not feel anything else."[6] In the absence of spiritual guides for Russians, Russian writers presented allegories in the guise of fiction, and this passage, which takes place in "infinite" space, surely has allegorical overtones.

Ultimately, the literary image of the poor clerk who is left coatless and shivering in the infinite spaces of St. Petersburg will erupt into life, as literary images in Russia have a way of doing. Although Russian literature did not, and could not, "reflect reality," as Soviet authorities liked to say, it could, and did, anticipate the future. Gogol's image of poor Akaky Akakiyevich prostrate in the snow proved prescient in the twentieth century when in the 1930s and 1940s hapless zeks were robbed and then dumped into the frozen wastes of Siberia without adequate food, clothing or shelter.

Gogol, genius that he was, surely sensed the importance of what he had done in "The Overcoat." But he surely also sensed that the dilemma of Russians living in post-Petrine Russia was not, and could not, be confined to St. Petersburg. This is why in *Dead Souls* he imaged the development of Russia as the most famous allegory in all the Russian classics, the image of the troika.[7]

> Hey, troika! Troika-bird, who thought you up? You know, you could only have been born to a perky people, in that land that doesn't like to joke…And there it rushed along, rushed along, rushed along…And it's visible in the distance that something is sawing and drilling the air.
> And you, Rus', rushing along like a perky uncatchable troika?…Rus', whither are you rushing? Give an answer. It doesn't give an answer.[8]

To this quotation may be added an equally well-known one, written at about the same time. Lermontov's late poem "I go out alone onto the road." (1841) gives poetic expression to Russians' emergence into the wide open spaces. Neither Gogol nor Lermontov can specify a destination for this motion.

In this book, I use the principle of binary oppositions first set forth by Claude Levi-Strauss[9] and wish to propose a binary opposition as a way of articulating the larger historical meaning of Gogol's troika. In binary analysis, the presence of one prominent image or element implies the presence of its opposite image or element. It is inadequate to posit the existence of a simple inside/outside opposition. In this case the opposite of movement in boundless space represented by the troika is stasis in a bounded space. In terms of Russian cultural geography, this means an opposition to the boundless steppe and the bounded monastery.

The post-Petrine boundless steppe across which Gogol's troika dashes works well as an image for the undefined cultural space in which the Russian classics found themselves, and to which their works constituted a response. There is a certain element of agoraphobia, the fear of public spaces in nineteenth-century Russian culture. The best known example is Tolstoy's short story "Notes of a Madman," which he published in 1884. There is general agreement that key passages are autobiographical, and refer to what is called the "Arzamas horror," a devastating panic attack, which he experienced during the night of 2/3 September 1869. Although the panic continued in his hotel room, it began in the open spaces of the steppe. As the narrator and his servant are riding along, "I dozed off, but suddenly woke up. I became frightened of something.……Suddenly it seemed to me that I didn't need to be riding into this open space (*v etu dal'*), that I would die there in a strange place." (12, 48) Here we have a personal account of a version of what it might have been like to ride in Gogol's troika. Significantly, the steppe brought on thoughts of imminent death.

A version of agoraphobia occurs in *Crime and Punishment* when Raskolnikov moves from the disorienting open space of St. Petersburg's streets and squares to the exculpatory enclosure of prison. The image of the boundless and therefore disorienting steppe has far-reaching implications for both the literary history of Russian literature and also for the social history of Russian literature.

The consistency between Russian literature and Russian art in this period is worth noting. When he was in Rome, Gogol befriended the painter Aleksandr Ivanov, and watched as he was working on the masterpiece that defined his career, *The Appearance of Christ to the People*. This painting may be understood in connection with Ilya Repin's *The Procession of the Cross in Kursk Province*. Both of these great paintings show people in open space, with no sign of human habitation anywhere. In Ivanov's painting the Teacher who will give meaning to the world approaches but has not arrived. In Repin's painting, which might be construed as a response to Ivanov's painting, the Russians have no savior in sight, and look like the twelve tribes of Israel wandering in the desert as penance for some unnamed sin.

For Pasternak's Yury Zhivago in 1917, the destination of the troika does not matter. What matters is the effect of the revolution, which he understood as toppling people off the troika. He tells Lara, "Just think: The roof has been torn off of all of Russia, and we with all of our people are left under the open sky."[10] After 1917, Russians who were sent to the gulag were forced to work in inadequate clothing and with inadequate tools on poorly planned projects of marginal economic importance such as the Belomor Canal. Other, less well-known, projects were begun with major publicity campaigns and then abandoned as the gulag metastasized. But as the boundless steppe in binary analysis implies its opposite, the bounded monastery, in the same way the issue of the zeks laboring under the open sky, as Zhivago puts it, implies its opposite, the issue of interior space. The organization of interior space became a deeply problematic issue after 1917. Russians were often crowded into communal apartments, with all the personal and sanitary issues that they caused, and into the perpetually crowded prisons. The Russians are as unprotected—and certainly as deprived of private space—as Akaky Akakiyevich was in the infinite space of s St. Petersburg square.

What Zhivago could not have known, and what Gogol did not know, was that the ultimate destination of the troika was Kolyma, the site of the concentration camps in the frozen wastes of northern Siberia, a hell on earth whose horrors Varlam Shalamov chronicled in his *Kolyma Stories*. As Zhivago says, after the

Revolution, the Russians were left under the open sky. That is where they were worked and starved to death.[11]

More generally, the unrestrained speed of the troika may be said to correspond to *stikhiinost'*, a Russian word that means something like "elemental force." It was this belief in the power of elemental force of the Russian people that would sweep all obstacles before it that motivated Dostoyevsky to oppose written laws. For his part, Lenin opposed not just written laws in general, but also a constitution for the Soviet Union. This absence of written laws and procedures in the first years of the Soviet Union gave free rein to a consummate bureaucrat named Joseph Stalin, who quickly realized that he could impose his own order on this formless system. In organizational terms, Gogol's troika is headed toward Stalinism, a system that was the culmination of Russian messianism, and was headed by a man whose mentality was formed by the period of almost four years that he spent studying to be a priest in an Orthodox seminary.[12]

If such authoritarianism represents imposed order in Russia, in literature we find historically determined disorder. Disoriented by the lack of cultural coherence in their society that the speeding troika represents, the Russian classic writers flailed about, and since they were so gifted, this flailing produced remarkable results. Russian aristocratic writers could not/would not use the middle-class novel as it was being practiced in the West at the time, and had no usable literary past of their own that would have provided them with precedents, so they coped with this situation in a variety of creative ways.

Although Russians are accustomed to discussing the lyrical digressions in the Russian classics, they do not seem to realize how unusual these digressions are. In fact, there is nothing like them in the work of Western novelists such as Dickens and Flaubert. We may conclude, then, that Russian writers felt free to break the frame of fiction by inserting digressions, lyrical and otherwise, into their works. They did so because Russia had few guidelines for what could, and could not, be done in fiction. In fact, numerous examples of heterogeneous elements inserted into fictional works appear in the Russian classics. They include the diaries of Varvara and Makar in Dostoyevsky's *Poor Folk* and "The Legend of the Grand Inquisitor" in his *The Brothers Karamazov*. And then there is the matter of Tolstoy's historical essays in *War and Peace*. Tchaikovsky's use of bells and cannons in his "1812 Overture" provides a musical example of comparable heterogeneity in the use of materials.

The logical extension of this loose sense of literary form is that the Russian classics had recourse to a term without generic features, a form as formless as the Russian steppes themselves, a form that they could use for their own purposes.

I refer here to the free-form genre that they called "Notes," a word that appears in the title of various important works. One major thick journal was called *Fatherland Notes*, for example, and a major historical journal was called *Historical Notes*. Then, too, four of the Russian classic writers wrote a work that they called "Notes," as the following list shows.

Nikolay Gogol, "Notes of a Madman" (1834)
Ivan Turgenev, "Notes of a Hunter" (1852)
Leo Tolstoy, "Notes of a Billiard Marker" (1853); "Notes of a Madman" (1884)
Fyodor Dostoyevsky, "Notes from the Underground" (1864)

These writers realized that calling a piece of writing "notes," gave them a great deal of freedom. The stylistic and thematic differences between "The Notes of a Hunter" and "Notes from the Underground" may illustrate the point.

These general thoughts about the cultural agoraphobia that gripped Russia in the nineteenth and twentieth centuries[13] define the topics that the essays in this book will treat in more detail.

Thus, Essay I, "The Biological and Literary Fathers of the Russian Classics," addresses the issue of the relationships between fathers and sons, in both their psychological and their literary implications.

In Essay II, "The Arrival Motif and the Monoplot of the Russian Classics," I analyze in some detail the use of the arrival motif in the Russian classics as part of what I call the monopoly. Over and over again, from Griboyedov to Chekhov, Russia's classic writers created works in which a man[14] arrives, creates turmoil of various kinds, and then leaves. Griboyedov's *Woe from Wit* and Dostoyevsky's *The Idiot* offer exceptionally clear examples of the arrival motif and the monoplot that incorporates it.

In Essay III, "Metaphor is to Dostoyevsky as Metonymy is to Tolstoy," I make my contribution to the great game of Russian criticism. My version of the comparisons and contrasts between Tolstoy and Dostoyevsky derives from the work of Roman Jakobson. It also continues the discussion of boundaries, or the lack of them, in psychological rather than literal terms.

However, if the patterns of creativity for Russian writers have the general meaning that I claim for them, then they will appear in later periods as well. This is why, in Essay IV, "Why Are Russian Novels So Long?" I have some things to say about enduring popularity of long novels as responses to the various succession crises in Russian history, and the common patterns in the lives of the men who wrote them. It is for this reason that I extend the discussion into the twentieth century.

In Essay V, "A Proposed Periodization of Russian Literature, 1825-1918," Russian literary history shows considerable discontinuity created by death on one hand and by political upheaval on the other. Two examples will show the principles of this analysis. The Golden Age of Aristocratic Poetry, for example, may be said to begin in 1825, which was both the year of the ill-fated Decembrist Uprising, and the publication of the first chapter of Pushkin's *Yevgeny Onegin,* and ends in 1841, the year of Lermontov's death. The period between 1841 and 1856, the year Turgenev published *Rudin,* his first novel, may be called the Period of Preparations for Greatness, for it was during this period that Tolstoy, Dostoyevsky, and Turgenev served their literary apprenticeships.

Although the nineteenth century provided plenty of stress and anxiety for those who lived through it, we can readily understand why it seemed like paradise to later writers caught up in the Stalinist terror. And yet while the lived experiences of Russian writers varied wildly between the nineteenth and the twentieth centuries, there were nevertheless some striking commonalities created by the recurring patterns that characterize Russian history as a whole.

As a preliminary discussion of this issue, I address some of these commonalities in the Epilogue, "The Heart of Russian Literature: Two Poets, Two Novelists." Here I argue that Osip Mandelstam and Aleksandr Solzhenitsyn have importance for twentieth-century Russian literature that presents some key similarities to that of Aleksandr Pushkin and Leo Tolstoy in the nineteenth century. Mandelstam had an awareness of Pushkin as his predecessor that resembles Solzhenitsyn's awareness of Tolstoy as a comparable predecessor.

Notes

1 A.S. Pushkin, *Mednyi vsadnik* (Leningrad: Nauka, 1978), 30.

2 *Ibid.*

3 *Ibid.,* 31

4 *Ibid.,* 34.

5 Nikolay Gogol, *Sobraniye khudozhestvennykh proizvedenii v pyati tomakh,* 2nd ed. (Moscow, 1960), II, 123.

6 *Ibid.,* 126.

7 The Russians have known for a long time that the image of the rushing troika in Gogol's *Dead Souls* was powerful and important. They sensed that it told them something vital about their country's evolutionary process, and in the long history

of the interpretations of the image, they did everything that could think of to avoid figuring out what it was. Confronted with Gogol's image, Russians have taken refuge in abstractions like "the incarnation of the Russian spirit" and such phrases. See the important article by V.V. Maroshi, "Troika kak symvol istoricheskogo puti Rossii v russkoy literature XX veka." *Philology and Culture,* No. 2 (40).

8 Gogol, *op. cit.,* V, 231.

9 See Claude Levi-Strauss, *Structural Anthropology* (New York: Basic Books, 1974).

10 Boris Pasternak, *Doktor Zhivago* (Moscow: AST, 2020), 108.

11 The uses of the troika motif in the Soviet period deserve a separate investigation, obviously. However, here I can only mention Vladimir Vysotsky's "Skittish Horses" ("Koni priveredlivye") as an especially moving use of the motif by a great artist who inherited Blok's and Mayakovsky's intimations of doom. Here the singer, sensing that the troika is taking him to his death, begs his horses to slow down.

12 On the way Stalin's stay in the seminary affected him, see my book *Stalin's Soviet Monastery.*

13 One might speculate the various enclosures (prisons, camps) that the Bolsheviks created after 1917 constituted a response to the wide-open spaces of the steppes.

14 The only woman who arrives in a Russian classic is Natasha in Chekhov's *The Three Sisters.* It is a sign of his audacity that he created this situation.

III.

The Biographical and Literary Contexts of the Russian Classic Writers

All creativity takes place in contexts that can be defined in various ways, and in studying Russia's classic writers, we may divide these contexts into biographical contexts and literary contexts. The first part of this essay examines various aspects of the writers' biographies, such as birth order and problematic relationships with their fathers. The second part of the essay is devoted to the example of Dostoyevsky, who found a challenging and stimulating literary father in Nikolay Gogol.

Part 1

Although everybody agrees that the life experiences of artists have a determinative effect on their work, there is little agreement as to how and why this happens. The tendency to study great geniuses such as Shakespeare and Michelangelo in isolation, understandable though that is, has led to controversial conclusions because they have a reductionist quality. The issue of the relationship between biography and creativity is enticing because we believe that there must be some kind of connection between the two, which is why scholars have been studying it for a long time.

The lives of the artists who created the efflorescence of culture that occurred in nineteenth-century Russia can be subject to non-reductionist study. That is to say, as long as we do not search for a single factor that causes creativity, certain worthwhile conclusions can be drawn. The first thing to notice is that it does not make a lot of difference where, in their huge country, Russian artists were born. Pushkin was born in Moscow, and Tolstoy was born in the provinces. Most Russian Prominent artists were, in fact, born in the provinces (Ilya Repin and Pyotr Tchaikovsky, for example) and then made their way to Moscow and St. Petersburg because these cities offered educational opportunities that the provinces did not.

With regard to the cultural geography of Russia, it is worth noting that hardly any of the artists who set their work in St. Petersburg were born there. Both Pushkin and Dostoyevsky were born in Moscow, for example. In the twentieth century, Aleksandr Blok, Anna Akhmatova, and Osip Mandelstam, the trio of great poets, who wrote about the agony and the ecstasy of St. Petersburg/Petrograd/Leningrad, were all born, not in St. Petersburg itself, but on the periphery of the Russian empire. Blok and Mandelstam were both born in Warsaw and Akhmatova was born in Southern Russia near Odessa. All three of them came to the capital as young people. Remarkably enough, the first great poet who wrote about the city and who was also born there was Joseph Brodsky.

Although it is not appropriate to speak of simple cause and effect relationships in the study of creativity, several decades of psychological research have identified some biographical factors that are consistently associated with creativity. In the most basic way, creativity is an expression of a unique combination of genes. This fact explains why creativity runs through certain families, such as the Bach family of composers in Germany, and the Peale family of painters in America. Pablo Picasso's father was an art teacher, and Igor Stravinsky's father was an opera singer. More generally, it is difficult to examine the sustained richness of Italian art in the years from 1400 to 1800 without coming to the conclusion that there was something in the gene pool of northern Italy that predisposed men to excel in the visual arts.

I raise the matter of the gene pool in this discussion for the following reason. Although aristocratic men formed only a small percentage of the population in nineteenth-century Russia, they produced an astonishing array of geniuses, geniuses who produced an astonishing series of innovative masterpieces, from Pushkin's "novel in verse" to Dostoyevsky's polyphonic novel. I believe that this efflorescence of aristocratic culture in Russia in the nineteenth century is at least to some extent to be explained by the gene pool. And—to state the obvious—aristocrats had servants, so that they had abundant leisure for writing and thinking.

But if genes alone accounted for great bursts of creativity, then we would expect them to occur more or less continually, since the gene pool is continuously present. However, history tells us that this is not the case. Dean Keith Simonton, a leading researcher on creativity, cites anthropologist Alfred Kroeber on "emulation" as a partial explanation for especially creative periods.[1]

It is readily apparent that emulation played a role in the development of Russian culture. The reforms of Peter the Great motivated Russian aristocrats to emulate the luxurious lifestyle of French aristocrats in the eighteenth century. Then the upheavals associated with the War of 1812 and the beginnings of industrialization produced the social ferment that motivated them to compete with the artistic achievements of the West in the nineteenth century, thereby making the relationship between Russia and the West one of the "cursed questions" that bedeviled thoughtful Russians for many years. Russians wondered whether their country's poverty made them inferior to the West, and whether their abundant borrowings from Western culture relegated them to a subservient status among other countries.

However, there is another, admittedly speculative, explanation for the burst of creativity in all the arts in Russia between 1861 and 1917. We may say that artists are attracted to or stimulated by social dysfunction because it gives them something to work with.[2] Clearly, this concept of the origins of creativity explains more about twentieth-century Russian literature than about nineteenth-century Russian literature, but it seems important to have a single overarching concept.

Since virtually all the artists who will be discussed in this book were men, this discussion is a discussion of the construction of male gender roles. Aristocratic men in nineteenth-century Russia lived in a society that gave them a sense of entitlement that we can hardly imagine today. These men resembled their contemporaries in the American South in ways that make comparative studies richly rewarding.[3] One can find affinities among slave-holding societies such as ancient Rome, the American South, and Russia, for example. Csikszentmihalyi comments, "As in the slave-holding American South, fatal complacency [in ancient Rome] appeared as the inevitable dark side of the coin of material comfort."[4] Both in Russia and in the American South men owned slaves, and both groups believed that the sense of entitlement that resulted from this ownership gave them the right to have sex with them. Tolstoy had sex with peasant girls, and Tchaikovsky had sex with peasant boys.

Children sometimes resulted from these liaisons, and two illegitimate children appeared in the annals of Russian culture. The first of these was Orest Kiprensky, who became a major painter in the Romantic period and created the iconic portrait of Pushkin by which the poet is best known. And then there is Aleksandr Borodin, who would have been extraordinary in any country and time period; he had the strength of character to overcome the stigma of his illegitimacy and achieve distinction in not one, but two careers—one as a chemist and one as a composer.

Serfdom may also have had something to do with the obsession with gambling that dominated the lives of so many Russian aristocratic men.[5] This obsession was not restricted to the idle rich, such as the father of the brilliant polymath Aleksey Khomyakov, who gambled away almost all of his family's large fortune [6] as did the fathers of fictional characters such as Pushkin's Yevgeny Onegin and Pasternak's Yury Zhivago. In *War and Peace,* Count Rostov dissipates the family fortune and feels guilty about it when he dies. Among major writers, Tolstoy, Dostoyevsky, and Nekrasov were also caught in the grip of gambling mania.

Since so many Russian men were obsessed with gambling, it found literary expression. In Russian classic literature, gambling informs such classic works as Pushkin's "The Queen of Spades", Gogol's "The Gambler", Lermontov's "Stoss", and Dostoyevsky's "The Gambler." Gambling also appears in the Russian classics even when it is not the principal subject. In *War and Peace,* Nikolay Rostov loses an enormous amount of money at the card table.

Although any interpretation of the widespread gambling mania in imperial Russia by someone who is not a trained psychologist must remain speculative, it stands to reason that serf-owners would gamble.[7] The fact that they could force others to work in their stead removed them from the economic cause-and-effect relationships that governed the lives of businessmen in bourgeois Europe at the time. They may well have subconsciously believed that the entitlement that gave them so many rights, including the right to use women as they wished, also gave them the right to win at cards. The entitlement that resulted from this emancipation from cause and effect may well have led them to believe that they could also make money by gambling. It may also be true that they believed, at some level of consciousness, that no matter how much money they lost, their slaves would make more of it for them.

More specifically, it is worth noting that among artists it was only the writers who proved so susceptible to gambling mania. Gambling mania rarely appears in the lives of the artists and composers who were their contemporaries, and who belonged to the same demographic groups. Although they lived in the same country, and also came from aristocratic families, they did not generally gamble. One tentative explanation of this intriguing pattern is that writers produce neither physical things, as painters do, nor shared auditory experiences, as composers do. Writers write alone, and they hardly ever see others reading their work. They may thus compensate for their lack of engagement with the physical world by attempting to master it in the form of cards and roulette tables. However, I acknowledge that this is mere speculation; more thought clearly needs to be given to the psychological issues that distinguish writers from artists and composers, and that produce dysfunctional behavior in writers.

Like the American South, Russia was an honor culture, and in both places, men participated in duels to defend and satisfy their honor.[8] It is one of the enduring traumas of Russian culture that two of its great poets, Pushkin and Lermontov, were killed in duels. To speculate yet again on a point that deserves more investigation, it may well be that since aristocratic men did not need to find fulfillment in creating prosperity for themselves and their families, they took refuge in this abstract sense of honor for their identity.

These discussions of the social context in which the Russian classic writers created their great works may serve as an introduction to the all-important matter of family dynamics. The relationship between family dynamics and creativity has received much research attention. Studies have shown that some family configurations are related to creativity.

The relationship between birth order and achievement has attracted considerable scholarly attention. Simonton states in his book *Greatness. Who Makes History and Why*, that "one recent inquiry found that nearly half of all notable creators, leaders, and celebrities in the twentieth century were first-born children."[9] Birth order expert Kevin Leman adds, "Research bears out that first borns are more highly motivated to achieve than later borns. Of the first twenty-three Americans sent into space, twenty-one were first borns and the other two were only children."[10] The reasoning here is that first-borns acquire a sense of self-importance that tends to make them high achievers because they are at least initially bigger and stronger than their siblings, and thus acquire a sense of authority. First-borns also have a unique chance to bond with and imitate their parents in the absence of any competition for their attention.

However, these suggestive statistics refer primarily to scientists, political leaders, and others in non-creative professions. If we wish to ask about birth order and writers, we can turn to the standard source on the subject, a 1970 article by William D. Bliss, "Birth Order of Creative Writers." Although Bliss studied only American writers, his findings nevertheless apply quite well to Russian writers as well. Bliss concluded, "Among scientists a far greater proportion of only children and first-borns was found than among writers (61% vs. 23%)."[11] He speculates, "The advantage of a later-born over the first-born creative personality would seem to derive from his greater ability to work independently and tolerate isolation—surely qualities required of the artistically creative person."[12] Although Bliss's does not explain his reasoning, he seems to be thinking that in a multi-child household, parents simply do not have the time and energy to devote as much attention to middle-borns and last-borns as they do to first-borns and only children, even if they wish to do so. Like so many topics in research on creativity, this matter surely merits further investigation. Nevertheless, Bliss' findings provide a very useful context for analyzing the significance of birth order for the Russian classics.

Among the Russian classic writers, Mikhail Lermontov and Ivan Goncharov were only children, while Aleksandr Griboyedov was a first-born. However, as Bliss' findings would lead us to expect, they are in the distinct minority. Consider the following list:

- Aleksandr Pushkin was a middle-born. He had an older sister Olga and a younger brother Lev.
- Ivan Turgenev was a middle-born. He had an older brother Nikolay and a younger brother Sergey.
- Fyodor Dostoyevsky was a middle-born. He had an older brother Mikhail and a younger brother Sergey.
- Fyodor Tyutchev was a second-born. He had four younger siblings.
- Afanasy Fet was a second-born. He had an older sister Karolina.
- Leo Tolstoy was a fourth-born.

But perhaps it was not just Russia that was different when it came to birth order and achievement. Perhaps this is a matter of the difference between the nineteenth century and the twentieth century. For the sake of context, now consider the birth order of these three great contemporaries of the Russian classics:

- Gustave Flaubert was a second-born.
- Charles Dickens was a second-born (of eight children).
- Herman Melville was a third-born (of eight children).

Thus, in this admittedly selective group of men who were literary high achievers, the only children and the first-borns are in the distinct minority. Moreover, any grouping that brings together Tolstoy, Dostoyevsky, Flaubert, Dickens, and Melville surely tells us something about birth order and creativity, namely that great writers tend to be middle-borns.

The large families that were common in nineteenth-century Russia—families in which the father was often older than the mother—may well have created positive environments for the development of writers. Simonton says, "According to this view, large families are characterized by high interpersonal conflict and tensions both among siblings and between parents and offspring."[13] Although high interpersonal conflict and tensions among siblings do not usually make for happy childhoods, they may well prepare the psyches of gifted children to create rich characters and dramatic situations when those children mature as artists.

Nikolay Gogol offers an extreme but indicative example of the complex family dynamics that appeared in the nineteenth century. His mother gave birth twelve times. Strictly speaking, he was a third-born, but his two older brothers were stillborn, so he never knew them. Thus, he was in effect a first born—a first live born. Functionally, then, he must be considered a first-born—and thus a rarity among the Russian classics, along with Griboyedov. He also had a younger brother and sister who did not survive into adulthood. Then too he also had three considerably younger sisters who outlived him by many years.

Researchers have found that the extremes of family dynamics produce high achievers both in the arts and in the sciences. Csikszentmihalyi writes, "Highly creative individuals are likely to have had either very disrupted childhoods which they succeeded in overcoming or very early environments that provided stimulation and support."[14] It would appear that only three great Russian writers, Fyodor Tyutchev, Marina Tsvetayeva, and Boris Pasternak, experienced such nurturing environments in intact families when they were growing up. However, the overwhelming majority of Russian writers had what Csikszentmihalyi calls "very disrupted childhoods," and it is to the cases of these writers that we now turn.

A staple of psychological studies of creativity is that the early years of major artists often include an impaired relationship with the father. The word "impaired" is well-chosen, for it includes a multitude of possibilities—possibilities that are on display in the families of some key Russian writers.

Since Pushkin began so many things in Russia, a demonstration of this major pattern among the Russian classics may begin with him. One obvious form of impairment is that the father and the son do not spend much time together, and this is what happened to Pushkin and his father, Sergey Lvovich. In Pushkin's case, it was he, not the father, who left home. Pushkin left home at an early age to enter the Lyceum created by Aleksandr I to prepare boys for positions in the civil service. The young Pushkin was glad to leave home for the Lyceum, where he formed life-long friendships with his fellow students. We may suppose that these friendships compensated to some extent for the lack of closeness with his father.[15]

Another form of impairment in his relationship with his father became more serious as he matured. It appears that he and his father were never very close, and that Pushkin's rebellious ways in his twenties very nearly had serious consequences. When Pushkin returned from exile in the south to the family estate of Mikhaylovskoye in 1824, a certain Peshchurov proposed to Pushkin's father that he spy on his son. Pushkin was outraged, of course, and in a letter dated 31 October 1824, he wrote to his fellow poet Zhukovsky:

> The tendency to anger and the irritable sensibility of my father did not allow me to explain myself to him. I decided to be silent. My father began to scold my brother and tell him that I was teaching him godlessness….I go to my father and request permission to speak sincerely—not a word. My father got mad. I bowed, got on a horse and rode off. My father calls my brother and orders him not to associate *avec ce monstre, ce fils denaturé.*[16]

Clearly, any father who calls his son a *monstre ("a monster"),* a *fils denaturé* ("an unnatural son") has an impaired relationship with him. Since we know that the Decembrist uprising is only a year away, and that some of Pushkin's friends will take part in it, we tend to think of Pushkin's issues with his father as political ones. And while there is a certain truth to this, it is more likely that Pushkin's father—like most aristocratic men in Russia at the time—simply had little interest in art or literature and expected that his son would conform to the mores of his time.

It makes more sense to consider the issues between Pushkin and his father as resembling the issues usually referred to in Germany as the split between *Dichter und Philister,* between writer and philistine. This split had great resonance in Germany as well as in Russia; it greatly agitated Pushkin's close contemporary the German writer Joseph Eichendorff, for example. Ever since Pushkin's time, Russia has had her share of *Philister*—men like Pushkin's father, who simply lacked an artistic sensibility, and who mostly did not want to rock the boat of Russian society.

Lermontov presents a striking case of a situation in which a talented boy has an impaired relationship with his father.[17] By all accounts his mother had a nervous, morbid personality. As for the poet's father, Lermontov's biographer blandly and uninformatively describes him as capable of "crude, wild manifestations that went completely outside the limits of propriety."[18] After Lermontov's mother died of tuberculosis at an early age, Lermontov's father moved away and left his son to the care of the boy's grandmother.

Nikolay Nekrasov's father had a lot in common with Lermontov's father. He came from a large family, and his father's reckless behavior makes him seem like a real-life version of Fyodor Karamazov in *The Brothers Karamazov*. What it comes to is that Pushkin, Lermontov, and Nekrasov had complicated family situations and impaired relationships with their fathers that predisposed them both to creativity and also to alienation from their society.

By contrast, the poet Afanasy Fet did not just experience alienation from an unfeeling father; his father caused him a lasting trauma that overshadowed his whole life. When he was 14, he was told that his father's marriage to his German-born mother had been annulled, and that he himself was therefore stripped of his standing as a noble and also declared illegitimate. A greater psychological trauma in that society at the time can hardly be imagined. Although Fet later regained his social status, the effects of the trauma made him nervous and insecure for the rest of his life.

An impaired relationship with the father is one thing; the early death of the father is something else again. If one examines the first of the three tables presented above, one striking fact "throws itself into the eyes," as we say in Russian: The fathers of an overwhelming majority of these writers died when these writers were young. Consider the following list of nine Russian classic writers:

- Fyodor Dostoyevsky was 16 when his mother died in 1837, and he was 18 when his father died in 1839.
- Afanasy Fet was 18 when his father died in 1838.
- Nikolay Gogol was 16 when his father died in 1825.
- Ivan Goncharov was seven when his father died in 1819.
- Aleksandr Griboyedov was 19 when his father died in 1824.
- Mikhail Lermontov was 17 when his father died in 1831.
- Nikolay Leskov was 17 when his father died in 1848.
- Leo Tolstoy was about 11/2 years old when his mother died in 1830, and 9 when his father Nikolay died in 1837, leaving him an orphan.
- Ivan Turgenev was 16 when his father died in 1834.

Thus, the average age of these classic Russian writers when their fathers died was 15 years. This is, of course, a crucial age in a boy's sexual and psychological maturation. The fact that so many of Russia's classic writers suffered the loss of a father at a crucial stage in their adolescence is surely fraught with implications.

Before proceeding to those implications, however, we may pause to note another contrast with the lives of composers and painters. Strikingly, their fathers did not die when they were young. Pyotr Tchaikovsky was 40 years of age when his father died; Ilya Repin was 50 years of age when his father died. In short, this eminent composer and this eminent painter experienced the loss of their fathers when they were mature artists in mid-career. These men may have been saddened by this event, but it could hardly have affected their artistic development.

The same cannot be said for the young Tolstoy and the young Dostoyevsky, for example, so we may reasonably ask why the early death of the father is so much more common for writers than for painters and composers. If we agree that a crucial function of a father is to facilitate the socialization of his son, then this socialization takes place largely through language. To state the obvious, a writer uses language, and language is universally shared in society at large. Although great writers use language better than other people, they do share that language, using the same words and the same grammar, with other people in the same society. Note that this is not true of painters and composers. Painters and composers have very specific skills that are not widely shared in society at large. Most people cannot paint a representational painting or compose even a simple melody.

With regard to the psychodynamics of parental loss and creativity, J. Marvin Eisenstadt published an important essay, "Parental Loss and Genius" in 1978. An examination of the statistics he presented shows that the experiences of Russian writers conform to general patterns of parental loss in the West. Analyzing a list of famous individuals, Eisenstadt found that, by the age of 15, 24.8% of his subjects had lost their fathers.[19] Eisenstadt shared some thoughts about how gifted young people react to the loss of a parent. "The problem of mastering a charged and changeable environment can be translated into strivings for achievement, accomplishment, and power."[20] More generally, he supposes, "In the mastery of these personal problems and in the precociously felt need to master the environment, creative expression may have its deepest roots. The creative act is a restorative act."[21] Let us note that the concept of creativity as a "restorative act" has far-reaching ramifications for Russian literature. Among other things, it helps to explain both the origins of both Tolstoy's War *and Peace* and Solzhenitsyn's *The Red Wheel.*

Boys whose fathers die when they are adolescents and then go on to become important writers are artists who have experienced what the psychologists call "post-traumatic growth." In their book *Wired to Create: Unraveling the Mysteries of the Creative Mind,* Scott Barry Kaufman and Carolyn Gregoire make a point about such growth that has particular relevance to Russia. They write, "It is particularly the *meaning-making* aspect of creative thinking and expression that seems to contribute to growth after trauma."[22] Csikszentmihalyi says much the same thing, only more explicitly. He notes that "This pattern [of losing the father at an early age] is especially true for creative men." [23] He continues:

> A young boy deprived of a father may feel a great sense of liberation, a freedom to be and do anything he wants to; at the same time, he may feel the tremendous burden of having to live up to the expectations he himself has attributed to the absent father.[24]

Another comment on this subject by Csikszentmihalyi has great relevance here: "A fatherless boy has the opportunity to invent who he is."[25] It is not too much to say that the experiences of Tolstoy and Dostoyevsky in inventing who they were after both their parents died stood them in good stead when they came to inventing an identity when their society was struggling to find itself after the emancipation of the serfs. They were engaged in meaning-making, an activity that had preoccupied them since they were teenagers.

Neither in Russia nor in any other country did men in the nineteenth century talk about what they experienced when their parents died, so perhaps an analogy between a physical wound and an emotional wound will advance our understanding of this delicate matter. A cut in one's hand is literally an opening. The skin on a part of one's hand was closed, and the cut opened it. Analogously, we may say that an emotional wound opens people's psyches to the world. And if the people whose psyches are opened to the world are immensely gifted artists, then they are more open to taking in the world and making sense of it than they would have been if they had not been wounded. To be sure, emotionally wounded artists can, and do, take in various aspects of the world. Dostoyevsky took in the world in terms of literature, so his engagement with Gogol had a determinative effect on his career. Tolstoy, on the other hand, took in the world in terms of society, and no one has ever been able to write about social interactions with greater subtlety than Tolstoy.

Artists who were active in Russia after the emancipation of the serfs in 1861 were precisely engaged in making meaning, in creating situations and characters that helped Russians to find an orientation in a country without serfdom, which had lasted for several centuries, and without which most of them could not imagine their society. Csikszentmihalyi comments, "One typically turns to writing to restore order to experience."[26] It was precisely men who had lost their fathers at an early age, and who had to construct an identity for themselves, often without meaningful support from their siblings and relatives, who had the life experience that enabled them to create fictional versions of social order. One could say, for all their obvious differences, *War and* Peace and *Crime and Punishment* share the common goal of restoring order to the experience of life in Russia in the 1860s, where the social order had become problematic. The idea that great art comes into being as a response to the need for meaning-making in a society explains much about the extraordinary creativity that appeared in Russia in the 1860s and 1870s.

It is significant that it was the "orphans" Tolstoy and Dostoyevsky in addition to the gay man Gogol, who felt strongly the attraction of the monastery as the age-old center of meaning in Russia. Dostoyevsky made a monastery and the monastic way of life key elements in *The Brothers Karamazov*. Gogol and Tolstoy published confessions in which they repented of their secular way of life. Gogol did this in *Selected Passages from Correspondence with Friends*, and burned what he had written of a sequel to *Dead Souls*. Although Tolstoy was too much of an individualist to take monastic orders, he approximated doing so when he published his *Confession* and expressed his desire to renounce his literary works and to be celibate.

Tolstoy and Dostoyevsky have an affinity with another major figure in Russian history. Although it might seem that Tolstoy, Dostoyevsky, and Lenin have little in common, they do share, fatefully, the loss of the father during adolescence. Lenin's father Ilya Ulyanov died in 1886, when his son Volodya was 16. What that means is that Freud's oedipal complex really does work for Lenin. Deprived of a chance to work through his feelings of rage against his father, he deflected them onto his political mentor, Georgy Plekhanov, and then to the tsar. His approval of the murder of the imperial family in 1918 may be considered an ultimate act of rage against a parent.[27]

Part II

Although various nineteenth-century critics had commented on the relationship between Gogol and Dostoyevsky, modern treatment of the topic began with *Gogol and Dostoyevsky. On the Theory of Parody* (1921), by Yury Tynyanov. On the first page of his book, Tynyanov makes a statement that is fraught with implications for literary history. He says that in literary relationships, "There is no continuation of a straight line; there is rather a departure, a pushing away from a certain point—a struggle."[28] In the traditional way of thinking, the statement "X influenced Y" means "X resembles Y." In terms of symbolic logic, this statement implies monistic thinking, in which A=A. Tynyanov, however, construed literary history in a pluralistic way. He continues, "Any literary succession is primarily a struggle, a destruction of an old whole and a new arrangement of old elements."[29] Note here Tynyanov's use of the word "struggle," which was a trendy word at the time. Using this word gave him cover and made him sound like a would-be Marxist. A struggle must occur between two entities, and for awhile, using the word "struggle" allowed him to get away with thinking as a pluralist in a society that made monism an official government policy. (Filmmaker Sergey Eisenstein did much the same thing in his influential essays of the twenties and thirties.)

Although Tynyanov does not use the word "pluralism," he implies it when he describes what we would now call Dostoyevsky's use of intertextuality: "Dostoyevsky insistently introduces literature into his works."[30] That is to say, Dostoyevsky creates a literary pluralism by explicitly juxtaposing his own work to that of Gogol. Beginning with the discussions of "The Overcoat" in *Poor Folk,* Dostoyevsky will continue to develop intertextuality as an essential feature of his work until, in *The Brothers Karamazov,* he refers not just to specific works of literature but also to paintings and pieces of music.[31]

It is because of Dostoyevsky's literariness that Tynyanov can describe Dostoyevsky's works as parodies of Gogol's. His key point is that parody works only if the reader recognizes the work that is being parodied. Thus, "Parody exists insofar as a second element shines through the work."[32] This statement makes it clear why the young Tynyanov wanted to write this book on parody, a genre that juxtaposes one work to another, and thus requires pluralism.

Tynyanov devotes the second half of his book to a discussion of Dostoyevsky's *The Village of Stepanchikovo,* which he treats as a parody of Gogol's *Selected Passages from Correspondence with Friends.* Although the details of that discussion need not concern us here, a thoughtful reading of it makes it apparent that Tynyanov studied only part of the Gogol-Dostoyevsky relationship. As Dostoyevsky matured, his confrontation with Gogol developed into something deeper and richer.

We may begin a general discussion of this relationship, the most important relationship in Dostoyevsky's career, with psychology. Unlike the relationship between Tolstoy and Dostoyevsky, who were contemporaries, the relationship between Gogol and Dostoyevsky has some of the qualities of a father-son relationship, the first such relationship between two great writers in Russian literature. Indeed, Tynyanov notes, "Belinsky calls Gogol 'Dostoyevsky's father.'"[33] To be sure, Gogol, who was born in 1809, was only 12 years older than Dostoyevsky, who was born in 1821, but Gogol started his career earlier than Dostoyevsky. He had already established his reputation by the time Dostoyevsky came to St. Petersburg to enter Engineering School in 1837. Gogol had published his great play *The Inspector General* the previous year to widespread acclaim, and as a result an embryonic literary father-son relationship was formed. Gogol was already a celebrity when Dostoyevsky was still an unknown, and he remained the dominant figure in Dostoyevsky's literary consciousness throughout the latter's career. It is significant that Dostoyevsky quotes Gogol in the first sentence of his major pronouncement on literature, his Pushkin speech. (10, 442)

This quasi-paternal relationship between Gogol and Dostoyevsky illustrates a dynamic that sometimes occurs when the fathers of talented boys die when their sons are still young. Deprived of an actual father figure, the boy reaches out to the world in search of a man who can in some way substitute for the absent biological father. Sometimes a talented boy seizes upon, and bonds with, an accomplished figure in the art for which he has a talent. This surrogate father figure then stimulates the boy's abilities, and, in doing so, also gives him something to react against. To conceptualize this discussion and continue it in detail, we must turn to the work of American critic Harold Bloom.

Although Bloom may not have read Tynyanov, he in effect continued his work. Like Tynyanov, Bloom insists on two interrelated principles: the autonomy of the art work, which cannot be reduced to ideas or social problems, and conceptual pluralism as an expression of the inherent nature of literary history. For Bloom, as for Tynyanov, a literary relationship is a struggle. Although Tynyanov was the first critic to make this assertion, Bloom developed the concept in much greater detail, which is why his work leads to key insights into the Gogol-Dostoyevsky relationship.

A major advantage of Bloom's theory is that it gives coherence to literary history by transforming it from a static succession of writers and monuments (what Tynyanov once called "a history of generals"), as it is usually presented, into a series of dynamic processes in which writers establish themselves as strong writers.[34] Their work then causes younger writers to feel intimidated, or what Bloom calls the anxiety of influence. These younger writers, in turn, may become precursors in their own right if they have the talent—or the strength, as Bloom put it. Basically, what Bloom does in his now well-known book *The Anxiety of Influence*, which he first published in 1973, is to take Freud's theory of the oedipal complex and aestheticize it. That is to say, Bloom believes that an artistic version of an oedipal complex occurs between a literary father, an established writer, whom he calls a precursor, and a literary son, a beginning writer, whom he calls an ephebe. As in the classic psychological oedipal complex between a biological father and son, the son must prove himself to his father, so in the same way the literary son must prove himself by encountering and overcoming the literary father. Here is a key sentence from *The Anxiety of Influence*: "Poetic influence, or as I shall more frequently term it, poetic misprision, is necessarily the study of the life-cycle of the poet-as-poet."[35] If the proper study of the critic is the life-cycle of the poet-as-poet, and not of the poet as the subject of a biography or as a representative of social trends, then the critic is concerned with the poet's evolution, and thus with change. The most valuable change, the acquisition of what Bloom calls strength, comes about only through genuine achievement. Ephebes must show poetic strength to match the poetic strength of their precursors before they themselves can become precursors in their own right, as Dostoyevsky did, and as many other strong writers have done.

Applying Bloom's theory of the anxiety of influence to Dostoyevsky in his fateful encounter with Gogol, we can say that he first showed his own strength in this ephebe-precursor relationship by making fun of Gogol, or "lowering" him, as Russian critics might say. As Tynyanov shows, this is what he did by parodying Gogol in the early years of his career, beginning with "Poor Folk" and going through *The Village of Stepanchikovo*.

However, parody will take an ephebe only so far. It works as a way of encountering the precursor, but only in a superficial way. For the ephebe to achieve real strength, something more is needed. In his 1975 book *A Map of Misreading*, Bloom argued that ephebes necessarily misread, or misperceive, their precursors. Bloom's reasoning seems to be that if ephebes encounter their precursors on their own terms, the precursor's creative power will devastate them. Ephebes therefore misread their precursors as a creative way of dealing with them. In doing so, they figure out a way to overcome them by proclaiming their own strength, which is necessarily different from that of the precursor.

To this end, Bloom describes what he calls "Six Revisionary Ratios." These ratios are ways in which ephebes can engage their precursors by revising their work after the fact, as it were. That is to say, they can remain engaged with their precursors' work, while positioning their own in such a way as to show their own originality. If they do this successfully, it creates a new relationship between their work and that of their precursors. This new relationship forces readers to perceive the precursors' work differently.

Bloom's first revisionary ratio is a positive form of misreading. Bloom explains how an ephebe creates what he calls a clinamen:

> A poet swerves away from his precursor by so reading his precursor's poem as to create a *clinamen* in relation to it. This appears as a corrective movement in his own poem, which implies that the precursor poem went accurately up to a certain point but then should have swerved, precisely in the direction that the new poem moves.[36] (Bloom's emphasis)

In defining the clinamen relationship in this way, Bloom gives us a way of understanding how Dostoyevsky overcame his anxiety of influence from Gogol. To understand how this happened, let us recall the birth metaphor that was long attributed to Dostoyevsky, "We all came out of Gogol's overcoat."[37] Strictly speaking, it was Akaky Akakiyevich, in Gogol's "The Overcoat" who was forced out of his overcoat and left shivering in one of St. Petersburg's infinite squares. He has been deprived both of the physical warmth of the monastery as well as its spiritual warmth, and is thus having the ultimate secular experience.

Dostoyevsky agonized more acutely than most Russians over the inescapable historical dilemma that Gogol represents by casting his hero out into a cold secular world. It was, after all, a tsar who claimed quasi-divine status as a justification for his virtually unchecked power and relied on the Orthodox Church as the established church of his realm who had brought about this situation. This dilemma, this conflict between the sacred and the profane elements in the use of political power in Russia, caused Dostoyevsky endless agitation, and it was a paradox from which he never managed to escape. However, his attempts to resolve it bore extraordinary fruit in the form of his great novels, beginning with *Crime and Punishment*.

If Gogol posed the spiritual problem of secular isolation with its attendant suffering in "The Overcoat," Dostoyevsky structured *Crime and Punishment* in such a way as to suggest that Gogol in "The Overcoat" wrote "accurately up to a certain point but then should have swerved, precisely in the direction that the new poem moves." If in "The Overcoat" the characters are profoundly isolated, in *Crime and Punishment* Dostoyevsky creates a swerve from Gogol through the use of the characters who are intricately interrelated.

It was Mikhail Bakhtin who claimed to have discovered this essential feature of Dostoyevsky's work, although he does not connect it with Gogol. On the first page of his book *Problems of Dostoyevsky's Poetics,* he writes, "We consider Dostoevsky one of the most brilliant innovators in the realm of literary form. He created, we believe, a wholly new type of artistic thought, which we have conditionally called *polyphonic*."[38] Bakhtin understands the essential feature of Dostoyevsky's mature work as a polyphonic dialog between two interrelated people. Logically, then, he concludes, "Thus, Dostoyevsky's world is an artistically organized coexistence and interaction of a spiritual multiplicity, and not the stage of development of a single soul."[39] "Spiritual multiplicity" is one way to describe what Dostoyevsky created as a clinamen swerve in reaction to the secular isolation of Gogol's characters.

Like Bloom, Bakhtin does not ask about the origins of this spiritual multiplicity, but in the twenty-first century we may do so. There is a pervasive spirituality in Dostoyevsky's mature works, but it is a distinctively Russian spirituality called passion-suffering. Understanding it, and understanding the way it appears in Dostoyevsky, requires a brief digression.

One way to sum up the Gogol-Dostoyevsky relationship is to say that Dostoyevsky realized that if Akaky Akakiyevich was suffering on the frozen streets of St. Petersburg, then that suffering gave him something in common with Christ, who also suffered. In the hands of a brilliant novelist, secular suffering could then be converted into sacred bliss.

Christ imagery pervades *Crime and Punishment*, and a key to the overall interpretation of the novel is a centuries-old folkway, a widespread social construct that cannot be reduced to one of Dostoyevsky's ideas or to a social doctrine. I refer here to the folkway of the passion-sufferer (*strastoterpets*, in Russian), whose creation in the eleventh century had momentous, lasting consequences for Russian religious practices and thus for Russian society as a whole. It is in fact difficult to exaggerate the role that the folkway of the passion-sufferer has played through the centuries of Russian history.[40]

Appropriately, the incident that gave rise to the folkway of the passion-sufferer concerned an issue that the Russians have never been able to deal with successfully—succession. The situation in question is like a fairy tale. It is as follows. In 1015 there was a king named Vladimir Svyatopolkich, and this king had three sons, Svyatopolk, Boris, and Gleb. Svyatopolk was both ruthless and ambitious, and he decided to have his brothers killed in order to make sure that he would succeed to the throne. Whether out of cowardice or fear, Boris and Gleb did not put up a fight when Syatopolk's assassins arrived, and so they died, victims of fratricide. Such are the facts as they have come down through history. What matters, though, and matters immensely, is the way people made sense of their murder by assimilating it to an archetype.

In the "Myth and History" section of *The Myth of the Eternal Return*, Mircea Eliade explains the process that was at work in the canonization of Boris and Gleb, who had not lived especially pious lives. He says that in oral societies, "An object or an act becomes real only insofar as it imitates or repeats an archetype.

Thus, reality is acquired solely through repetition or participation; everything which lacks an exemplary model is 'meaningless,' i.e., it lacks reality."[41] The process of achieving meaning by imitating an archetype, and especially the key archetype of the suffering Christ, has overwhelming importance for understanding Russian culture.[42]

Eliade also refers to "the abolition of time through the imitation of archetypes and the repetition of paradigmatic gestures. A sacrifice, for example, not only exactly reproduces the initial sacrifice revealed by a god *ab origine*, at the beginning of time, it also takes place at the same primordial moment; in other words, every sacrifice repeats the initial sacrifice and coincides with it." [43] If in oral societies the imitation of archetypes "abolishes time," as Eliade puts it, the time that it abolishes is linear time—the measurable sequence in which one thing comes after another. Eliade calls this kind of time "profane time, which is without meaning."[44] In oral societies such as Russia, profane time, which consists of one moment after another in a rigid, unique sequence, is opposed to archetypal time, which is endlessly repeatable.

Thus, by refusing to defend themselves, Boris and Gleb acted as Christ had acted in the Garden of Gethsemane when he did not resist the Roman guards who came to arrest him. In keeping with the logic of archetypes, then, Boris and Gleb became Christ figures. Because they suffered the passion of Christ, they received the honorific title "passion-sufferers."

As Michael Cherniavsky, the first scholar who described the genesis of passion-suffering, pointed out, the folkway has two different roles: saintly princes and princely saints. Cherniavsky writes, "As the passion-sufferers in a symbolic way emulated Christ in their passivity and submission, the active warrior-princes, such as Alexander imitated Christ by fulfilling the highest potential of their princely status."[45] Moreover, Cherniavsky makes a key point when he discusses the way passion-suffering took on general meaning. "The myth of the saintly princes and princely saints was sufficiently comprehensive so that one would expect to find virtually all Russian princes sheltered under its wings. And, in fact, when we turn to all the available lists of saints, canonized or not, we find that our expectations come very close to being fulfilled."[46] He continues: "Basically, in Russian popular tradition and in Russian political theology, all princes were seen as saintly through their actions or their being, mediators between God and their people in life and in death, and in that sense true images of Christ."[47]

It took Dostoyevsky's synthesizing genius to realize that he could use the idea that it was not just princes who could become passion-sufferers. For him, as for the peasantry at large, anybody who suffered could acquire the status of a passion-sufferer, and in this way achieve the status and gravitas of a Christ figure. Dostoyevsky took the sensationalism of the murder trials that he followed avidly and applied the principle of interbeing to create his characters as passion-sufferers.

The action in *Crime and Punishment* has plenty of sensationalism. It begins when an impoverished young student named Rodion Raskolnikov kills an old woman who is operating a pawn broking business in her apartment. When he goes to see her, he takes two things with him, the axe with which he will commit the murder and a package. He tells her that it is a silver cigarette case that he wants to pawn, but in fact it is just a piece of wood and a piece of metal that he has tied together. "crosswise [*krest-nakrest*]." (5, 75)[48] Thus, when Dostoyevsky writes, "The old woman took the item" (5, 83), he is doing more than referring to a commercial transaction. As he often does, he is transforming the profane into the sacred. What the old woman is doing is accepting the cross; she is also accepting suffering, and thereby achieving the Christ-like status of a passion-sufferer. The larger point, though, is this. If we recall that Dostoyevsky's characters are all interrelated, we realize that she and Raskolnikov are both passion-sufferers. Anybody who causes suffering also experiences suffering, so what the pawnbroker experiences is what Raskolnikov will also do after a great deal of mental anguish. Much more, of course, can be said about what has been called interbeing as a structural principle in *Crime and Punishment* and indeed in Dostoyevsky's work in general, but for the moment let us sum up by saying that his use of interbeing creates a clinamen in opposition to the isolation of the characters in Gogol's work as a whole.

In *Crime and Punishment* Dostoyevsky uses the folkway of passion-suffering to initiate his life-long project of resacralizing Russia, and thus Raskolnikov experiences something like a Russian version of *Pilgrim's Progress*. Raskolnikov suffers, because he himself has caused suffering. He has sinned, and must therefore suffer to expiate his sin. He suffers in a particular way that relates the great moral drama of the novel to the greater spiritual dilemma of St. Petersburg, and thus to that of secularized post-Petrine Russia as a whole. In the powerful climactic moment, he goes to Haymarket Square: "He knelt in the middle of the square, bowed to the earth and kissed this dirty earth with enjoyment and happiness." (5, 550) By accepting suffering, Raskolnikov becomes a Christlike passion-sufferer, and this is why a drunk who sees him yells, "He's going to Jerusalem." (5, 552) Having performed this cleansing ritual, he then goes to the police station and confesses.

When Raskolnikov kisses the dirty ground of Haymarket Square, he is giving sanctity in the sense of form and meaning to the infinite and therefore featureless squares such as the one in which Akaky Akakiyevich was robbed—and to the formless steppes along which Gogol's troika races. Only an artist with a certain messianic streak would attempt something as grandiose as the resacralization of his country, but Dostoyevsky accepted this task as the burden that his genius imposed on him. He took on the task of resacralizing Russia as what humanistic psychologists would call his dominant life theme.[49]

Since Bakhtin could not imagine a viable cultural context for Dostoyevsky's work, when he appropriately discusses the very great importance of dialog in his work, he also cannot imagine a subtext for these dialogs. Given Gogol's importance for Dostoyevsky, it makes sense to say that Dostoyevsky's literariness would lead him to incorporate Gogol into *Crime and Punishment*. He needed to do so, because it was the first expression of his strength as an artist—a strength that he achieved precisely by encountering and overcoming his anxiety about Gogol's influence. With his flair for drama, he dramatized this encounter.

Dostoyevsky found a passage in *Dead Souls* that has the effect of a precursor-ephebe encounter, and realized that he could adapt it for his own purposes. The passage in question occurs when, like the con man that he is, Chichikov explains to a landowner named Nozdryov that he wants to buy up his dead souls—serfs that have died but are still listed as belonging to him.

> "'What to say to him?' thought Chichikov and after a moment's thought announced that he needed the dead souls to gain status in society, that he did not have big estates so until that time he had had only a few souls. 'You lie [*vryosh'*],' said Nozdryov, without letting him finish. 'You lie, brother!'"[50]

The scene continues for a few more lines, and every time Chichikov says something Nozdryov silences him with a powerful Russian monosyllable: "You lie!" [51]

For a critic who has taken over Bloom's terms, this scene can be interpreted as an ephebe's ultimate nightmare, a scene in which a powerful, supremely confident precursor says, "You lie!" to any utterance by the ephebe. The scene thus dramatizes the ephebe's deepest fear, namely that an intimidating precursor will so overpower him that he cannot say anything at all.[52]

Dostoyevsky's literariness enabled him to sense the possibility of this scene. In an act of surpassing boldness, he took it over and reworked it in *Crime and Punishment* in the three crucial encounters between the detective Porfiry Petrovich and Rodion Raskolnikov.[53] The multi-leveled participants—characters within characters—are these: Gogol the precursor/Gogol's character Nozdryov on one hand; and Dostoyevsky the ephebe/Dostoyevsky's character Raskolnikov/Chichikov on the other.[54]

Notably, Raskolnikov and Chichikov are both criminals; equally notably, their interlocutors, Porfiry Petrovich and Nozdryov, know that they have committed crimes. Dostoyevsky carries over this key element of the confrontation between Nozdryov and Chichikov when, during Raskolnikov's first dialog with Porfiry Petrovich, Raskolnikov thinks to himself: "He knows." (5, 260) Dostoyevsky makes this statement part of the metaphysical aura of his novel, because we never learn told how Porfiry Petrovich knows, or—for that matter—how Raskolnikov knows that he knows. But he does know.

The investigation comes to a head in the third encounter (significant events occur in threes in Dostoyevsky), when, after a two-page monologue by Porfiry Petrovich, Raskolnikov asks him, "Who committed the murder?" and Porfiry replies, "'Who committed the murder?' he said as though he didn't believe his ears. 'You committed the murder, Rodion Romanovich! You did it.' he added almost in a whisper, in a completely confident voice." (5. 476) He tells Raskolnikov to get some fresh air and makes his status as a passion-sufferer explicit when he adds, in an off-handed way, "Suffering is also a good thing. Suffer." (5, 479)

Like everything else in *Crime and Punishment*, the murder has multiple levels, beginning with the fact that when Raskolnikov kills the pawnbroker, he also kills himself and must undergo a metaphysical death and resurrection. But if *Crime and Punishment* is about, among many other things, the oedipal relationship between Gogol and Dostoyevsky, between the literary father and son, then murder must in some sense also be patricide, the murder of the father by the son. Although Gogol remained a presence in Dostoyevsky's life, Dostoyevsky was no longer in thrall to Gogol after *Crime and Punishment*. He had worked through his anxiety of influence, and thus had killed his precursor insofar as his precursor had blocked his development. Another way of saying this is that Dostoyevsky killed off the ephebe in himself, the part of his literary consciousness that told him that he was inferior to Gogol, and always would be.[55]

In "The Overcoat," Gogol defined the terms in which Dostoyevsky's career would unfold. In the intense Gogol-Dostoyevsky dialectic, it is as though Gogol challenged Dostoyevsky to find meaning in the secularized Russia that Peter the Great had created. Dostoyevsky responded to this challenge by undertaking a project that only a genius would even consider. All of Dostoyevsky's mature career, from *Crime and Punishment* and *The Idiot* through *The Brothers Karamazov* can be interpreted as nothing less than a project to resacralize Russia.

Notes

1 Dean Keith Simonton, *Genius, Creativity and Leadership. Historiometric Inquiries.* (Cambridge and London: Harvard U. Press, 1984), 34.

2 American literature offers a striking example of the way social tensions stimulate creativity. America's two greatest nineteenth-century poets, Emily Dickinson and Walt Whitman, did their best work during the traumatic decade 1855-65.

3 For a rare example of such a historical study, one that deals with both the South and Russia, see Peter Kolchin, *A Sphinx on the American Land: The Nineteenth-Century South in Comparative Perspective* (Baton Rouge: LSU Press, 2003).

4 Csikszentmihalyi, *Creativity*, 322.

5 See Ian Helfant, *The High Stakes of Identity. Gambling in the Life and Literature of Nineteenth-Century Russia.* Evanston: Northwestern U. Press, 2002. See also Ian Helfant, "His to Stake, Hers to Lose: Women and the Male Gambling Culture of Nineteenth-Century Russia." *The Russian Review*, Vol. 62, No. 2 (April 2003), 223-42

6 B. F. Yegorov, *Ot Khomyakova do Lotmana* (Moscow: Yurayt, 2018), 77.

7 Gambling is a problem in many different societies, not just in Russia. For a general treatment of pathological gambling, see *The Wiley-Blackwell Handbook of Disordered Gambling* (Hoboken: Wiley, 2014).

8 On duels and dueling, see Irina Reifman, *Ritualizirovannaya agressiya. Duel' v russ-koy kul'ture i literature* (Moscow: NLO, 2002). See also the collection of essays in *Men and Violence* (Columbus: Ohio State U. Press, 1998).

9 Dean Keith Simonton, *Greatness. Who Makes History and Why* (London: The Guilford Press, 1994), 167.

10 Kevin Leman, *The New Birth Order Book. Why You Are the Way You Are* (Grand Rapids: Fleming R. Revell, 1998), 18.

11 William D. Bliss, "Birth Order of Creative Writers." *The Journal of Individual Psychology*, Vol. 26 (1970), 202.

12 *Ibid.*

13 Simonton, *Genius, Creativity and Leadership*, 28.

14 M. Csikszentmihalyi and L. S. Csikszentmihalyi, "Family Influences on the Development of Giftedness," *The Origins and Development of High Ability* (Chichester: John Wiley and Sons, 1997), 200-16.

15 Male bonding, which first appears in Russian literature in Pushkin's friendships that he formed in the Lyceum, has such exceptional but little-noticed importance that it justifies some comments here. In the next generation, a short-lived but intense grouping occurred in Moscow around the short-lived Nikolay Stankevich (1813-40). By all accounts Stankevich was a charismatic man who left little in the way of a literary legacy but who had an overwhelming impact on the lives of his distinguished admirers, who included Vissarion Belinsky, Ivan Turgenev, the historian Timofey

Granovsky, and several other Moscow intellectuals. Two points may be made about male bonding in Russia, as it appears in Pushkin and his Lyceum friends, and in the Stankevich circle. It may well be that this male bonding, which did not occur to a comparable extent in European countries, is a carryover from monastic practices. It may well also be that sexual orientation played a certain role in this matter. Critic Yury Mann says, for example, that when Stankevich noticed that a young woman was interested in him, he acted in such a way as to convert her infatuation into a "friendly attitude." (Yury Mann, *Gnezda russkoy kul'tury (kruzhok i sem'ya)*. Moscow: NLO, 2017), 203. Turgenev never married, and Belinsky married only late in life.

16 Quoted in A. M. Skabichevsky, *Pushkin. Yego zhizn' i lteraturnaya deyatel'nost'* (St. Petersburg, 1891), 78.

17 On Lermontov, see David Powelstock, *Becoming Mikhail Lermontov. The Ironies of Romantic Individualism in Nicholas I's Russia.* (Evanston: Northwestern U. Press, 2011).

18 A. M. Skabichevsky, *M. Yu. Lermontov. Yego zhizn' i lteraturnaya deyatel'nost'* (Noginsk: Osteon-Press, 2015), 83.

19 J. Marvin Eisenstadt, "Parental Loss and Genius," *American Psychologist* (March, 1978), 214.

20 *Ibid.*, 220-21.

21 *Ibid.*, 221.

22 Scott Barry Kaufman and Carolyn Gregoire, *Wired to Create: Unraveling the Mysteries of the Creative Mind* (New York: TarcherPerigee, 2015), 155.

23 Csikszentmihalyi, *Creativity*, 167.

24 *Ibid.*

25 *Ibid.*, 168.

26 *Ibid.*, 262.

27 I have discussed Lenin's disappointment in Georgy Plekhanov, and its lasting implications in *Stalin's Soviet Monastery. A New Interpretation of Russian Politics* (New York: Peter Lang, 2020), 119-21.

28 Yury Tynyanov, *Dostoyevskii i Gogol' (K teorii parodii)* (Petrograd: "Opoyaz", 1921), 5.

29 *Ibid.*, 6.

30 *Ibid.*, 22.

31 These references make Dostoyevsky an exceptionally demanding writer. Throughout his career, from *Poor Folk* through *The Brothers Karamazov*, Dostoyevsky was intensely engaged with the work of other writers in a way that has no counterpart in Tolstoy's works, for example.

32 *Ibid.*, 26. Note the similarity of Tynyanov's statement to this line from the First Dedication in Anna Akhmatova's *Poem Without a Hero*: "Someone else's word comes through" ("Chuzhoye slovo prostupayet"). (Anna Akhmatova, *Polnoye sobraniye*

poezii i prozy v odnom tome (Moscow: Alfa-Kniga, 2009), 429) Boris Eichenbaum was Akhmatova's long-time champion; he often introduced her at her now legendary poetry readings, and wrote the first book about her work. In general, a discussion of the affinities between the Formalists' writings and Akhmatova's poetry would be worthwhile.

33 *Ibid., 7.*

34 Tynyanov suggests as much, and gives a hint as to the kind of literary history he could have written when he refers to, "The silent struggle of almost all of the Russian literature of the nineteenth century with Pushkin." Tynyanov, *Ibid.*, 15.

35 Harold Bloom, *The Anxiety of Influence* (New York: Oxford U. Press, 1973), 7.

36 *Ibid.,* 14.

37 Simon Karlinsky says that the authorship has been traced to the turn-of-the-century writer Melchior de Vogué. See Simon Karlinsky, *The Sexual Labyrinth of Nikolay Gogol* (Chicago: U. of Chicago Press, 1992), 134.

38 Mikhail Bakhtin, *Problemy poetiki Dostoyevskogo* (Moscow: Khudozhestvennaya literatura, 1972), 3.

39 *Ibid.,* 44.

40 On passion-suffering in Russia, see Daniel Rancout-Laferriere, *The Slave Soul of Russia. Moral Masochism and the Cult of Suffering* (New York: NYU Press, 1995).

41 Mircea Eliade, *The Myth of the Eternal Return* (New York: Bollingen Foundation, 1954), 34.

42 For a general discussion of Raskolnikov and myth, see Roger B. Anderson, "Raskol'nikov and the Myth Experience," *ASEEJ*, Vol. 20, No. 1 (Spring, 1975), 1-17.

43 *Ibid.,* p. 35.

44 *Ibid.*

45 Michael Cherniavsky, *Tsar and People. Studies in Russian Myths* (New Haven and London: Yale U. Press, 1961), 22.

46 *Ibid.,* 30.

47 *Ibid.,* 32.

48 Volume and page numbers after quotations from Dostoyevsky refer to this edition: Fyodor Dostoyevsky (Moscow: Gosudarstvennoye izdatel'stvo khudhozhestvennoy literatury, 1956-8).

49 See M. Csikszentmihalyi and O. Beattie, "Life themes: a theoretical and empirical exploration of their origins and effects." *The Journal of Humanistic Psychology*, Vol. 19 (1979), 45-63.

50 N.V. Gogol', *Sobraniye sochinenii v devyati tomakh* (Moscow: "Russkaya Kniga," 1994), 6, 327.

51 Nozdryov's accusation anticipates the accusations of lying, i.e., not "reflecting reality" that Soviet authorities would later direct at artists.

52 This scene between Nozdryov and Chichikov also makes sense as an anticipation of the wave of guilt that swept over Gogol for writing secular fiction at all. In *Selected*

Passages from Correspondence with Friends he says that he wishes to do penance to expiate this guilt.

53 On Pofiry Petrovich, see the interesting observations in Marina Turkevich Nauman, 'Raskol'nikov's Shadow: Porforij Petrovich." *SEEJ*, Vol 16, No. 1 (Spring, 1979), 42-54.

54 Dostoyevsky may have known, or suspected, that Gogol was gay. This may explain why Porfiry Petrovich is described as having "something feminine" (5, 259) about him. He encompasses both male and female elements.

55 In my essay, "Ephebes and Precursors in Chekhov's *The Seagull.*" *Slavic Review*, Vol. 44, No. 3 (Fall, 1985), 423-38, I make the argument that we find a comparable dynamic in Chekhov's first great play when he kills off the ephebe in himself by having Treplev commit suicide.

IV

The Arrival Motif and the Monoplot of the Russian Classics

To understand the proposition advanced in this essay, we must begin with the assumption that various aspects of a given work can be analyzed more or less independently of each other. Vocabulary, for example, might or might not be related to character relationships. As a case in point, this essay discusses the beginnings and endings of the best-known Russian classics, which differ widely in other respects. It cites abundant evidence for an overall pattern in them. The overwhelming majority of them feature events and characters that are suspended, as it were, between an arrival, or arrivals, and a departure or departures.

In his book *The Irony of the Ideal*, Mikhail Epstein makes a relevant comment about the significance of patterns in Russian literature. He writes, "There occurs something like the revolution of literature around its own axis, around one and the same problems."[1] In connection with this proposition he cites Mandelstam's poetic version of the same idea in his 1918 poem "Tristia": "Everything was in the past; everything will be repeated again;/Sweet is only the moment of recognition."[2] This essay is dedicated precisely to what Mandelstam called "the moment of recognition," to the recognition that in the nineteenth century at least, Russian literature did indeed "revolve around its own axis," repeating the same pattern time after time. Since this was an organizational pattern that created macro-structures, it allowed for the development of great thematic and stylistic diversity, and thus for the dazzling variety of the masterpieces that constitute the Russian classics. The following discussion shows how a non-reductionist treatment that can incorporate these recurring patterns into the relationship between Russian literature and the social order is possible.

For all their thematic and stylistic variety, the Russian classics use what I propose to call a monoplot, a recurring plot that uses an arrival motif as an instigating element. The monoplot of the Russian classics may be summarized as follows:

> A man arrives into a settled social environment. He interacts with the people who live in that environment such a way as to cause agitation. He then leaves.

Three comments are in order here. First, there is only one Russian classic in which a woman arrives and causes agitation; this is Natasha in Chekhov's play *The Three Sisters*. All the other characters who arrive are men, so this is the exception that proves the rule. To be sure, Anna Karenina arrives in Moscow at the beginning of the novel that bears her name, but she soon returns home to St. Petersburg, which is where the agitation begins. Second, this summary of the arrival motif is sufficiently general to allow it to apply to works as different as Griboyedov's *Woe from Wit* and Dostoyevsky's *The Idiot*. Third, it is fair to say that the literature of no other country offers such a remarkable combination of consistency and richness.

We find a clue to the dynamics of the Russian classics in the way Dostoyevsky triumphantly exclaims in his Pushkin Speech that even Pushkin's first poems were "not an imitation." (10, 443) Indeed they were not, but the very fact that Dostoyevsky considered it necessary to make the point shows that imitation was a sore issue for the Russians. After all, their monastic heritage had left them without a literary heritage to guide them in their work. They lacked what Henry James called "a usable past." Second- and third-rate writers did indeed imitate Western models, but the great writers rejected them with varying degrees of vehemence. It is important to understand that it is inadequate to consider this rejection a matter of national pride, or of nationalism in any meaningful sense. Rather, Russia's literary geniuses sensed that there was something esthetically unsatisfying for them about taking literary structures that arose in a region that had been transformed by the Protestant Reformation and then using them in a country such as theirs, which had hardly been affected at all by the Protestant Reformation.

Before proceeding to a discussion of the monoplot of the Russian classics, therefore, it will be helpful to define some general characteristics of the Western novel, against which they were reacting by creating the monoplot. To understand the uniqueness of what we do find in the Russian classics, we must begin with what we do not find in them.

What is at issue here is the broadened understanding of the familiar opposition of Russia versus the West that I proposed in the Introduction. If we restrict the discussion to Russian writers versus Western writers, we can make this opposition and thus more useful by rewriting it as "Aristocratic Orthodox men versus Middle-class/Bourgeois Protestant men." (Note that I use these religious affiliations not to indicate personal belief or religious observances, but rather to indicate the presence of what I have called "churchiness"—social practices that derive from religious beliefs.) This version of the matter makes it possible to apply Csikszentmihalyi's very useful principle of cultural development: "Every domain has its own internal logic, its pattern of development, and those who work with it must respond to this logic."[3] To understand the dynamics of the development of the Russian classics, it is essential to understand what Csikszentmihalyi calls the "internal logic" of the key domain of the time, the nineteenth-century novel in France and England.

The American critic Lionel Trilling defined a key element of the internal logic of this domain in the following way:

> *The Princess Cassamassima* [by Henry James] belongs to a great line of novels which runs though the nineteenth century as, one might say, the backbone of its fiction. These novels, which are defined as a group by the character and circumstances of their heroes, include Stendhal's *The Red and the Black*, Balzac's *Pere Goriot*, and *Lost Illusions*, Dickens' *Great Expectations,* Flaubert's *Sentimental Education*; only a very slight extension of the definition is needed to allow the inclusion of Tolstoi's *War and Peace* and Dostoevski's *The Idiot*. The defining hero may be known as the Young Man from the Provinces.[4]

With all due respect to Trilling's well-deserved reputation as a sensitive, well-informed critic, his reference to *War and Peace* and *The Idiot* is nonsense. Young Man from the Provinces Novels are precisely what they are not. As a matter of fact, there are no clear examples of that genre at all among the Russian classics. When men arrive in the Russian classics, they arrive either from the West (as in *Woe from Wit* and *The Idiot*), or they leave the big city for the provinces (as in *Yevgeny Onegin* and *Fathers and Sons*).

Trilling inadvertently explains why there are no Young Man from the Provinces Novels among the Russian classics when he makes the definition of his hero more explicit:

He need not come from the provinces in literal fact, his social class may constitute his province. But a provincial birth and rearing suggest the simplicity and the high hopes he begins with—he starts with a great demand upon life and a great wonder about its complexity and promise. He may be of good family but he must be poor. He is intelligent, or at least aware, but not at all shrewd in worldly matters. He must have acquired a certain amount of education, should have learned something about life from books, although not the truth. [5]

If Trilling's young man from the provinces "must be poor," then the major male characters from *War and Peace* and *The Idiot* cannot possibly qualify as young men from the provinces. Andrey Bolkonsky and Lev Myshkin are princes, after all. In any case, no novel to which Trilling refers is anything like as long and complicated as *War and Peace*.

Trilling's Young man from the Provinces Novel did exist in the West, though, and his definition of the genre advances our understanding of the French and English novels that exemplify it. However, this is a situation in which the phrase "Russia is different" really means something. There were no Young man from the Provinces Novels in Russia because aristocratic writers had no interest in using the themes of social mobility that occur in them.

To be sure, Raskolnikov in *Crime and Punishment* has some of the features that Trilling describes. However, Dostoyevsky may have written his first great novel in part to undercut the conventions of the Young man from the Provinces Novel. Although Raskolnikov is a poor young man who has recently come to the big city and has acquired "a certain amount of education," in Trilling's phrase, he does not find fame and fortune. In fact the point of the novel is that his story reverses the plot of the genre that Trilling defined. In a long-standing Russian tradition, he becomes a passion-sufferer, and goes off to Siberia to expiate his crime by suffering.

To understand in more detail why the Russian classics did not write like their French and British contemporaries, we may begin with something that I mentioned in the Introduction, namely that the novel as it developed in the nineteenth century, was not a historically neutral genre. The novel in England and France arose from, and incorporated in its plots and characters, the effects of the Protestant Reformation and the French Revolution. The long-term effects of these momentous events had the effect of loosening social structures so that an enterprising young man could have great expectations about his future. Thoughtful writers who wished to chronicle their times seized upon the literary potential of this situation.

Before describing in detail the more or less ubiquitous arrival motif in the Russian classics, it will be helpful to specify what does not happen in them. These are features that do occur in the Western novel and ultimately derive from the social structures of Western countries, especially England and France, of course.

In the West, one of the things that an enterprising young man and an enterprising young woman could have great expectations about was marriage. In the novels of Jane Austin, and not only there, the characters talk incessantly about marriage. Young girls gossip among themselves about possible marriage partners and flirt with attractive young men. And of course the plots of the novels themselves end in marriage.

Nothing like this ever happens in the Russian classics. There are only a few marriages in the Russian classics, and those that do occur do not represent the culmination of the plot, if there is one. Raskolnikov's sister gets married in a minor episode of *Crime and Punishment* and Levin gets married in *Anna Karenina*. In *Fathers and Sons* Arkady Kirsanov marries Katya, and his father marries his peasant mistress. Yet the thing to notice about these marriages is that they do not occur as a result of intrigue and they do not resolve any tension or uncertainty that is essential to the plot of the novel, as marriages do in Western novels.

To be sure, people do get married in *War and Peace*, but here too the weddings do not serve as a culmination of anything and in any case occur offstage. Moreover, there are no sincere proposals in *War and Peace*, and some of the characters get engaged without the man ever proposing to the woman at all, as in the case of Pierre and Hélène at the beginning of the novel and also of Nikolay and Marya at the end. After a tense scene in which they cannot say what is on their minds, Marya turns around and leaves. Here is Nikolay's non-proposal:

> "Princess! Stop, for God's sake," he shouted, trying to stop her. "Princess!"
> She looked around. For several seconds they silently looked into each other's eyes, and what was distant and impossible suddenly became near, possible, and inevitable.. (7, 285)

The ellipsis is Tolstoy's. It is a device that he uses several times to imply something at the extremes of existence that is so important that it cannot be said.

Pierre never proposes to Natasha, either. First comes the very moving scene in which he realizes that he loves her, and the next thing we know, in The First Epilogue, they are married with children. In *Anna Karenina* the very fact that Vronsky tells Anna that he is attracted to her is a sure sign that they will not get married.

This discussion of marriage provides a useful context for understanding two of Tolstoy's statements about the novel. The first, previously mentioned, is one that was cited in the Introduction. In a letter dated 3 January 1865, Tolstoy wrote to his publisher Mikhail Katkov and begged him "not to call my composition a novel." That is to say, Tolstoy did not believe that *War and Peace* was a composition that anybody would read like a detective story, to find out how things turn out in the end. Tolstoy's genius was so configured that he needed to portray open-ended processes, not stories with discrete beginnings and conclusions.

Tolstoy's opposition to marriage as the appropriate conclusion for a novel was something of an *idée fixe* with him, and stayed with him for a long time. As late as 30 August 1894, he wrote in his diary:

> Novels end with the hero and the heroine getting married. One must begin with that, and end with them getting divorced, that is emancipated. But to describe the life of people in such a way as to break off the description with a wedding is like describing the journey of a man and break the description at a place where the traveler falls into the hands of robbers. (19, 508)

Since this was a diary entry, he was not trying to convince anyone or to make a public statement. These thoughts are his own private musings, and all the more persuasive because of that. His sense of himself as a Count, as the *barin* of Yasnaya Polyana, was so strong that he could never articulate his bone-deep opposition to the social mobility that marriage in the nineteenth-century novel in England and France presupposed. Opening a school for peasant children was one thing; approving the social mobility experienced by middle-class couples was something else entirely.

Tolstoy's visceral reaction against social mobility may explain a unique passage in *Anna Karenina*. After Anna grows impatient with the English novel she is reading, a narrative comment summarizes it in the following way: "The hero of the novel was to achieve his greatest happiness, a baronetcy and an estate." (8, 122) That is to say, the subject of the novel is social mobility, and the experienced reader of Tolstoy cannot miss the irony in the phrase, "his greatest happiness."

To pursue this matter further, we may consult again the classic book that relates the Western novel to the social structure that produced it, Ian Watt's *The Rise of the Novel*. In it Watt comments about Daniel Defoe's *Robinson Crusoe* that:

> Crusoe's original sin is really the dynamic tendency of capitalism itself, whose aim is not merely to maintain the *status quo*, but to transform it incessantly.

> Leaving home, improving on the lot one was born to, is a vital feature of the individualist pattern of life.[6]

Leaving home and improving on the lot that one was born to was generally perceived as a threat to the quasi-feudal social structure of nineteenth-century Russia, and was treated as such by the aristocrats who wrote the literature of the time. One could say, for example, that Napoleon in *War and Peace* is the ultimate example of a young man who leaves home with the goal of improving his lot in life—and we know how Tolstoy treats him, and what happens to him. The fictional character in the Russian classics who most closely resembles a Young Man from the Provinces in a Russian classic is Bazarov in *Fathers and Sons*, and he dies an early, untimely death without either getting married or improving his lot in life.

Watt has some insightful things to say about eighteenth-century novelist Samuel Richardson, the author of the immensely popular novels *Pamela* and *Clarissa*. In particular, Watt notes Richardson's "emphasis on private experience."[7] In his book *The English Middle*-Class *Novel*, T. B. Tomlinson goes so far as to refer to "The pervasive tendency to split personalities, individuals, away from their society in which, after all, they must live and act."[8] The presentation of private experience in West novels relied on the split between the public and the personal to which Tomlinson refers. This split ultimately derived from the new-found ability to read the Bible in private, and to keep a private journal, as so many Puritans did.

It is the fixation on private experience that generally distinguishes characters in western novels from those in the Russian classics. Of course, Tolstoy depicts the private experience of his characters with exquisite skill, but they take on such depth because they experience a rhythm, an interchange, between the public and the private. Commitment to social concerns is followed by withdrawal to private interests; characters as different as Natasha in *War and Peace* and Levin in *Anna Karenina* follow this pattern. In the West, the Protestant Reformation had legitimized private experience for representation in the novel. This did not happen in Russia.

A major reason for the absence of marriage in the Russian classics is the presence of male bonding in them, an under-appreciated social phenomenon that appears both in fiction and in politics.[9] One readily identifiable expression of male bonding in the Russian classics is the importance of intense conversations between men. The intense conversations between Stolz and Oblomov in *Oblomov*, between Andrey and Pierre in *War and Peace*, between Porfiry Petrovich and

Raskolnikov in *Crime and Punishment*, between Myshkin and Rogozhin in *The Idiot,* and between the various Karamazov brothers in *The Brothers Karamazov*—to name some obvious examples—have few, if any counterparts in the Western novels of the time.

Perhaps enough has been said to show the relevance of another of Csikszentmihalyi's principles, namely that "A domain generates novelty only when there is a convergence between instability within it and the mind of a person who is able to cope with the problem."[10] We may understand "instability" here to mean a cognitive dissonance between the most common features of the French and British novel of the nineteenth century on one hand and the minds of Russia's classic writers on the other. As it happens, they were very able indeed to "cope with the problem."

If the Russian classics chose not to write novels that ended in weddings and did not feature Young Men from the Provinces, how did they organize their work? They used the motif of arrival and departure, or the arrival motif, as I will call it for the sake of simplicity. The great advantage of motif study in the present context is that it treats the work as a dynamic whole; rather than isolating characters, it shows the interactions of characters in their dynamic context.

A study of the arrival motif in Russian classic literature shows that we have a series of works in which somebody arrives, causes agitation, and then departs. The first and most obvious thing to say about this literary practice is that it was in part dictated by geography. Russia is an enormous country, so writers needed to bring their characters together in order to create interesting interactions. Having somebody arrive from outside a family circle is a useful way to do that. But surely there is more to great literature than the exigencies of geography.

As an initial statement of the historical significance of the arrival motif, one can say that the people who arrive represent the forces of secularization. Although they are not Protestants, they usually embody a secular version of the individualism that historically accompanied Protestantism in the West. The character who arrives has a divisive attitude that produces tensions and conflicts—and thereby gives writers something to work with. Note that this generalization applies to characters as different as Chatsky in *Woe from Wit* and Bazarov in *Fathers and Sons*. And of course in their different ways Tolstoy's two characters who arrive in Moscow, first Napoleon and then Anna Karenina, are both individualists who act in such a way as to satisfy their personal desires no matter what the cost to the social order.

The characters who arrive do not change, even if they come to no good end, as Bazarov does in *Fathers and Sons*. The characters who receive the arrival do not change, either, although they may progress through various life stages, as the characters in *War and* Peace do. As a result, the major feature of the work—its principal emphasis—is character revelation.

But to make general statements such as these is only to begin the discussion. The larger argument here is that the arrival motif had the power to stimulate so many different literary minds because it replicated the actions of the tsarist government. It is in this connection between the separate but related social features of art and history, between literature and politics, that the enduring power of the Russian classics resides.

In analyzing this connection, we may again begin with the determinative fact about Russia, its geography. A fundamental, enduring, and inescapable fact about the exercise of political power in Russia is that those who wield that power, whether they are called tsar, General Secretary, or President, must wield it at great distances. Ever since the Grand Princes of Muscovy used the term "the gathering of the Russian lands" to justify their imperialistic policies, the Russian government has sent emissaries, often in the form of soldiers, out from the capital into the countryside to carry out its edicts. And usually the effect of those edicts was to fragment existing local structure in one way or another.

This is precisely the dynamic that appears in Denis Fonvizin's 1782 play *The Minor*, the first major Russian work that uses the arrival motif and that therefore has great relevance in this discussion. *The Minor* is the first work of Russian literature that shows how the government's policies carried out the fragmentation of local structures. Moreover, it specifically ties these policies to the reforms of Peter the Great. It therefore merits a brief discussion as an introduction to the arrival motif.

As one reads the list of the *dramatis personae* in *The Minor*, it immediately becomes obvious who the good characters are, and who the bad characters are, because the "telling names" indicate their primary qualities. Thus, we have Pravdin (from *pravda*, truth), and Starodum ("old thought"), two older men who represent the ideals of Peter the Great. (Starodum's father served under Peter the Great.) The ingénue is Sofiya, and her future husband is Milon (from *milyi*—nice). Opposed to Pravdin, Starodum and Milon are the Prostakovs (from *prostoy*—simple). They are provincial aristocrats, and their family consists of a husband and wife and their son Mitrofan, the minor.

The Prostakovs perk up their ears when they learn that Sofiya will inherit 10,000 rubles. However, Starodum announces that he plans to take her to Moscow, where he has found a match for her. This news upsets Milon and Sofiya, not to mention the Prostakovs. So Mrs. Prostakova decides to do the only thing she can think of, which is to abduct Sofiya. In his manly way, Milon draws his sword and foils the plot.

But the real denouement comes when Milon calls the Prostakovs together and makes the following announcement:

> In the name of the government, I order you to gather immediately your servants and peasants for the reading of an order in which the government orders me to take over your house and village because of the inhumanity of your wife, which your extreme weak-mindedness led to.[11]

Presumably, Mrs. Prostakova has been abusing her peasants, although we see nothing like this on stage. In a moment of genuine, if perverse, emotion that briefly brings her character to life for a brief moment, Mrs. Prostakova screams, "What am I good for if my hands are not free in my own house?"[12] The Prostakovs are vanquished, and Milon and Sofia live happily ever after.

Despite its use of cardboard characters and stiff conventions, *The Minor* has the great merit of doing what later remained implicit in the Russian classics. The play makes explicit the effects of the government's policies and explicitly associates them with the reforms of Peter the Great. Beginning the study of the arrival motif with *The Minor* shows us what goes underground, so to speak, when Russia's great writers want to incorporate the social processes of their time into their work in personal terms.

The best way to show just how pervasive and important the arrival motif was, how it gives an overall structure to the Russian classics is to present the works in which it appears in chronological order. This necessarily cumbersome list follows:

The Arrival Motif in the Russian Classics

- Aleksandr Griboyedov, *Woe from Wit* (1818-24). Aleksandr Chatsky arrives from Europe, causes agitation in Moscow society, and leaves.
- Aleksandr Pushkin, *Yevgeny Onegin* (1825-31). The story begins in Chapter Two, when Onegin arrives in the countryside. After a disastrous non-relationship with Tatyana, he leaves for Europe. He returns briefly, only to find out that Tatyana is married.
- Nikolay Gogol, *The Inspector General* (1835). Gogol combines the two possibilities of arrival in this clever play. First a false inspector general arrives, and then leaves after accepting money from the provincial officials. Then

the real inspector general arrives, and will presumably fragment official-dom by imposing punishment.

- Nikolay Gogol, *Dead Souls* (1846). As is usually the case in picaresque novels, Chichikov, the principal character and an accomplished con man, arrives at a succession of different places.
- Mikhail Lermontov, *A Hero of Our Time* (1842). The hero in question, Grigory Pechorin, arrives at various places, such as Taman, with varying effects.
- Ivan Goncharov, *An Ordinary Story* (1847). At the beginning of Chapter Two, Aleksandr Aduyev arrives in St. Petersburg to begin government service. After a complicated series of events, he becomes disenchanted with St. Petersburg, returns home, and then arrives in St. Petersburg a second time.
- Ivan Turgenev, *A Month in the Country* (1854). In what might be called a naïve arrival, young Aleksey Belyayev, a tutor, arrives at an estate, causes considerable agitation, and leaves.
- Ivan Turgenev, *Rudin* (1856). Rudin arrives at an estate, proposes to Natasha, is refused permission to marry her, and leaves. The Epilogue tells us that he was killed on the barricades of Paris.
- Ivan Turgenev, *Fathers and Sons.* (1862). Yevgeny Bazarov arrives—on the first page of the novel! —causes agitation, and leaves. He soon dies.
- Ivan Goncharov, *Oblomov* (1859). Various people arrive and visit Oblomov, then Andrey Stoltz arrives, but none of them persuades Oblomov to get out of bed.
- Leo Tolstoy, *War and Peace* (1865-68). As we would expect in a novel that has over 300 recognizable characters, this novel has multiple arrivals and departures. The two key arrivals are the arrival of Pierre Bezukhkov in St. Petersburg, in the opening scene, and of course, later the arrival of Napoleon in Russia. Napoleon causes considerable agitation, and not just agitation, but also suffering and death, before he leaves.
- Leo Tolstoy, *Anna Karenina* (1875-77). Again Tolstoy uses two arrivals, but this time he places them both at the beginning of the novel. Anna Karenina arrives on the train, ironically to make peace between her brother Stiva and his wife. Konstantin Levin arrives after a stint as a mediator in agricultural disputes, and thus offers a classic example of the vacillation between private happiness and social commitment that Tolstoy's characters experience.
- Fyodor Dostoyevsky, *Crime and Punishment* (1866). In his breakthrough novel, Dostoyevsky uses an imbedded arrival, since the arrival of Rodion

Raskolnikov occurs before the beginning. This is Russia's closest approximation to a novel about a young man from the provinces, but Raskolnikov most emphatically does not make his fame and fortune, since he leaves as a convict headed for Siberia.

- Fyodor Dostoyevsky, *The Idiot* (1868-69). As the novel begins, Prince Myshkin is on a train riding to St. Petersburg. Dostoyevsky might have called his novel *Woe from Sanctity*, because it follows in some way the plot of *Woe from Wit*. Like Chatsky, Myshkin causes agitation—and ultimately murder—and then returns to Europe.

- Fyodor Dostoyevsky, *The Devils* (1872). Nikolay Stavrogin, an "enigmatic and romantic" personality arrives in Dostoyevsky's first full novel set outside of St. Petersburg, in the provinces. Stavrogin slaps Shatov and has a duel with Artemy Gagarin. After causing widespread agitation among both the men and the women, Stavrogin hangs himself.

- Fyodor Dostoyevsky, *The Brothers Karamazov* (1879-80). In his swan song, Dostoyevsky returns to what he did in *Crime and Punishment*. He uses the imbedded arrival, in that Ivan Karamazov's arrival precedes the beginning of the novel, and the agitation resulting from it has already begun.

- Anton Chekhov, *The Seagull* (1895-96); *Uncle Vanya* (1896); *The Three Sisters* (1900); and *The Cherry Orchard* (1904). No Russian classic used the arrival motif more consistently than Chekhov. Each of his four great plays begins with an arrival and ends with a departure. *The Seagull* features the arrival of a writer, Trigorin, who inadvertently causes the suicide of Treplev, a younger writer, and has an affair with the seagull herself, Nina, which results in her professional and emotional maturity. It is appropriate, therefore, that it is Chekhov who brings the grand cycle of classic works that use the arrival motif to a close. In several classic works, such as *Fathers and Sons* and *War and Peace* the man who arrives threatens the social order, and then leaves. In *The Cherry Orchard*, however, Lopakhin arrives at the estate where he grew up as a peasant, and eventually buys it for himself.

Clearly, then, the arrival motif informs (gives structure to), the grand sweep of the Russian classics for about 80 years, from *Woe from Wit* to *The Cherry Orchard*.

To discuss the use of the arrival motif in this dazzling array of works, we may begin by distinguishing between instigating arrivals and imbedded arrivals. It is only Dostoyevsky who uses imbedded arrivals, by which I mean arrivals that take place considerably before the beginning of the work. In *Crime and Punishment,* Raskolnikov arrives in the city long enough before the novel begins so that the city has had time to affect him. Similarly, in *The Brothers Karamazov* Ivan arrives in Skotoprigonevsk long enough before the action of the novel to influence Smerdyakov, who will ultimately murder his father. Generally, though, arrivals occur either at the beginning of the work (sometimes literally on the first page, in the case of *Fathers and Sons*), or in an early scene, as in Pierre's appearance that Anna Pavlovna Scherer's salon in the first scene of *War and Peace.*

Perhaps because Raskolnikov's arrival is imbedded, he is a rare major character who arrives and who also changes. Of course, he undergoes radical changes when he confesses to his crime and is sent to Siberia. But note the contrast with the works written in the first half of the nineteenth century. In those works, Onegin, Pechorin, Khlestakov, and Chichikov all arrive and depart without undergoing any apparent change. Men as different as Bazarov and Myshkin don't change, either. Although one cannot say that Stavrogin in *The Devils* changes (despite his confession), he does commit suicide.

The overall structure provided by arrivals and departures facilitated the use of a certain episodic quality in the work of the Romantic generation in Russia— Griboyedov, Pushkin, Lermontov, and Gogol. In addition to convenience, their use of arrivals and departures may well be related to the fact that they all died so young. Griboyedov died when he was 34; Pushkin died when he was 36; Lermontov died when he was 27. Gogol was the only member of this generation to reach 40. He died when he was 43, but by that time he had done no creative writing for several years. It is fair to say that all four of them died at the height of their powers, after careers that lasted only a little over a decade after they reached literary maturity. They simply did not have time to build on what they had done, and craft unified longer works.

So what, then, did the next quartet of Russian classics—Goncharov, Turgenev, Tolstoy, and Dostoyevsky—do? After all, they lived long enough for us to assess the beginning, middle, and end of their careers. For one thing, they started out with short stories. Turgenev's *Notes of a Hunter* is a collection of short sketches, like Lermontov's *Hero of Our Time*. Tolstoy and Dostoyevsky also began their careers by publishing shorter works before they were ready to tackle a novel.

Unlike his literary contemporaries, Goncharov began his career, not with a collection of short works, but with a novel, *An Ordinary Story*. This is the closest thing in Russian classic literature to a Young Man from the Provinces novel. In it Aleksandr Aduyev arrives in St. Petersburg to make his fame and fortune. But he is hardly an adventurer, an upstart out to make his way in the world, and we would not expect Goncharov, who belonged to one of Russia's most distinguished families, to create such a character. Young Aduyev comes from a comfortable land-owning gentry family. He is willing to enter government service, but he also wants to write poetry on the side.

Thus, Goncharov was the first writer to address in a novel the issue of how his main character changed, if at all. One might say that Aduyev changes mostly by maturing and giving up his youthful dreams. He returns home, and accepts his society for what it is, and then arrives in St. Petersburg a second time.

If the point of the Young Man from the Provinces Novel was to follow the changes that occur when an outsider comes to the big city with great hopes for social advancement, what changes can occur when this genre is absent? A sympathetic reading of *An Ordinary Story* finds that the contrast between what happens to Aduyev and what happens to later literary characters raises some recurring questions for the characters in nineteenth-century Russian literature, such as: "Do the characters change at all? If they do change, how and why do they change?"

Turgenev is the Russian classic who is usually associated with social change. The story goes that the future tsar Aleksandr II read Turgenev's *Notes of a Hunter* at an impressionable age, and was so moved by the portrayals of the peasants in that work that he was later sympathetic to the emancipation of the serfs in 1861.

Although Turgenev was too much of an aristocrat to write a Young Man from the Provinces Novel, he did write several works in which the story line reverses the direction of the movement. These works could be described as "Young Man Goes to the Provinces" novels. These were his play *A Month in the Country* and his novels *Rudin* and *Fathers and Sons*.

A Month in the Country may be the best play written in the middle of the nineteenth century, which was not a great period for drama. In this proto-Chekhovian work, a young tutor, Belyayev, arrives, and is so young that he has a minimal sense of the emotional cross-currents that he sets off. He leaves, setting the stage for two key works by Turgenev, *Rudin* and *Fathers and Sons*.

For a full appreciation of Turgenev we may discuss his work in terms of the microcosm as well as the macrocosm. In terms of the microcosm—in terms of sentences and paragraphs—Turgenev was an exquisite stylist, and his descriptions of nature can sustain detailed analysis—and have, in countless essays written in Russian schools. However, if we wish to understand the macrocosm of the organization of his work and of the interaction of the characters in them, a historicist interpretation makes a great deal of sense.

If Turgenev's sensitivity to nature had sensitivity to social trends as its macrocosmic counterpart, then he could only create characters that represented the current state of social development in Russia. As a result, they were stuck between the arrival and departure—the ultimate departure in the form of death, in the cases of Rudin and Bazarov.

They were stuck in an early stage of individualism that they had acquired from books, in isolation from their social milieu, and thus their interactions with women proved as disastrous as Tatyana's interactions with Onegin. They had little if any cultural rationale for explicitly reciprocating a woman's feelings and then marrying her. Barbara Heldt comments that in Turgenev's work, "The female, whole and perfect in herself, is to the male a fragment or missing piece of himself."[13] Speaking of "whole and perfect" women, it is helpful here to recall Dostoyevsky's fixation on Raphael's Sistine Madonna as a clue to the dilemma of the Russian male characters who cannot express their feelings to, much less embrace, a woman.

It makes historical sense to say that just beyond Turgenev's consciousness as he created his female characters was the image of the perfect, and therefore ethereal and untouchable Madonna as depicted in Western paintings, or the Mother of God, as she is known in Russia and depicted in icons.

In the novel that bears his name, Rudin approaches Natalya as a worshipper might approach an icon. As a result, he can interact with her only verbally, and never physically. Church rituals have direct relevance here because they separate words from actions. This is another, more general, way of saying what Heldt says, namely, "The man and heroine, both Russian and usually of the same social class, are actually from different worlds, the male and female."[14] Although Turgenev did not create characters with religious interests, the radical separation of male and female worlds to which Heldt alludes ultimately derives from the way the walls of the monastery separated words from action, and thereby produced a heritage of lasting divisions of various kinds.

No writer benefitted more from the social divisions in Russia than Tolstoy—Count Tolstoy, that is. Count Tolstoy could take his time writing and rewriting *War and* Peace because (unlike Dickens at this time), he had an assured income from his large land holdings, so he did not need to make money from his work. Yet since Tolstoy was who he was, he had a delicate sensitivity to the way social divisions were evolving in the 1860s.

As we know, men who arrive also depart. In the terminology that I have used, Alyosha Karamazov's entry into the monastery is an embedded arrival. He is the only character in the Russian classics whose departure is more important than his arrival, because his departure from the monastery is a quasi-allegorical act that has far-reaching implications for Russian society.

After Father Zosima tells Alyosha Karamazov that he must leave the monastery, He then dies, and his body begins to stink, bringing on the greatest trauma of Alyosha's life. That trauma leads to the last arrival in a Russian classic novel, Alyosha's arrival in Skotoprigonevsk from the monastery. In a quasi-feudal society whose enduring image is the static, two-dimensional icon placed within a church within a monastery, a change of environment such as this one has great potential significance.

At the beginning of the section "The Boys," the narrator says:

> Here let us mention, by the way, that Alyosha had changed greatly since we left him: he had discarded his cassock and now wore a beautifully cut suit coat, a soft round hat, closely cropped hair. All that enhanced his appearance, and he looked like quite a handsome man. (10, 30)

Although Alyosha's suit coat marks him as a man of the world, and not a priest, he is in the world, but not of it. His arrival is only a partial one, so to speak. He is in a liminal state, and we know that because we never see him in private space. In fact it is unclear where he lives, or how he will support himself. He is no more capable of establishing a relationship with Grushenka or any other woman than Father Zosima was.

Alyosha finds himself confronting, not the boundless space of the steppe, but a limited version of the steppe in the open space of the streets of a provincial town. It is here that he serves as something like a counselor to street urchins—boys who would in the 1920s be called *besprizorniki*, boys without anyone to take care of them.

Like Levin, then, Alyosha has lost his defined place in the world, and has only a limited function in the world. He spreads good will and gives thoughtful advice to young Kolya Krasotkin, who eerily resembles a real boy who was living in a real provincial town at the time—a boy named Volodya Ulanov, who will become Vladimir Lenin. However, if we ask, "How will Alyosha make a living?" we realize that he is lost in the undefined space of post-reform Russia in a way that has some analogies to the plight of Levin and his fellow aristocrats.

It was left to Chekhov to address the question of how Russians would live in the world without the institutions of the monastery and the estate, which had given Russian life coherence and stability for centuries. Each of Chekhov's four great plays begins with an arrival and ends with a departure. Like his aristocratic predecessors, he used the arrival motif to organize his plays so that he could rely on mini-dramas and atmosphere rather than plot. In doing so, he created a revolution in modern drama and became the most frequently staged and most influential playwright of the twentieth century.

Another feature of his plays that makes him part of the modernist movement and that is so important and pervasive that it requires a separate book-length treatment is his use of intertextuality. Although I cannot give this topic the detailed discussion it deserves here, it must suffice to say that, as I showed in an earlier article,[15] Chekhov was intensely aware that his outsider status made him an ephebe in the world of aristocratic Russian literature.[16] However, he had the strength of his genius and in his first great play, *The Seagull*, he took on two awe-inspiring precursors, Shakespeare and Turgenev.

Chekhov seems to have sensed that by using the play within the play and other references to the plot of *Hamlet* he had done enough to come to terms with Shakespeare. First Turgenev, and then Tolstoy, were another matter, however. Chekhov had a life-long engagement with them, and his plays are shot through with references to their works.

Unlike his aristocratic precursors, Chekhov experienced exceptional social mobility. A Young Man from the Provinces Novel could be written about the 11-year period in his life between his departure from Taganrog in 1879 and his purchase of a house in Moscow in 1890. He came to the city, found fame and fortune, and married a beautiful, talented woman. He himself had experienced enormous change, as had several of his artist friends, such as the painters Konstantin Korovin and Isaac Levitan. It therefore makes sense to examine the issue of how characters evolve in his plays.

In *The Seagull* Trigorin arrives and departs twice. He is so self-involved that he does not realize that his treatment of Nina has caused her great pain, which in turn has forced her to mature. Similarly, he is not aware that the inescapable difference between his achievements and Treplev's failures leads, through no fault of his own, to Treplev's suicide.[17]

In *Uncle Vanya* it is Serebryakov who arrives and causes so much agitation that Uncle Vanya takes a shot at him. Very little change occurs, though.

Chekhov wrote four great plays, and they divide nearly into two pairs. In the first pair, *The Seagull* and *Uncle Vanya*, change remains internal and is contained. In the second pair, *The Three Sisters* and *The Cherry Orchard*, change grows until it sweeps everything before it. What is at issue is the fate of the manor house and of the way of life that it represents.

In *The Three Sisters*, Natasha arrives and eventually takes over the house. (Here Chekhov is playing off his Natasha against Tolstoy's Natasha.) However, the play is kept in balance by the fact that the three sisters themselves do not change, and at the end are shown living their lives very much as they did in the beginning.

In *The Cherry Orchard* the charming but weak Gayevs, Leonid and Lyubov', arrive, as does the energetic entrepreneur Yermolay Lopakhin. When he announces that the Gayevs are saved, because they can sell off their land and turn it into a housing development, they are aghast. Here Lopakhin is the irresistible force launching himself at the immovable object, the Gayev family. Radically, for the first time in Russian literary history, Chekhov creates characters, all of whom are immune to change, and thus remain the same at the end as they were in the beginning. The effect of doing this is to displace change onto to the estate itself, which Lopakhin buys.

A moment's reflection will show the sale of the estate represents the culmination of a long-term literary process. As far back as the 1860s, Bazarov had offered a cultural critique of the estate, but then died. Levin had acknowledged that he and his fellow aristocrats are like ancient vestal virgins, who have lost their functional role in society. And then, finally, it is because they have lost their functional role in society, i.e., their connection with their society, that the Gayevs lose their house and land.

As early as 1904, the year of the premiere of *The Cherry Orchard*, people recognized the social implications of the ending, and Soviet productions of the play presented it as a foreshadowing of the revolution. And so it was, but not quite in the way Soviet directors and critics thought.

Chekov did not live to see the 1905 revolution, so he felt optimistic about Russia's future. He believed that soon Russia would have a constitution. And one implication of Lopakhin's success in buying the estate is that the age of the aristocracy had passed, and that the future of Russia lay in the hands of men like him. This was half true, of course.

Indeed, the age of the aristocracy was passing, as Levin acknowledged, and the real-life equivalents of Lopakhin, such as Sergey Shchukin, a smart, hardworking Moscow businessman who made a lot of money, did appear. (Shchukin was also a major art patron, a friend of Picasso and Matisse.) However, Shchukin resembled Levin in *Anna Karenina* in that he confined himself to his immediate world of business. Around 1916 or so, Shchukin and the other movers and shakers of Russia's business world belatedly realized that Nicholas II was incapable of guiding Russia through a time of crisis, but by then it was too late.

Literature erupted into history with the most important arrival in Russian history, the arrival of Lenin and his fellow Bolsheviks at the Finland Station in the famous sealed train in April of 1917. If ever there was a Russian man who believed he knew what to do in the world, it was Lenin. He made a lasting impression on the Russians because he did something that no other Russian leader had ever done—he went out into the open spaces of Petrograd streets and made impassioned speeches. He certainly had as much energy as a Lopakhin, his immediate literary predecessor, and had Lopakhin's confidence. In connection with Lenin we may recall Yeats' ominous line that sums up so much of authoritarianism, "The worst are full of passionate intensity."

As it turned out, Lenin proved incapable of doing the one thing that really mattered if revolutionaries are to carry through on their promises, namely create a stable, lasting government. In his infamous Testament he showed himself to be as solipsistic as Levin. In his Testament, he said that he, and he alone, could govern the Soviet Union. On his deathbed it did not matter to him that he was, by his own admission, leaving a state that no one could govern. His self-absorption was as complete as Tolstoy's, and left a vacuum in Russian politics.

That vacuum was quickly filled by someone who, like Alyosha, had left the monastery. However, he was amoral enough to know very well indeed how to function in the world. This was Joseph Stalin, of course, and the gulag that he created was thus the logical destination of Gogol's troika. He often left people in the wide open spaces and forced them to work on poorly planned projects of marginal economic significance, such as the Belomor Canal.

Notes

1 Mikhail Epshteyn, *Ironiya ideala. Paradoksy russkoy literatury* (Moscow: NLO, 2015), 200.

2 Osip Mandel'shtam, *Stikhotvoreniya,* 163. (Moscow: Eksmo, 2006), 135.

3 Czikszenmihalyi, *Creativity,* 87.

4 Lionel Trilling, *The Liberal Imagination* (New York: The Viking Press, 1950), 61.

5 *Ibid.*

6 Watt, *The Rise of the Novel,* 64.

7 *Ibid.,* 190.

8 T.B. Tomlins, *The English Middle-Class Novel* (New York: Harper and Row, 1976), 102.

9 To recapitulate briefly some matters that I discussed in *Stalin's Soviet Monastery,* the first major instance of male bonding in Russian occurred in the Stankevich circle in Moscow. One prominent member of that group, the critic Vissarion Belinsky, formed an especially close bond with Gogol, and then when Gogol disappointed him by publishing his autobiographical *Selected Passages from Correspondence with*

Friends, Belinsky in his famous "Letter to Gogol," proclaimed that he had loved Gogol, and that Gogol had betrayed him. We have no reason to believe that he ever had a physical relationship with Gogol (although Gogol would probably have welcomed that). Strikingly, the same situation played itself out when Lenin and Georgy Plekhanov were in exile in Switzerland. After experiencing what he perceived as a slight from Plekhanov, Lenin wrote an essay in which he vehemently proclaimed that he had loved Plekhanov, had had "extremely intimate" (*intimney-shiye*) relations with him, and that Plekhanov had betrayed him. For details on these examples of male bonding in Russia (and there are surely others) see *Stalin's Soviet Monastery*, 120.

10 *Ibid.*, 339.

11 Denis Fonvizin, *Nedorosl'* (Leningrad, 1952), 43.

12 *Ibid.*, 44.

13 Barbara Heldt, *Terrible Perfection. Women and Russian Literature* (Bloomington and Indianapolis: Indiana U. Press, 19887), 19.

14 *Ibid.*

15 See James M. Curtis, "Ephebes and Precursors in Chekhov's *The Seagull.*" *Slavic Review*, Vol. 44, No. 3(Fall, 1985), 423-38.

16 Chekhov's clever short play *The Proposal*, which he wrote in 1888, may be interpreted as a dramatized allegory of his entry into the aristocratic world of Russian literature. In it, an over-dressed suitor, Ivan Lomov, enters a manor house to propose to a young woman. Lomov's name comes from the verb *lomat'*, "to break." In creating Lomov, Chekhov was breaking and entering. Moreover, the woman to whom Lomov wish to propose just happens to be named Natasha. Of course, Natasha is a common name for women in Russia, but given Chekhov's intense historical awareness and his knowing use of names, there is only one Natasha that matters, the Natasha of *War and Peace*. Asking for Natasha's hand is thus not just a romantic gesture; it is also Chekhov's way of asking for admittance to the ranks of the Russian classics.

17 *The Seagull* contains numerous personal references to Chekhov's life and work. In terms of Chekhov's evolution, we may say that in killing off Treplev, he killed off the ephebe in himself. The same may be said of the way Lermontov kills off Grushnitsky in *A Hero of Our Time*..

V.

Metaphor is to Dostoyevsky as Metonymy is to Tolstoy

Ever since the 1860s, when Dostoevsky and Tolstoy established their reputations with *Crime and Punishment* and *War and Peace* respectively, lovers of Russian literature have been aware that these giants of literature complemented each other in various ways. Thus, a key question in Russian literary history is this: How are we to understand the relationship between Tolstoy and Dostoyevsky? Although various Russian critics have addressed this issue, around 1900, their works on the subject primarily have historical interest today.[1]

The two best-known books in English on Tolstoy and Dostoyevsky are Isaiah Berlin's *The Hedgehog and the Fox. An Essay on Tolstoy's View of History,*[2] and George Steiner's *Tolstoy and Dostoyevsky. An Essay in Contrast.*[3] Both of these consummately well-educated, cosmopolitan scholars quite understandably perceived Tolstoy and Dostoyevsky as outliers, and proposed in their different ways to integrate them into European thought and culture. Berlin did this by citing a Greek adage. Allegedly, the hedgehog knows one thing, and that is surely Tolstoy. The fox, however, knows many things, and that is Dostoyevsky.

Unlike Berlin, Steiner treats Tolstoy and Dostoyevsky as writers, but he too assimilated them into the legacy of Greek culture. For him, Tolstoy's works belong with epic poetry, whereas Dostoyevsky's works belong with tragic drama. In lesser hands, these analogies might have remained impressionistic, but Caryl

Emerson gives Steiner credit for "the high degree of theoretical sophistication" in the book.[4]

Steiner and Berlin both wrote their books in the 1950s. At the time, another equally brilliant scholar, Roman Jakobson, was also writing about Tolstoy and Dostoyevsky. Throughout his extraordinary career, Jakobson unequivocally aligned himself with the analytical side of the analytical/impressionist opposition. For this reason his theoretical ideas, derived from linguistic principles, have the potential to introduce logical rigor into discussions of the contrasts between Tolstoy and Dostoyevsky. This rigor makes it possible to apply Jakobson's ideas both to a global understanding of the distinctive features of their genius, and also to detailed readings of individual scenes.

Here I wish to apply to Tolstoy and Dostoyevsky Jakobson's ideas about metaphor and metonymy in his 1953 essay "Two Aspects of Language and Two Aspects of Aphasic Disturbances," which has exceptional historical significance. Leon Surette goes so far as to say that Jakobson's article "has fundamentally altered the way literary critics use the terms 'metaphor' and 'metonymy.'"[5]

As the title of this essay indicates, it makes the argument that, as Jakobson uses the terms, metaphor is to Dostoyevsky as metonymy is to Tolstoy. That is to say, the argument is that these are the predominant modes in the major works by these authors. It enriches our understanding of Tolstoy to notice how consistently and frequently he uses metonymical devices, and it enriches our understanding of Dostoyevsky to notice how frequently he uses metaphorical devices. That is not to say, however, that Tolstoy is exclusively a metonymical writer, or that Dostoyevsky exclusively a metaphorical writer. It is obviously the case that Tolstoy, especially the later Tolstoy after his crisis in 1880-81, uses metaphorical devices such as parables, and that Dostoyevsky sometimes uses metonymical devices. What is at issue is a matter of recurring tendencies, and how these tendencies explain major features of the major works of these authors.

Moreover, one can say that these recurring tendencies recur so frequently that they constitute an aesthetic system. They thus invite systemic analysis, as in the work of Vera Zubaryova. In her book on Chekhov, she discusses books such as Ludwig von Bartanlaffy's *General Systems Theory*, [6] and concludes, "In a systems approach the description of the whole must *precede* the analysis of individual components."[7] Note that this principle is completely consistent with linguistic analysis in general and in particular with Jakobson's theories such as his theory of the Russian verb.

Moreover, this consistency with linguistic theory has vital implications for one's understanding of creativity and thus for critical procedure. If one assumes with linguists that native speakers of a language cannot articulate the structure of their language because it remains at an unconscious level, so in the same way I would argue that artists cannot articulate in any meaningful way their intentions in creating their art, because creativity arises from the creative unconscious. This is why I do not presume to extrapolate from Tolstoy's works to his intentions in creating them.

To apply Zubaryova's point to Tolstoy and Dostoyevsky, one can define their aesthetic systems as metonymical and metaphorical respectively, and then proceed by explicating specific images and characters in those terms. All the available evidence of these writers' long careers suggests that metonymy was an essential feature of Tolstoy's creative unconscious, just as metaphor was an essential feature of Dostoyevsky's creative unconscious. This is why Tolstoy's creative unconscious generated works in which metonymy predominated, and why Dostoyevsky's creative unconscious generated works in which metaphor predominated. With these global definitions in mind, let us proceed to the specifics of terminology, and applications of that terminology.

We may begin by examining what Jakobson said about metaphor and metonymy. In the section of the essay that has relevance here, he begins:

> The development of a discourse may take place according to two different semantic lines; one topic may lead to another either through their similarity of their contiguity. The metaphoric way would be the most appropriate term for the first case and the metonymic way for the second, since they find their most condensed expression in metaphor and metonymy respectively.[8]

A little later in the essay, he applies the opposition of metaphor and metonymy to literature in a well-known and much-cited passage:

> Following the path of contiguous relationships, the realist author metonymically digresses from the plot to the atmosphere and from the character to the setting in space and time. He is fond of synecdochic details. In the scene of Anna Karenina's suicide Tolstoj's artistic attention is focused on the heroine's handbag; and in *War and Peace* the synecdoches "hair on the upper lip" and "bare shoulders" are used by the same writer to stand the for the female characters to whom these features belong.[9]

For the sake of clarification, I cite here the passage from *Anna Karenina* to which Jakobson refers. As Karenina prepares for her ride on the train, we are told in passing that she has a "red handbag." (9, 384)[10] And then she gets on the train: "She went up the high step and sat down alone in the compartment on the spotted, springy seat that had once been white. Her handbag trembled on the springs, [and] came to rest." (9, 385)

In the synecdochic mode, in which a part stands for the whole that is characteristic of metonymy, Tolstoy is able to imply that Karenina's handbag stands for her—its color attests to her adultery—and the fact that the handbag comes to rest on the seat anticipates that she too will come to rest in death. Although Jakobson does not mention it, the seat on which she sits also has metonymical significance. It was once as white as her wedding dress, but is now stained, as she is.

The subtlety of Tolstoy's technique comes from the fact that none of this is ever made explicit. Although people who are reading the novel for the first time may not register the significance of these details, they—and many others like them—have a subconscious, cumulative effect. Such synecdochic details recur again and again in key scenes in *War and Peace* and *Anna Karenina*. [11]

Thus, metonymy is a system characterized by synecdoche, in which the part stands for the whole. A key implication of metonymic, or synecdochic, systems is that there is a consistency between the part and the whole. The part and the whole are not just related to each other; they partake of the same nature.

Jakobson says, "The researcher possesses more homogeneous means to handle metaphor, whereas metonymy, based on a different principle, easily defies interpretation." [12] In discussing Tolstoy's use of metonymy, as the previous discussion has shown, what matters is not so much interpretation as indentifying individual synecdochic details, not as random elements of a scene, but rather as constituent parts of an overall symbolic system. In terms that Jakobson would have appreciated, the study of metonymy is comparable to phonology, whereas the study of metaphor is comparable to morphology.

If in metonymy the part stands for the whole, and it necessarily partakes of the same nature, the opposite is true of metaphor. In metaphor, as Jakobson defines the term, and as I will be using it in this chapter, two dissimilar, heterogeneous entities are juxtaposed. A case in point might be the expression "the winds of change." Whereas winds are a natural phenomenon, change is a social phenomenon. The image is thus metaphorical in Jakobson's sense.

It is the general thesis of this chapter that the creative unconscious of some great artists has a deep structure, and that an examination of the patterns in their work make it possible to define that deep structure. More specifically, I will argue that the deep structure of Dostoyevsky's creative unconscious was metaphorical, and that this is why he consistently juxtaposed dissimilar entities in his work. The deep structure of Tolstoy's creative unconscious, on the other hand, was metonymical, and this caused him to establish connections between entities and people, as in the case of Karenina's handbag.

These assumptions explain a great deal about what Tolstoy and Dostoyevsky do, and what they do not do. They explain, for example, why Dostoyevsky refers to famous paintings and incorporates them into the symbolic structure of in his short stories and novels. Images are different from words, so Dostoyevsky's references to famous paintings are thus metaphorical. The opposition of Dostoyevsky's words and other artists' images makes sense only in a heterogeneous, metaphorical system By contrast, Tolstoy as a metonymical writer hardly ever refers to a famous painting.[13]

As a metaphorical writer, Dostoyevsky creates clashing juxtapositions that push his characters from their immediate circumstances outward toward the future, as in the cases of characters as different as Rodion Raskolnikov and Alyosha Karamazov. These juxtapositions also push his characters toward the consciousness of others, and not just in the dialogs that Bakhtin emphasized, as well as to other novels and art forms.

On the other hand, as a metonymical writer, Tolstoy establishes the integration of things, and shows how like eventually matches like, which is the state that exists when the parts of the society are in a metonymical relationship. He begins *War and Peace* with a statement that the social order is threatened politically, and he begins *Anna Karenina* with a statement that the social order is threatened personally. This disturbance of the peace becomes a social conflict (Napoleon's invasion, Anna's affair with Vronsky), which is then resolved (Napoleon's defeat, Anna's suicide). In both novels, the effect of these resolutions is to establish a genuinely peaceful social order (life on the Russian estate), yet the threats to the social order never disappear completely.

Understanding a great artist's oeuvre as a unified, coherent system with a deep structure that the artist did not—and indeed could not—articulate makes it possible to characterize the evolution of Tolstoy and Dostoyevsky in a general way before proceeding to more detailed discussions. A reading of Tolstoy's and Dostoyevsky's first works shows how the creative matrix of metonymy and metaphor respectively was operating in their psyches from the very beginning.

In Tolstoy's first published work, his short story, "Childhood," he uses first-person narration, which lends itself to metonymy because the narrator describes his familiar environment and experiences. It is significant that Tolstoy began his career by publishing two trilogies of short stories, "Childhood"; "Boyhood"; and "Youth"; and "Sevastopol in December"; "Sevastopol in May": and "Sevastopol in August." As a metonymical writer, Tolstoy could not compose plots in the usual sense of the word, in which conflicts of various kinds arise and are then resolved at the end. Rather, as he matured, what he did was to create juxtapositions of increasing subtlety and complexity and then resolve them.

By contrast, *Poor Folk* is a strikingly literary work, and not just because it is an epistolary novel that contains the correspondence between Makar Devushkin and Varvara Dobroselova. Two features mark Makar as a character created by a writer with a metaphorical sensibility. First, he has a "telling" name. Devushkin is related to *devushka,* "girl." Devushkin is not a manly man, and Dobroselova will be taken from him by a man named Bykov, from *byk,* "bull."

Devushkin is a strikingly literary character in a strikingly literary work. He is engaged with literature, something beyond his immediate experience. He thinks of buying a friend the first posthumous edition of Pushkin's work, and talks about Gogol's "The Overcoat." This reference begins Dostoyevsky's life-long engagement with Gogol and his work.

The general point is that nothing like this ever happens in Tolstoy's works. As in "Childhood," his characters are caught up in their immediate experiences and those of the people around them. Literature, as well as the other arts, hardly exists for them. If Tolstoy's characters ever write anything, they write letters and diaries. No Tolstoy character ever imagines that he might be a poet, as Devushkin does.

We find a rare example of a Tolstoy character who does read fiction, only to reject it, in the scene in which Karenina is returning from Moscow, where she had met Vronsky, to St. Petersburg. She opens an English novel and begins to read. (Note that Tolstoy does not give the name of the novel and relate it to Karenina's situation, as Dostoyevsky would have.) "Anna Arkadyevna read and understood, but it was unpleasant for her to read, that is, to follow the reflections of the life of other people. She herself wanted to live too much." (8, 121) Anna, like her literary grandmother Natasha Rostova, has too much manic energy to sit still and read. She feels restless because—although she doesn't realize it—she has fallen in love with Vronsky.

Earlier I cited the work of Anna Berman as having some analogies to the methods of descriptive linguistics. The same applies to Robert Louis Jackson's essay, "Breaking the Moral Barrier: Ann Karenina's Night Train to St. Petersburg," in which he explicates this scene. For Jackson, the basic unit of the novel is the character, and he offers no global understanding of the novel, or of Tolstoy's work in general. Indeed, he might well deny that any such understanding is even possible.

Fortunately for Jackson, Tolstoy's prose is so rich that almost any scene in *Anna Karenina* could be explicated as Jackson explicates the scene of Anna's ride on the train and of her nighttime encounter with Vronsky. In fact, Gary L.

Browning also explicates this scene, and does so in a very similar way. Rather than interpreting Anna's environment as consisting of metonymical analogies, he interprets it as consisting of symbols. Thus, he writes, "The storm [at the train station] encapsulates Anna's approaching relationship with Vronsky."[14]

In a long tradition of explicating Tolstoy, Jackson uses the text to arrive at a generalization about him: "In Tolstoy's view, we are never separate from the world around us."[15] If we rewrite this principle as "Literary characters are never separate from the world around them," it is the essential principle of metonymy. I would generalize from what Jackson says to argue that Tolstoy's characters are "never separate" from each other, and for that matter, never separate from other characters in other works by Tolstoy. I will presently show that a psychological, rather than a moral, interpretation of Anna Karenina makes sense once one understands her as a further development of Natasha Rostova in *War and Peace.*

It clarifies the unusual nature of the case being made here for metonymy as a defining feature of Tolstoy's genius to notice what happens when a scholar makes radically different assumptions. I noted earlier that Gary Saul Morson, in *Hidden in Plain View*, his book on *War and Peace*, assumes Tolstoy stands apart from his novel, and that his intentions necessarily determined our interpretations of it. Analogously, Morson assumes that the characters in *War and Peace* do not cohere into an integrated system. Thus, he writes, "Pierre and Andrei, like all the characters in *War and Peace,* are identified by their approaches to planning, and by the kind and degree of personal responsibility that their individual approaches permit."[16] If what matters about Pierre and Andrey is their personal responsibility, then no network of character relationships into which they might fit, exists. If, however, we assume that a network of metonymical relationships exists in *War and Peace*, then we may say that understanding Pierre and Andrey requires us to understand how they fit into this network.

It may very well be that, as Jakobson says, metonymy defies interpretation; but it does not defy description. Since critics have devoted so little attention to metonymy in Tolstoy, it is worthwhile to describe in some detail here the metonymical connections between and among the characters in his two great novels.[17]

Tolstoy's numerous characters are not isolated, unique individuals. Connections exist that connect individual characters to their families, and that connect families to cities. To anticipate some more general discussions, I can say here that Tolstoy's use of synecdoche here and elsewhere enables him to enrich his narrative by doing something that is essential to his art—connecting the characters to their milieu. He does this more, and in more complex ways, than any other writer in the Western canon. Tolstoy's ability to create synecdochic details that form an all-embracing system for an entire novel is a key feature that makes him a great writer.

It is the always intuitive Natasha who gives us a vital clue about characterization in Tolstoy. In the First Epilog she says Sonya will remain unmarried, and explains why. 'She is a *sterile flower*, you know, like in a flower bed?" (7, 291) (Tolstoy's emphasis) What she is saying is that Sonya's life experiences—what Russians would call her "fate"—represent an unfolding of an inner essence. The major characters, and a number of the minor characters as well, have such an inner essence, so that there is a through line that connects the individual to the family as well as to the milieu. It is one of the miracles of *War and Peace* that Tolstoy is able to show how each of the characters manifests this inner essence in speech, behavior, and even clothing over the long course of the novel.

War and Peace begins with two set pieces that demonstrate this through line in which characters manifest their inner essences. These set pieces bring together most of the major characters in the novel—first in St. Petersburg, and one in Moscow. It matters where the characters live because the characters that live in a certain city embody its characteristics. Take, for example, the first scene, which shows Anna Pavlovna Scherer's soirée in St. Petersburg. The straight streets and rectilinear buildings of St. Petersburg that haunt Raskolnikov so much have their psychological equivalent in the emphasis on propriety that dominates this scene. It has a mechanical quality: "Anna Pavlovna's soirée was launched. From various sides the spindles were making noise incessantly and regularly. (5, 8)

By contrast, in chapter 10, which shows Natasha's name-day in Moscow, a folksy democratic ethos, which markedly differs from the formality of St. Petersburg prevails. Count Rostov's first speech is a microcosm of Moscow attitudes. "Very, very grateful to you, *ma chére* or *mon cher* (he said *ma chére* or *mon cher* to everyone without exception without the slightest shadings to people who stood above him or beneath him)." (5, 23) The key to understanding the network of synecdochic connections in *War and Peace* is that the characters embody in their speech and actions the characteristics of their city or estate, as they case may be. Space does not allow for a detailed discussion of even a small percentage of the 300 identifiable characters in *War and Peace*, so this discussion must be confined to the five major characters.

The five major characters in *War and Peace* may be arranged in the following way:

St. Petersburg	Moscow
The Bolkonsky Family	The Rostov Family
Andrey Bolkonsky	Nikolay Rostov
Pierre Bezukhov	
Marya Bolkonskaya	Natasha Rostova

Each of Russia's two capitals has a brother-sister pair, and in each case the brother and the sister share family characteristics. However, because Pierre Bezukhov is the exception that proves the rule about connections, let us begin with him.

Pierre is the illegitimate son of the old count Bezukhov, and his ambiguous status is shown in his French first name and Russian surname. Thus, unlike the other major characters, Pierre is betwixt and between. He is perpetually out of place; he searches for his identity and his place in the world until he marries Natasha. Pierre shows the way Tolstoy endows each of his characters, even down to the minor ones, with a deep structure that generates their speech and behavior.

Thus, it is not enough that Pierre's name indicates his outsider status. Tolstoy consistently had his characters relate to their milieu in the overall arrangement of themes. If Napoleon poses a threat to the political order, as the first sentence in *War and Peace* indicates, Pierre poses a threat to the smooth functioning of Anna Pavlovna Scherer's *soirée*. Here is Tolstoy's description of his introduction to St. Petersburg society:

> This fat young man was the illegitimate son of the famous *belmoge* from the Catherine era, Count Bezukhov, who was now dying in Moscow. He didn't serve anywhere; he had just arrived from abroad, where he was educated, and was in society for the first time. Anna Pavlovna greeted him with a bow appropriate for the people of the very lowest hierarchy in her salon. But despite this greeting of the lowest sort, anxiety and fear were expressed on Anna Pavlovna's face at the sight of Pierre as he came in. (4, 5)

Thus, Pierre is out of place in multiple ways. He has just arrived from Europe, is not in government service, and does not know how to behave in society. "Pierre was awkward…He didn't know how to enter a salon, and still less did he know how to leave one." (4.6)

Being out of place is an essential element in the deep structure of Pierre's character. And, characteristically, Tolstoy shows us how out of place he is indirectly, through his clothing. When Pierre goes to the Battle of Borodino, where he is out of place because he is not a soldier, "Everybody with almost naïve curiosity looked at Pierre's white hat and green frock coat." (6, 216) Pierre will remain a searcher, wandering through life, good-hearted but confused and disoriented, until he finds his place with Natasha.

A classic example of what may be called an anticipatory microcosm of a character appears in this description of Andrey Bolkonsky when he first appears at Anna Pavlovna's *soirée*. "Everything in his figure, beginning with his tired, bored gaze to the quiet measured step presented the sharpest opposition to his small lively wife." (5, 4) To use the title of a play by Tolstoy that has become a common Russian expression, Andrey is a living corpse, and it is one of the finer ironies in *War and Peace* that his wife Liza, who is presented as literally full of life (she is pregnant), will die before he does.

One might say that the Andrey-Natasha story is at the heart of *War and Peace*, so it is useful to note the corresponding anticipatory microcosm of her first appearance: "A thirteen-year-old girl ran into the room holding something in her short muslin skirt and stopped in the middle of the room." (4, 34) Natasha's lively spontaneity is a defining feature of her personality and keeps her in the middle of things. Her singing will bring life to Andrey, and Tolstoy provides the synecdochic detail of the tree that comes to life as he leaves the Rostovs' estate.

Dancing is a recurring motif in *War and Peace*, and when Andrey and Natasha dance during the magnificently written ball scene, which brings together a number of the major characters, their behavior is determined by the characteristics of their respective cities. In yet another of the exquisite ironies of character development in *War and Peace,* it is Pierre who asks Andrey to dance with Natasha. Andrey is talking to a Baron about a matter of diplomacy, and responds in a very St. Petersburgish way. "'Sorry,' he said to the baron, 'We'll finish this conversation in a different place, but at a ball one must dance.'" (5, 226) As a sophisticated man of society, Andrey knows what is proper in any given situation, and what is proper at a ball is dancing.

Natasha, a Rostov, has a radically different experience at the ball. For her part, Natasha frets because she is out of place, as a Moscow girl in St. Petersburg, and as a wallflower at the ball. As she enters, her metonymical sensibility creates a merger between her and the other people there. "Natasha looked in the mirrors and in the reflection she couldn't distinguish herself from the others." (5, 221) But to her distress none of the men will dance with her, and her isolation makes no sense to her. "But they must know how much I want to dance, how excellently I dance and how nice it would be for them to dance with me." (5, 225) Dancing might be said to be the key Rostov activity, since it requires a lively spontaneity. This is why both Natasha and her brother Nikolay are excellent dancers, of course. The various scenes in which they dance simply glow with life.

Tolstoy was too great a writer not to sense the implications of Natasha's impulsiveness. Sexually and emotionally frustrated by Andrey's long absence, this young woman who needed immediate emotional release, lets herself be drawn into Anatole Kuragin's plot and agrees to elope with him. Fortunately, however, a servant intervenes. "Gavrilo, Marya Dmitriyevna's enormous man servant met Anatole. 'Please see the lady of the house,' he said in his bass voice, blocking the way to the door." (5, 395) And that is that, except that Natasha has put the Rostovs to shame and attempts suicide.

Still, Natasha and Andrey are star-crossed lovers, although they never sleep together. After Andrey is wounded, Natasha nurses him. Andrey and Natasha are deeply in love, and they both know that Andrey is dying. These chapters belong among the most moving in all of world literature, and are comparable in their effect to the last act of *Romeo and Juliet*.

A key moment occurs when Andrey's sister Marya comes to see him, and Natasha rushes to greet her, just as she ran into the room where her mother was in her first appearance in the novel.

> On her agitated face when she ran into the room was only one expression—an expression of love of *boundless* love for him, for her, for all that was dear to the man she loved, and expression of pity, of suffering for others and the passionate desire to give all of herself over to help them. (7, 65) (My emphasis)

Natasha's love is *boundless*—that key word for nineteenth-century Russians, who have emotions to match the landscapes that surround them. Natasha's unified metonymical sensibility will not allow her to put boundaries between herself and others, or to distinguish between herself and others, as she could not distinguish between her reflection and that of others at the ball in St. Petersburg.

Whereas Natasha's sensibility is boundless, Andrey's sensibility is bounded. The spaces of St. Petersburg enclose him, as do his sense of propriety and his pride, which will not let him fall to the ground when he sees the bomb during the battle of Borodino. This is why he alone, of all the characters in *War and Peace*, achieves transcendence. He has a key dream that images his enclosure. In it he is in the room he is actually in. He attempts to lock the door, i.e., maintain his separateness from others. "And an agonizing fear seized him. And this fear was the fear of death: behind the door was standing *it…it* came in, and it was *death*.

And Prince Andrey died." (7, 75) (Tolstoy's emphasis) But in Russia, as in other Christian countries, death implies resurrection, and in fact death and resurrection constitutes one of the overarching themes in Russian culture. Thus, after Andrey symbolically dies, he wakes up and says to himself, "'Yes, that was death. I died—I woke up. Yes, death is awakening!" (7, 75)

One word in this passage requires special commentary, the word the "it" that breaks through the door—*ono*. Russian is an inflected language, so nouns, pronouns, and adjectives have gender. *Ono* is not the usual generic word for "it," *eto*, but rather the pronoun for a neuter noun. Tolstoy uses a neuter pronoun here because it implicitly refers to the neuter noun *telo*, "body." Unlike the Rostovs, the Bolkonskys do not inhabit their bodies, and are in fact alienated from them as well as from other people. Thus, for Andrey, when *it* comes through the door, it means that he has accepted his body, and is ready to die. As he says, he has both died and awakened.

Natasha's brother Nikolay shares with his sister some of the traits that mark him as a Rostov. In keeping with his principle of using an anticipatory microcosm for a character's first appearance, Tolstoy writes of Nikolay that when he and the other young people in the Rostov household follow Natasha into the Rostovs' living room, "Nikolay blushed as soon as he entered the living room. It was apparent that he was searching for something to say and couldn't find anything." (4, 36) Like his sister Natasha, Nikolay has a metonymical sensibility. Here and later, he has so completely merged with his family milieu that he can't manage to say anything about it.

These discussions of the use of metonymy in presenting the Rostovs in action provide a useful context for understanding what Formalist critic Viktor Shklovsky famously called "estrangement (*ostraneniye*)." Shklovsky first used the term in his well-known essay "Art as Device," where he defines it in the follow way:

> The device of estrangement in L. N. Tolstoy consists of his not naming a thing by its name, but describing it as if seen for the first time, and an incident as if it had happened for the first time, while using in the description of the thing not the names of its parts that are accepted, but calling them the corresponding parts in other things.[18]

As an illustration of estrangement, Shklovsky cites two passages from *War and Peace* that have since become textbook examples of the device. The first involves Natasha's perception of the opera in Moscow: "In the center of the stage sat some girls in red bodices and white skirts. One very fat girl in a white silk dress sat apart on a low bench, to the back of which a piece of green cardboard was glued." (5, 360) Shklovsky's second example is Nikolai Rostov's thoughts during his first experience of battle. In a manner consistent with the anticipatory microcosm of his first appearance, Nikolay finds it difficult to say anything about the situation. He looks at some French soldiers and thinks, "'Are they really running toward me? And why? To kill me? *Me*, whom everybody loves so much?"' (4:255) (Tolstoy's emphasis) In his book on *War and Peace*, Shklovsky generalizes from these examples: "Tolstoy extends the distrust of ordinary perception to all his characters, and one can say that Tolstoy's characters have traditional perception only when their perception is not analyzed."[19] With all due respect to Shklovsky, and his substantial contributions to critical theory, to Tolstoy scholarship, and to Russian culture in general, this statement is not true. It is not true that all of Tolstoy's characters experience estrangement. It is primarily the Muscovites Nikolay and Natasha Rostov who experience estrangement, and the preceding discussion will help to explain why.

If we ask what common element the scene of Natasha at the opera, and of Nikolay in his first battle, share, the answer is obvious. Both the opera and the battle divide people into two groups. In the opera, the performers on stage are divided from the people in the audience. Similarly, in the battle the combatants are divided into the Russian army and the French army. And it is precisely division, the separation of people into distinct groups that Nikolay and Natasha simply cannot understand. Nikolay cannot understand why the French soldiers would want to shoot at him any more than Natasha at the ball in St. Petersburg can understand why the men do not understand why she wants to dance so much.

Although we first meet Pierre in St. Petersburg, Natasha says that he has a good heart, and she of course marries him. So there exists an affinity between Pierre and the Rostovs. This affinity helps to explain why Tolstoy uses Pierre to create estrangement in battle scenes.

Jakobson's comment on the implied metonymical relationship between Anna Karenina and her purse mentioned earlier has important implications for Tolstoy's battle scenes. If contiguity implies affinity, then the following sentences have larger implications for the meaning of war:

> It was only now that he [Pierre] noticed wounded men staggering or being carried on stretchers. On that same little meadow with rows of fragrant hay over which he had ridden the day before, a soldier was lying athwart the rows, with his head turned awkwardly and his shako off."(6, 261)

Note that we are not told that this is a corpse; we must *conclude* that this is a corpse because the head is "turned awkwardly." We are therefore dealing with yet another example of estrangement in Pierre's perception of the battlefield. But merely characterizing the passage as estrangement does not explain why the corpse is lying on fragrant hay. The first reference to "fragrant hay," a phrase with positive associations, occurs when Pierre rides with Benningsen to survey the field on which the battle will be fought the next day: "From Gorki, Benningsen descended the high road to the bridge which, when they looked at it from the hill, the officer had pointed out as the center of our position, and where rows of fragrant new-mown hay were lying by the bank."(6, 228) Such recurring phrases always have significance in Tolstoy's work, but we understand the significance of this one only when we relate it to the later one.

If in Tolstoy's work as a whole, the juxtaposition of things implies an affinity between them, then we may infer an affinity between the corpse and the hay. And if-as the historical essays argue-war is a natural phenomenon, then it is reasonable to conclude that both the soldier and the hay have been cut down as part of the ongoing, immutable rhythms of life. Tolstoy needs to establish that war has an organic quality, because then he can deny Napoleon the role of a great strategist. In Tolstoy's imagination, that which is foreordained is natural like mowing hay. Thus, in the larger scheme of things, the death of the soldier is as natural as, and of the same nature as, the mown hay.

The opera and the battle divide people into groups because of the social definition of the situation. The ultimate division of people into groups is biological—the division of people into men and women. Tolstoy's characters are unable to overcome this division when it comes to the crucial situation of marriage proposals.

A detailed discussion of the marriage proposals in *War and Peace* would show that none of them are sincere. In fact, the limitations of Tolstoy's metonymical sensibility prevented him from creating a situation in which a man expresses desire for a woman and then marries her. The mere fact that Vronsky expresses his desire for Karenina means that their relationship is doomed.

Although Pierre gets married twice, he does not propose either time. Early in *War and Peace,* when Pierre proves incapable of proposing to Hélène, Count Kuragin takes matters into his own hands, rushes into the room, and pronounces them engaged. Pierre does not propose to Natasha, either. In the Epilogue we are simply told that they are married.

The through line in Nikolay Rostov's behavior from the beginning of *War and Peace* to the end is very clear, and appears in his marriage proposal. In his very first scene Nikolay Rostov does not know what to say, and very late in the novel, he does not know what to say when he wants to propose to Marya Bolkonskaya, either. His non-proposal is worth examining again. He and Marya talk past each other for a while, and finally Marya gives up on him, and she turns to go.

> "Princess! Stop for God's sake—," he shouted, trying to stop her. "Princess!"
> She looked around. For several seconds they silently looked into each other's eyes, and what was distant and impossible suddenly became near, possible, and inevitable. (7, 285)

Nikolay is never more the quintessential Rostov than when he tries to explain his love for his wife and distinguish it from typical Romantic love. "Well, do I love my finger? I don't love it, but try to cut it off…" (7, 299) The Rostovian inability to distinguish between self and others produces his outrage when he learns of Pierre's participation in a secret society in St. Petersburg, which we understand to be the genesis of the December plot:

> If you create a secret society, begin to oppose the government, no matter what it's like, I know that it is my duty to obey it. And if Arakcheyev orders me to attack you with a squad and cut you up—I won't think for a second and I'll go. (7, 319)

In interpreting this statement, everything depends on context. If we take it by itself, Nikolay unmasks himself as the most complete proto-Stalinist in Russian classic literature, and his tirade must figure into any serious discussion of the connection Russian literature before 1917 and after 1917.

On the other hand, Nikolay is a Rostov, and the Rostovs' charm and spontaneity are of a piece with their complete lack of self-awareness. Nikolay does not remember that he made similar bellicose statements before the battle of Austerlitz, only to express his puzzlement as to why French soldiers are attacking him when the longed-for battle actually begins. In short, as his very first appearance in the novel indicates, he is so inarticulate that he can't say what he really means. The idea of a division between the government and the people upsets him as much as, and for the same reasons, as the division between the performers and the audience causes estrangement when Natasha attends the opera.

And what of Marya Bolkonskaya, the woman who saves Nikolay's psyche and restores the family's finances, which Nikolay damaged because of his gambling debts? She is quite literally an outlier among the five principal characters in that she spends virtually the whole novel, from beginning to end, on the Bolkonsky estate of Bald Hills. She says to Andrey, "I don't ask for another life, so I can't wish for one, because I don't know another life." (5, 241) She does not know another life, and she never will know another life. Nikolay and Natasha Rostov, as well as her brother Andrey, travel a good deal, but Marya stays put. She spends her entire life on her family's estate, first as the dutiful daughter of her father, and then as a dutiful wife of her husband. In the first sequence in which she appears, during which we meet her father, Andrey brings his pregnant wife Liza to the estate. He then leaves, in a scene filled with metonymical microcosms that anticipate in some detail what will happen.

The relationship between Andrey and his sister Marya is a sibling bond, of course, and Anna Berman has performed a great service to Russian literature by drawing attention to the previously neglected topic of the significance of sibling bonds in it.[20] As she shows in her article on sibling bonds in *War and Peace* siblings have "a deep understanding of each other."[21] In the article, she convincingly shows that this is the case between Natasha and Nikolay Rostov.

A careful reading of Berman's work suggests something that she, like other Tolstoy scholars, does not quite articulate. She properly points out that the early death of Tolstoy's mother made him tend to idealize, i.e., de-sexualize, women, all his life. Hence, he tended to portray sibling bonds as ideally close. However, all sibling bonds by definition occur within a family, and if we take family bonds rather than sibling bonds, as the basic unit of the work as this chapter has done, then sibling bonds take on a different character. Assuming that family members share defining characteristics motivates us to notice how these characteristics manifest themselves over the generations. For the Bolkonskys a key characteristic is the difficulty in establishing empathy with others.

Thus, a certain lack of authenticity obtains among the residents of the Bolkonsky estate, Bald Hills, beginning with old Prince Bolkonsky, who is a (mostly) benign despot, and whose behavior will become increasingly erratic as the novel progresses. He is so brittle that maintaining his daily schedule is essential to his welfare. It is indicative that although he wants his daughter to be educated, he teaches a most abstract subject, geometry, as opposed to the practical subjects that she will later need when she has to run the estate.

Marya is the only one of the major characters who is consistently associated with reading and writing. Tolstoy tells us that her desk was "covered with notebooks and books." (5, 230) Like a true Bolkonsky, Marya relates to the world through the written word, not through direct interaction with others.

The sequence in which we meet her includes a letter to her from Julie Karagina that fatefully mentions that Nikolay Rostov has left the university to enroll in the army. In making such references, Tolstoy is planting a narrative seed that will come to fruition after hundreds and hundreds of pages. It is Nikolay who will later quell a revolt among the peasants at Bald Hills, of course. As a result by the time of Nikolay's non-proposal to her, the two of them have been brought together in such a way as to make their marriage seem inevitable in retrospect. And it starts with a casual reference in a letter by Julie Karagina.

Marya doesn't just reach out into the world by writing. As a woman, she has more understanding of others than her brother and her father. She looks at her brother with "both love and sadness." (5, 250) Like a Dostoyevsky character, she anticipates what will happen to her brother. She tells him, "You are good to everyone but you have a certain pride of thought." (5, 253) And it is of course this pride that will prevent him from saving his life by falling down when the bomb hits. Sensing all this, she gives him an icon to wear.

Old Prince Bolkonsky's obsessive need to maintain order at all costs bespeaks a certain death of the spirit. This death of the spirit is of a piece with the literal death that will come to both his son and his daughter-in-law. Although Liza is not a Bolkonsky, she intuits her death, as her sister-in-law intuits the death of her brother. She confides in Marya, and tells her that "She anticipates an unfortunate labor, is afraid of it, and she complains of her father-in-law, and her husband." (5, 340)

In the First Epilogue, Nikolay enters his and his wife's bedroom and sees that she is sitting at her desk and writing. What he does not realize, and what we the readers realize, is that when she does so, she is doing what she did in her first scene when she wrote a letter to Julie Kuragin after the unpleasant geometry lesson with her father. The engagement with literacy that appears in her first scene also appears in her last one. Now, however, as a wife and mother she is not writing a letter to her girlfriend. She is doing something that shows her to be her father's daughter, despite the obvious differences in their personalities. Her father held her at a distance and had a domineering attitude toward her. She treats her children as her father treated her.

As Berman says, "Mariya's children become the center of her life after the marriage."[22] Indeed they do—and they are the worse for it. When Nikolay asks Marya what she is writing, she replies that it is a diary. But it is not a personal diary; rather it is a diary of her experiences with her children. With a typical Bolkonskian lack of awareness of the consequences of her behavior on others, she had written in her diary that when her older son Andryusha was stubborn one morning, "Then I took it on myself; I left him and along with the nanny started getting up the other children, *and I told him that I didn't love him.*" (7, 321) (My emphasis) Just as her father imposed his will on her regardless of the consequences, so in the same way she imposes her will on children, blissfully unaware that when a mother withholds her love because of a child's behavior, and tells the child that she is doing so, it has terrible consequences for the child's development.

But there is more. She reminds her children that she holds herself at a distance from them, always watching and evaluating them. She wants them to know that she is always ready to give or withdraw her approval at any minute. She does this by giving them slips of papers every night with grades on them.

As it often happens with the work of important scholars, Berman's work on the ideal, and idealized, sibling bonds in Tolstoy suggests a conclusion beyond that she specifically says. This conclusion concerns the elusive, mostly mysterious nature of his creative process. Berman is surely right to say that the early death of Tolstoy's mother made him tend to portray sibling bonds as ideal because they were not sexual. However, we may suppose that there was always a tension between his need to idealize siblings on one hand and his need to endow families with general traits on the other. And as his principal characters aged and had families of their own, as they do in the Epilog, he overcame his need for idealization and let the traits that they had inherited from their parents manifest themselves—sometimes with less than optimal consequences.

Keeping in mind that Tolstoy's overarching theme is the relationship between the social order and the threats to that order, we may in the Epilogue construe social order as coming from the Rostovs, from Natasha's obsessive domesticity and Nikolay's authority in running the estate. The threats to that order are associated with St. Petersburg, which harbors the secret society to which Pierre belongs. The Bolkonskys embody the attitudes of St. Petersburg, and they pose the ultimate threat to the social order—death. We are to understand that Andrey's son Nikolenka will be executed as a Decembrist, and we may conclude that some form of emotional death awaits Marya and Nikolay's children because of her manipulative treatment of them.

If it is true that Tolstoy carried over his practice of metonymical characterization from *War and Peace* to *Anna Karenina* as part of his remarkably unified literary evolution, and I believe it is, then it is possible to create an imaginary genealogy for his characters. For example, we are told that Natasha was 13 in 1806, so she was born in 1793. Then, in the First Epilogue of *War and Peace* we learn that at the age of 20, "Natasha got married in the early spring of 1813, and by 1820 she had three daughters and one son." (7, 298) Although we have no more details about her children, we may suppose that if one of her daughters was born in, say, 1818, she would have been 30 in 1848. Her social position as a

Rostov would have made it possible for her to meet and marry a certain Arkady Oblonsky. A daughter, Anna Arkadyevna Oblonskaya, could have been born in 1848, and could have married Aleksey Karenin around 1868 when she was 20. His position in government would have made him seem like a good match. It is reasonable to suppose, then, that Anna Karenina is in her late twenties during the action of the novel that bears her name. Anna's brother Stiva could have been born a few years earlier or later. (We never learn the relative ages of Anna and Stiva.)

It helps to understand the unity of Tolstoy's evolution if we suppose that he gave a further development in *Anna Karenina* to some of the literary personalities that he introduced in *War and Peace*. If we think of Anna and Stiva as Natasha Rostova's grandchildren, we have Anna and Stiva as a brother-sister pair corresponding to Natasha and Nikolay and continuing Rostovian personality traits. As brother and sister, Nikolay and Natasha share the Rostov metonymical sensibility. As brother and sister, Stiva and Anna also share a characteristic—the proclivity to adultery.

More specifically, we may surmise that Tolstoy's creative unconscious realized that it is only something external—the intervention of a servant—that saves Natasha from the social disgrace that Anna's affair with Vronsky brings down on her. I believe that Tolstoy realized in the depths of his creative unconscious that such an external intervention deprived his character of her autonomy, and that this was ultimately an unsatisfactory treatment of the behavior of an impulsive, passionate woman.

In Anna, Tolstoy allowed the full implications of Natasha's personality to play themselves out. If Natasha cannot see anybody in the mirror at the ball except herself, Anna becomes increasingly self-absorbed and paranoiac. She separates herself from Vronsky and from the external world in general. The progression in the forms of suicide that they chose shows an indicative development. The standard manual of the American Psychiatric Association, the *Diagnostic and Statistical Manual of the Mental Disorders*, makes the following useful comment about the various forms of suicide: "Suicidal behavior is often categorized in terms of violence of the method. Generally, overdoses with legal or illegal substances are considered nonviolent in method, whereas jumping, gunshot wounds, and other methods are considered violent."[23] Thus, the fact that Natasha ingests arsenic while Anna throws herself under a train shows the progression of despair in the forms of suicide that they choose, and thus the development from grandmother to granddaughter.

It is noteworthy that the establishment of a connection between Natasha and Anna undercuts the common rhetoric about fate and destiny in Anna's suicide. Jackson speaks of her freedom, and says, "This freedom lies in the conscious choice of a tragic destiny."[24] Remarkably, no one speaks of destiny with regard to Natasha's suicide attempt, and indeed it is not necessary to do so, just as it is not necessary to do with regard to Anna.

In his book *Culture and Explosion*, Yury Lotman describes the process (a favorite word of his) of ascribing inevitability to something that has happened. He writes, "Thus, the moment of the explosion creates an unpredictable situation. Further there occurs a highly curious process: the event that has occurred creates a retrospective glance backwards."[25] To put it more simply, the fact that something has happened means that it was inevitable; it was pre-determined by fate that it should happen. This is a process that often occurs in discussions of Russian literature, but it is a process of assertion, not a process of reasoning.

In *A Labyrinth of Linkages*, his book on *Anna Karenina*, Gary L. Browning emphasizes the recurring image of the peasant, such as the one who is killed when Karenina arrives in Moscow. He writes, "From the text I will marshall evidence to demonstrate how the peasant *allegorically* represents a degraded Karenin, and then Vronsky, and on the *symbolic* level, a more universal, metaphysical desecration and perversion of human law."[26] (Browning's emphasis.)

Two responses to this interpretation may be recorded here. First, it is not necessary to limit the meaning of *Anna Karenina* to the novel itself. To take up Browning's idea of allegory, it is perfectly reasonable to interpret the death of the peasant as an allegory of the way the train and the social changes that it represented was destroying the peasant way of life. This interpretation is bolstered by an application of T.S. Eliot's observation that new works change our perceptions of old ones. Thus, Solzhenitsyn's massive historical novel *The Red Wheel*, to be discussed in the Epilogue, in which the wheel of a locomotive symbolizes the destructive forces that Lenin erroneously thought he could control. There is thus a continuity, a development, from the death of the peasant at the Moscow train station in *Anna Karenina* to the death of Russian society in *The Red Wheel*. An awareness of this continuity enriches our understanding of the deep bond between Tolstoy and Solzhenitsyn as a key aspect of the development of Russian literature in the modern world.

As so many critics have done, Browning believes that he can articulate "Tolstoy's deepest and most essential message," which concerns "the utter futility of seeking enduring happiness in even the most defensible and sincere adulterous relationship."[27] Here too the application of a twenty-first century sensibility makes a difference. If this message is indeed what Tolstoy believed, and it is therefore appropriate to reduce *Anna Karenina* to it, then he makes it easy for people to dismiss him as a prisoner of his time, as an ill-tempered misogynist whose work does not and cannot address the complexities of intimate relationships in our time.

However, it is possible to interpret *Anna Karenina* without allegory and morality, thereby preserving its standing as a work of genius that does speak to our time. A satisfactory psychological explanation of Anna's life and death goes like this: Anna had an inherent psychological imbalance, which did not become apparent as long as she lived in a stable environment. When, however, she stepped outside of that environment, as when she stepped outside of the railroad car, her instability rendered her less and less capable of coping with her circumstances. Her justly famous monolog during the ride to the train station, an extraordinary piece of writing, shows her to be a paranoid schizophrenic. She then commits suicide, as paranoid schizophrenics often do.

Russians often think, and say, that one must resign one's self to one's fate. There are numerous Russian proverbs to this effect, such as "Whatever happens, it's all for the best" (*Chto ni delayetsya, vsyo k luchshemu.*) However, just because Russians believe this, that imposes no obligation on anyone to take it at face value. In this interpretation, *Anna Karenina* shows us an unflinching, exquisitely detailed, portrait of an unstable woman whose circumstances lead to derangement and suicide. It is possible, but by no means necessary, to interpret her suicide as the result of fate or predestination.

A purely psychological interpretation of Anna's suicide has two advantages. First, it brings *War and Peace* together with *Anna Karenina*, thus treating Tolstoy's work as a coherent whole. Second, it relies only on the available evidence; an interpretation of Anna's suicide as the result of fate relies on unproven and unprovable metaphysics.

The same understanding of the continuity of Tolstoy's creative process also justifies treating Konstantin Levin as Nikolay Rostov's grandson. We are told that Nikolay and Marya get married in the fall of 1814, and thus they could have had children of about the same age of those of Natasha and Pierre. One of those children could have been the parent of young Kostya Levin in the 1840s. Both Nikolay Rostov and Konstantin Levin, grandfather and grandson, are occasionally irritable, have limited social skills, and know that life on an aristocratic estate as the only possible one for them. Both are deeply engaged with the life of their peasants.

It makes sense that as a descendant of a Rostov, Konstantin Levin would have such a unified metonymical sensibility that he finds himself tongue-tied in the presence of the woman to whom he wants to propose. In a rare scene in a Tolstoy novel that strains credibility, he writes the first letters of the words of a question in chalk on a tablecloth. Although "There was no possibility that she could understand this complicated phrase." (8, 465) They play this chalk game for a while, but the words do not really matter. Just as his grandfather's inarticulateness did not matter at the crucial moment of proposal, so Levin's does not matter, either. "He couldn't put in the words she meant; but in her beautiful eyes shining with happiness he understood everything that he needed to know." (8, 466) and—such is the metonymical harmony between Tolstoy's characters—Kitty understands him.

After Konstantin and Kitty are married, they eventually have their first quarrel, and his response to it makes perfect sense if we recall Nikolay Rostov's implication that his wife is like his finger. Konstantin states his unified sensibility quite explicitly in Tolstoy's clearest statement of the ultimate quasi-metaphysical unity of husband and wife:

> Then he clearly understood for the first time what he didn't understand, when he led her out of the church after the wedding. *He understood that he was not only close to her, but he now didn't know where she ended and where he began.* He understood that by the agonizing feeling of bifurcation that he experienced in that moment. (9, 59) (My emphasis)

"The agonizing feeling of bifurcation" is what Natasha Rostova experienced at the opera, and what her brother experienced on the battlefield. For his part Konstantin Levin experiences something similar in social situations that create separation, and thus what Shklovsky called estrangement.

Konstantin above all wants to avoid bifurcation and thus the separation of people into classes. This is the emotional subtext of this participation in the wheat harvest. As it happens, this scene offers an exceptionally clear example of the connection between *War and Peace* and *Anna Karenina*.

Before the battle of Austerlitz in *War and Peace*, Kutuzov's chef, a man named Tit (Russian for Titus) appears. And, to relieve the tension before the impending battle, a fellow soldier jokingly says to him "*Tit, stupay molotit'.*" (4, 334) The translation 'Tit, go thresh" loses the pun between the name *Tit* and the verb *molotit'*. An English equivalent that retains the rhyme would be "Titus, sit beside us." The implied comparison is between cutting down soldiers on the field of battle and cutting down stalks of wheat.

In a brief episode that shows both the continuity and contrast between *War and Peace* and *Anna Karenina* Tolstoy retains the character named Tit who sharpens a scythe, but transforms him into a peasant who sharpens Levin's scythe (8, 291) and shows him how to use it. When he merges with the work, he experiences what Natasha experiences when she is dancing: "In his work there now began to occur a change that brought him enormous enjoyment. In the middle of his work minutes during which he forgot what he was doing came over him."[28] (8, 297) In the image of harvesting wheat Tolstoy uses the same image to progress from the war of *War and Peace* to the peace of *Anna Karenina*.

Let us pause here to note that Tolstoy's metonymical sensibility made him unique in his time, and that it created a contrast between his work and that of his contemporaries in the West. In addition to *Anna Karenina*, there is one other famous nineteenth-century novel about adultery, Flaubert's *Madame Bovary*. In it we find the following description of Charles Bovary's cap:

> It was a headgear of composite order, containing elements of an ordinary hat, a hussar's busby, a lancer's cap, a sealskin cap and a nightcap: one of those wretched things whose mute hideousness suggests unplumbed depths, like an idiot's face. Ovoid and stiffened with whalebone, it began with three convex strips; then followed alternating lozenges of velvet and rabbit's fur, separated by a red band; then came a kind of band, terminating in a cardboard-lined polygon intricately decorated with braid. From this hung a long, excessively thin cord ending in a kind of tassel of gold netting. The cap was new; its peak was shiny.[29]

While one may consider this a virtuoso piece of writing, and surmise that it shows the effects of preparing compositions in the *lycée*, it is too over-written to function as a synecdochic detail. (Notice that Tolstoy gives us only one detail about Karenina's handbag, its all-important color.) Various critics have called this a dunce cap, and it may well be that. What it is not is one example among many in a book suffused with synecdochic details, as *Anna Karenina* is, because there is nothing like it in the rest of the novel. That is to say, M. Bovary's cap could function as a metonymic detail, like Karenina's handbag, only if it belonged to a system of other metonymical details in the novel that reveal character either by suggesting patterns of behavior or connections between characters and their environment. Flaubert's novel does neither of these because his novel is about alienation and separation. Metonymy would not have served his purposes and was in any case foreign to his artistic sensibility.

If Tolstoy's novels are principally concerned with the relationship between the social order and the threats to that order, Dostoyevsky's novels deal in one way or another with the relationship between the individual and the transcendent order. Thus, the plots of *Crime and Punishment* and *The Brothers Karamazov* are set in motion by dreams of individualistic assertion by Rodion Raskolnikov and Ivan Karamazov, respectively. Although these dreams lead to the reality of murder, they conclude with assertions of transcendent order (Raskolnikov's sentence in Siberia, which is presented as a pastoral idyll).

Thus, *Crime and Punishment* ends far from the city, in the open spaces of Siberia. *The Brothers Karamazov* also ends with an outdoor scene. This scene, entitled "Ilyushechka's Funeral. The Speech at the Rock" shows Alyosha Karamazov and the boys from the town who gather near a rock after Ilyushechka's funeral. The general tone is ecstatic; the boys vow to remember their dead comrade, and Kolya Krasotkin articulates the theme of death and resurrection that the epigraph states when he asks Alyosha, "Will we rise from the dead and come to life and see each other again, and everybody and Ilyushechka?" Predictably, Alyosha answers, "We'll definitely rise." (10, 338)

This dense, symbolically fraught scene has naturally attracted the attention of Dostoyevsky scholars, and their comments about it show the effect of implicit assumptions in interpretation. Thus, Anna Berman in her article "Siblings in *The Brothers Karamazov,*" says that Dostoyevsky "Emphasizes the sibling relationships because he sees its expansion to all of humanity as a solution to many of the ills he depicts in society."[30] She goes on to say that in this final scene, "This new family is a family of siblings."[31] Since her subject is sibling relationships, she is very concerned to explicate various passages to show the nature of the love that the brothers do, or do not, have for each other.

Also relevant here is Robert Louis Jackson's essay, "Alyosha's Speech at the Stone: 'The Whole Picture'."[32] Like Berman, Jackson believes in explicating the words on the page, to the exclusion of historical context. He concludes, "The speech of Alyosha, and the chorus of voices at the end of the novel (shared in all its purity and joy), form a momentous and symbolic moment."[33] Thus, Berman and Jackson associate themselves with the long line of people who have read Dostoyevsky in a specific, limited way in order to arrive at general conclusions.

If, however, we make different assumptions, we arrive at different conclusions. To begin with, there is the matter of what Russian critics like Bakhtin call Dostoyevsky's poetics. As we know, throughout his career, from *Poor Folk* to *the Brothers Karamazov,* Dostoyevsky created dialogic connections between his work and other literary works. Concentrating on the words on the page to exclusion of everything else makes it easy to forget this essential feature of his work, and to miss a key example of allusion in this scene. Keeping this key fact about Dostoyevsky in mind and incorporating it into an interpretative strategy, we may conclude that he was not a writer who would leave so important a moment as the ending of his last novel without an allusion. As it so often happens in Dostoyevsky, this scene takes on greater importance when we understand its implicit reference.

The Brothers Karamazov begins with the quotation from the Bible, so it is fitting that it ends with a Biblical allusion. (One might say that Dostoyevsky's novels cohere in dialog with the cultural works that gave rise to them.) Dostoyevsky gives us a clue in the title "The Speech at the Rock." This reference to a rock, presumably, a large rock, is an anomaly because we hardly learn anything else about the physical features of Skotoprigonevsk, the provincial town where the novel takes place. So when the final, symbolically fraught scene mentions a physical feature, we have reason to sense the presence of an allusion.

In fact, the allusion is to Matthew 16:18, in which Christ says to Peter, "And I tell you that you are Peter, and on this rock I will build my church, and the gates of Hades will not overcome it." The phrase "the gates of Hades" refers to death, and thus the end of the novel takes us back to the epigraph that begins it, which asserts the dialectic of death and resurrection. Furthermore, the implicit comparison of Alyosha to Peter suggests that Alyosha's ministry in the world may serve as a model for the future of the Orthodox Church.

If one believes that this novel—and in fact any novel—does not consist exclusively of words on the page, but that, rather, readers and scholars may appropriately bring to bear on it their general understanding, then a historicist interpretation emerges.

In *The Brothers Karamazov* Dostoyevsky deals with the situation in which Russians confronted the outside world by moving the monastic ideal into the world. In doing so, he confronted the intractable problem of the relationship between the monastery and the world. Roughly speaking, Alyosha and the boys represent the next generation of the Zosima/Alyosha relationship. Moreover, Berman says, "Dostoevsky emphasizes the sibling relationship because he sees its expansion to all of humanity as a solution to the many ills of society."[34] Strictly speaking, the word "sibling" is too general here. Sibling relationships usually refer to brother-sister relationships, but of course there are no sisters here. These are fraternal relationships in an all-male society, like that of a monastery.

One can reasonably ask about Alyosha and the boys, who supposedly represent the future of Russia, "What is to be done?" Alyosha is in the world, but not of it. He has no job, or anything like what we would call job skills. We never learn where he lives. In short, despite all the good feelings of the moment, we cannot believe that this is a viable community that can be expanded to all of humanity.

The obvious reason that this is not a viable community is that it has no women. Dostoyevsky was a great writer, and he could create women as potential saints, like Sonya Marmeladova in *Crime and Punishment*, victims like Nastasya Fillipovna in *The Idiot*, or objects of lust, like Grushenka in *The Brothers Karamazov*. What he could not do, and what Tolstoy could do so well, was to create married couples. He could create intense, non-sexual relationships between men, but not sexual relationships between men and women.

If we carry through the Biblical quotation implied in "The Speech at the Rock" to its logical conclusion, and bring to bear on it what we know about nineteenth-century culture, then we can conclude that what the scene implies is a celibate utopian community like the Shakers in America. But of course celibate communities cannot create a viable future, and Dostoyevsky, a married man himself, must have had some awareness of this.

In general, the metaphorical element in Dostoevsky, as I have defined it, admits of numerous literary applications. The following discussion will show that it is inadequate to say, as Bakhtin does, that "Everything in Dostoyevsky's novels comes down to dialog, to the dialogic opposition as its center."[35] There is much more to Dostoyevsky than dialog, important though it is. Bakhtin emphasized that the essence of dialog is difference, and to achieve a fuller understanding of Dostoyevsky, one has only to subsume dialog into the list of devices by means of which Dostoyevsky creates heterogeneity, that is to say metaphor. For example, he sometimes does so by beginning a work in one style or genre and then inserting a piece of material in a contrasting style or genre. Like many other recurring features of Dostoyevsky's style, this tendency appears in his very first work of fiction, the parodistic epistolary novel *Poor Folk*. After Makar and Varvara exchange a number of letters, we come upon Varvara's diary, which seems intrusive because it has neither the ironic implications nor the literary associations of Makar's letters.

We find such contrasting styles and genres frequently in his mature work, as in the often-noted differences between parts 1 and 2 of "Notes from the Underground." In *The Idiot* we have Ippolit's "Necessary Confession"; the best-known example is of course "The Legend of The Grand Inquisitor" in *The Brothers Karamazov*. This insertion of chapters with great dramatic intensity and thematic significance that often differ significantly in tone and style from the texts surrounding them is a key indicator of Dostoyevsky's metaphorical imagination.

More generally, one can say that Dostoyevsky's metaphorical creative matrix manifests itself in the fact that he is a profoundly literary writer. It is not just that he is engaged with literature; as we know, Dostoyevsky's characters are engaged with literature, as Tolstoy's characters never are. From *Poor Folk* to *The Brothers Karamazov* Dostoyevsky cites works of literature and incorporates them in increasingly complex ways into his work.

Dostoyevsky gives names symbolic significance, he inevitably creates a contrast, and thus a heterogeneity, between the reader's associations with the writer in question and the reader's experience of Dostoyevsky's text. Dostoyevsky responded intensely to the literature of the past, and he drew on writers as different as Jean Racine and E. T. A. Hoffman, but he really begins and ends with Pushkin and Gogol. Pushkin's symbolic role begins with Pokrovsky's anxiety about the edition of the poet's work in *Poor Folk*. It continues in various ways throughout Dostoyevsky's career: the incorporation of the plot of "The Queen of Spades" in *Crime and Punishment*, the quotations from "The Covetous Knight" in *The Idiot*, and the references to *Yevgeny Onegin* in *The Brothers Karamazov*. In *Poor Folk*, Dostoyevsky is, of course, writing against, and replying to, Gogol's "The Overcoat." *The Brothers Karamazov* makes explicit its combinations of heterogeneous elements in its complex systems of interrelated chapter titles.

In *The Idiot*, Myshkin finds a copy of *Madame Bovary* in Nastasya Filipovna's room; this is both an *hommage* to Flaubert, and a hint at Nastasya Filipovna's infidelity. Similarly, Aglaya Yepanchina laughs when she puts a note from Myshkin in a copy of *Don Quixote*, because she understands the resemblance between them.[36] It is fair to say that no other nineteenth-century writer uses intertextuality as consistently and as ingeniously as Dostoyevsky.

In virtually all Dostoyevsky's major works, he is not content to contrast his own work with that of other writers; he also contrasts literature to visual images, a practice known as ekphrasis. Examples of ekphrasis in Dostoyevsky's work range from the early reference to Karl Bryullov's "The Last Day of Pompeii" in *Poor Folk* through his uses of Hans Holbein's *Madonna* in *The Idiot*.

The ultimate example of his use of painting occurs in *The Brothers Karamazov*, where we read the following in a passage about Smerdyakov: "The painter Kramskoy has a remarkable painting called 'The Contemplator' (*Sozertsatel'*)." There follows a fanciful description of the painting, which shows a peasant walking in the woods, and which concludes with the comment, "There are enough contemplators among the simple folk. One of such contemplators was surely Smerdyakov, and was surely accumulating his impressions with greed, almost not knowing why himself." (9, 161-2). I submit that this is an extraordinary, and probably unique, passage—as unique as the equation in *War and Peace*. I know of no other nineteenth-century novel that includes an explicit comparison between a character in the novel and an actual painting. Dostoyevsky's association of Smerdyakov and Kramskoy's painting bears witness to the novelist's extreme sensitivity to visual stimuli.

Dostoyevsky's use of architecture is related to his use of painting and literature. All three of these art forms have a physical existence outside the pages of his books. He had an extraordinarily intuitive sense for the symbolic potential of windows, which juxtapose public and private space and therefore play an exceptionally important role in his work. From the window through which Makar Devushkin looks at Varvara's window—on the first page of his first published work of fiction! —to the emblematic window in Snegiryov's hut in *The Brothers Karamazov* Dostoyevsky used windows in a variety of creative ways.

As a case in point, consider the following passage from *Crime and Punishment*:

> Raskolnikov passed directly to the -sky Bridge, stopped in the middle, at the railing, leaned on it with both elbows and began to peer outward. After saying goodbye to Razumikhin, he had gotten so weak that he hardly made it this far. He wanted to sit down or lie down somewhere on the street. Leaning over the water, he mechanically looked at the last pink gleam of the sunset, at a row of houses darkening in the gathering twilight, at one distant window somewhere in a garret on the left bank, which was gleaming as though in flame from the last ray of the sun, which struck it for a moment, at the darkened water of the canal and seemed to look attentively at this water. (5:47)

The reference to this window may seem like nothing more than a detail that makes the narrative vivid, but to assume this is to underestimate Dostoyevsky's genius at integrating the elements of his narrative. Dostoyevsky did not just open his work to something heterogeneous, like a painting. He opened his work to the entire city of St. Petersburg, which is why it is helpful to read *Crime and Punishment* with a nineteenth-century map of the city at one's side. A careful reading of this passage combined with a scrutiny of the map shows that this is not just any window. In fact, this is the window in Sonya's room.

Let us consider this passage carefully. In it Raskolnikov is standing on the Ascension (Vosnesensky) Bridge, which takes Ascension Prospect across the Yekaterina Canal, for which Dostoyevsky uses the slang name by which it was known at the time, "the Ditch" (*Kanava*). If Raskolnikov is watching the reflection of the sunset on a window, he must be standing with his back to the sun, and therefore he must be facing east. People who stand on the Ascension Bridge and face east will have on their left the side of the Ditch, on which Carpenter Lane (Stolyarny Pereulok)—the street on which Raskolnikov lives—is located.[37]

With this knowledge, we can return to the text of the novel; in the scene in which Svidrigaylov makes his first appearance, he follows Sonya after she leaves Raskolnikov, and we read, "When Sonya came out onto the Ditch, they were alone on the sidewalk.... Going as far as her apartment house, Sonya turned into the gate... (5, 253). Thus, Sonya lives on the left side of the Ditch from the Ascension Bridge. When we learn, just before Raskolnikov confesses, that the outer wall of Sonya's room, with its symbolic three windows, "faced onto the Ditch" (5, 327), we can be certain that it is Sonya's window that Raskolnikov is looking at in the scene quoted above. Sunshine and water are associated with her here, as elsewhere, because she represents life and salvation. The fact that the ray of sunlight, which symbolizes grace, from her window catches his eye provides a condensed version of the narrative to come. It means that he will ultimately go to her apartment, confess his crime, and take upon himself the suffering which, so the Christ imagery implies, leads to resurrection. Thus, this window beckons to Raskolnikov and foreshadows the extraordinary scene in which Sonia will sit in that room and read the Bible to him, thus bringing him to repentance.[38] What such connections between the text of the novel and the geography of St. Petersburg mean is that heterogeneity appears in Dostoyevsky not just in the juxtaposition of his work to other works of literature, but even in the juxtaposition of his work to the physical spaces of St. Petersburg.

The following exceptionally important narrative comment at the beginning of *The Brothers Karamazov* shows how the late Dostoyevsky developed the elements of the window and the setting sun from the embryonic scene in *Crime and Punish*ment quoted above: "He [Alyosha] recalled a quiet summer evening, an open window, the slanting rays of the setting sun (he remembered the slanting rays most of all), an icon in a room, in a corner, before it a lighted votive lamp, before the icon his mother, sobbing on her knees as if in hysterics, with screechings and wailings." (9, 26) Having received grace through a window here, Alyosha then transmits it in various ways, as when he knocks at the window to end Ivan's nightmarish encounter with the devil and to tell him that Smerdyakov has hanged himself. (10, 180)[39]

The contrast between public and private space that the window represents has an analogy in the recurring motif of the private letter read in public. In *Poor Folk*, Ratazyayev reads one of Devushkin's letters to Varvara aloud to his friends, to his extreme embarrassment. In *Crime and Punishment*, Svidrigailov's wife finds Dunya's letter to her husband, and she turns her public readings of it into a regular concert tour. And of course in *The Brothers Karamazov*, Katya produces a sensation during the trial scene when she produces Mitya's letter in court.

Dostoyevsky's juxtaposition of the heterogeneous elements of private and public experience creates his famous scandal scenes, as I have said, but this juxtaposition appears most clearly in "Notes from the Underground." We may think of Part 1 of that work as the private underground man, which is then undercut by the public underground man in Part 2. This juxtaposition becomes all the more dramatic because of the contrast between his excruciating self-consciousness in part 1 and his naiveté about himself in Part 2.

Part 1 of "Notes" only seems like a monologue.[40] Bakhtin's conclusions are thus consistent with what Jakobson says about someone who has a pronounced tendency toward metaphor: "It is particularly hard for him to perform, or even to understand, such a closed discourse as the monologue."[41]

The generalization has equal validity the other way as well; if there are no monologues in Dostoyevsky, they abound in Tolstoy. After all, as Gleb Struve showed, Nikolay Chernyshevsky coined the term interior monologue to describe the thought processes of Tolstoy's characters in the Sevastopol stories.[42] Moreover, some of the most memorable passages in *War and Peace*, such as Andrey's ruminations on the nature of glory the night before the battle of Borodino, are monologues.

Even when Dostoyevsky gives his characters internal monologues, they are not pure trains of thought, as those of Andrey Bolkonsky are. Dostoyevsky uses metaphoric narrative in the sense that the present and the past, the past and the future, are often juxtaposed in his characters' minds, as in this passage from *Crime and Punishment*: "Suddenly he shuddered: one thought, also yesterday's, again passed through his head. But he shuddered not because this thought passed. After all, he knew, he had a presentiment [*predchuvstvoval*], that it would indeed 'pass' and was already waiting for it; and this thought was not yesterday's thought at all." (5:51) A close analysis of Dostoyevsky's use of the key verb *predchuvst-vovat'*—"to anticipate, to have a presentiment" — will show that his characters often anticipate the future and that the present and the future thus tend to merge in their consciousnesses.

Thus, after Raskolnikov's first visit to see the pawnbroker, he goes to a tavern, and has various thoughts about his agitation. "But even in that moment he distantly anticipated [*predchuvstvoval*] that this receptivity was also morbid." (5, 13) After reading his mother's letters about, among other things, his sister's disdain for Luzhin, he had a thought. "After all he knew, he *anticipated [predchuvstvoval]*, that it would definitely 'fly by' and he was already waiting for it; this thought was not at all yesterday's thought." (5, 51) (Dostoyevsky's emphasis) Later, after he has seen Porfiry Petrovich, we learn of him that "He sort of anticipated [*pred-chuvstvovalos'*] that at least for today he could *almost* certainly consider himself safe." (5, 370) (My emphasis). "Almost" is another word that Dostoyevsky used to undercut meaning, and make everything tentative.

But, of course, Raskolnikov is not the only character who anticipates. His double Razumikhin does, too. He tells Raskolnikov's sister, "I am his friend, so I am your friend as well. I want it like that. I anticipated [*predchuvstvoval*] this last year, there was a moment like that..." (5, 208) However, as a man of reason (*razum*) he is not privy to Raskolnikov's sense of interbeing, of connection, so he immediately undercuts what he says: "I didn't anticipate it all, though, because it is as though you dropped out of the sky." (5, 208)

Such mergers of the present and the future occur rarely if at all in Tolstoy, whose characters are caught up in the moment. As she goes to her first ball, "Natasha had not had a minute of freedom from the morning of that day and had not once managed to give a thought to what awaited her."(5, 221) Tolstoy's characters are often surprised by what happens to them; Dostoevsky's rarely are.

Perhaps it was the complexity that results from merging the present and the future that prompted Dostoyevsky to create one of his most radical innovations—narrative uncertainty. This topic deserves a separate discussion, but here I can cite only one example.

When in *Crime and Punishment* Porfiry Petrovich, while interrogating Raskolnikov, asks him to write a statement. Raskolnikov responds by asking if he should write it on plain paper. Here is Porfiry's response and the narrative comment about it:

> "Oh, on very plain paper, sir!"-and suddenly Porfiry Petrovich somehow looked at him in an obviously mocking way, as he squinted and somehow winked. This, perhaps, only seemed that way to Raskolnikov, though [*vprochem*], because it lasted a moment. At least there was something like that. Raskolnikov would have sworn that he winked at him, God knows what for. (6, 72)

And if we ask, "Did Porfiry Petrovich in fact wink at Raskolnikov?" we find that this question admits of no definite answer. The word *vprochem* that is used here becomes a leitmotif that appears again and again in narrative comments, allowing Dostoyevsky to make emphatic statements and then undercut them in the next clause or the next sentence. The result is that statements are made, only to be turned into possibilities and suggestions. Narrative uncertainty in

Dostoyevsky's works reaches a peak, of course, in *The Brothers Karamazov*, which uses two incommensurable narrative styles and is filled with words like "though" and "perhaps."

In addition to undercutting the distinction between what did and did not happen, Dostoyevsky also undercuts a distinction so essential that no one thinks to discuss it, namely the distinction between individuals. As a result, what has been called interbeing exists between some of his characters. However, the connections between individuals are not metonymical family resemblances, as in Tolstoy's work, but are more general.

Thus, in the scene in which Porfiry Petrovich may—or may not—have winked at Raskolnikov, we read "'He knows!' flashed in him like lightning." (5, 260) In their third and final encounter/dialog/duel, Raskolnikov asks Porfiry, "Who committed the murder?" Porfiry replies:

> "Who committed the murder?" he repeated as thought not believing his own ears "Well, *you* committed the murder, Rodion Romanich. You committed the murder, sir" he added almost in a whisper, in a completely convinced voice. (5, 476) (Dostoyevsky's emphasis)

Yes, Porfiry Petrovich knows, and presumably he has always known, ever since the first time Raskolnikov went to see him.

The question of how Porfiry Petrovich knows remains a mystery, and thus *Crime and Punishment* is as unique in its time as *War and Peace* is. They are both distinguished from other novels written in the 1850s and 1860s by their coherence, although they treat coherence in radically different ways. There is nothing like the through line of character-family-place that we find in Tolstoy either in Western novels written at the time, or in Dostoyevsky. Only in *The Brothers Karamazov* did Dostoyevsky treat family relationships in detail, and even then they are not connected to a particular place.

Dostoyevsky creates multiple kinds of coherence in *Crime and Punishment* by undercutting the usual distinctions between one character and another, and between the past and the present. Although the characters of the novel are as much creatures of St. Petersburg as Tolstoy's Bolkonskys are, they have not fully internalized its mores. It remains an external environment to them. This is why we can follow their movements on a map. One might say that St. Petersburg inhabits the Bolkonskys in *War and Peace*, whereas the characters of *Crime and Punishment* inhabit the city.

The differences between Tolstoy and Dostoyevsky appear clearly in the different ways in which they started their longest novels. Tolstoy begins *War and Peace in media res*, with dialog (in French, to be sure) about Napoleon's latest exploits. He then uses Anna Pavlovna's soirée to introduce some of his principal characters and to create the ambience of St. Petersburg. By contrast, it takes Dostoyevsky a full 36 pages of dense exposition to get to his first dialog. It is as though he uses this exposition as a test that the reader must pass in order to get to the novel proper.

This is what Dostoyevsky does, though, and there is more to the opening pages of *The Brothers Karamazov* than that. Here is the first sentence of the novel:

> Aleksey Fyodorovich Karamazov was the third son of a landowner of our province, Fyodor Pavlovich Karamazov, so famous in his time (and still remembered among us) because of his tragic and dark demise, which occurred exactly 13 years ago, and about which I will communicate in its place. (9, 11)

This sentence carries as much thematic weight as the first sentence of Solzhenitsyn's *August 1914*. Since Karamazov's "tragic and dark demise" is still remembered among us, then the novel as a whole represents the merger of the past and the present. No longer does Dostoyevsky need to do that through the presentiments of individual characters.

There are no murders in Tolstoy's work before the 1880s. Even during his battle scenes, no soldier ever aims a rifle and kills a member of the opposing army. Dostoyevsky differs strikingly from Tolstoy on each of these points. Because of his metaphorical imagination, Dostoyevsky needs fewer characters and fewer places than Tolstoy; the passage of time has relatively little significance. One might say Dostoyevsky's need for metaphorical juxtapositions creates a centrifugal force in his characters, which then meets the centripetal force of family and society-most obviously in *The Brothers Karamazov*, but in other works as well. On the other hand, Tolstoy's need for metonymical relationships creates a centripetal force that pulls his characters away from art and memory, drawing them toward hearth and home. If families define Tolstoy's characters, they confine Dostoyevsky's characters; a comparison and contrast of these two authors' treatments of families may serve to bring this essay to a close.

The differences between the two writers' treatments of families are as systemic as their other differences. With respect to family groups, Dostoyevsky uses relationships between brothers-either biological brothers in the obvious example of *The Brothers Karamazov*, or spiritual brothers as in the case of Raskolnikov and

Razumikhin in *Crime and Punishment*, and Myshkin and Rogozhin in *The Idiot*. To take the obvious example again, Dostoyevsky depicts a brother and sister in Rodion and Avdotya Raskolnikov, but Avdotya is a much less important character than her brother, although they share the family trait of pride. There are no female Karamazovs at all, of course, and Dostoyevsky's most powerful female character, Nastasya Filipovna in *The Idiot*, has no significant family relationships. By contrast, it would appear that Tolstoy's metonymical imagination allowed him to use brother-sister pairs in his most important works precisely because their personalities were similar enough to balance out their gender differences.[43] He could present these siblings as the result of the natural processes of birth and growth, processes that produced people with similar behaviors.

Unlike Tolstoy's epic chronicles, Dostoyevsky's major novels usually take place in one place during a limited period. As if in compensation, however, his characters often evoke the past through their stories about it and reach beyond the place of action with their artistic references. Again, unlike Tolstoy, Dostoyevsky often creates a direct confrontation of opposites. This conflict, which is verbal at first, often leads to murder. Although several of Dostoyevsky's characters commit suicide, they invariably do so after first committing murder.

Although this long chapter has not said everything that could be said about the comparisons and contrasts between Tolstoy and Dostoyevsky, it may come to a conclusion by acknowledging the limits of scholarship and of scholarly inquiry. The appearance of genius will always remain a mystery, although we can say various things about the life circumstances that shape it in one way or another. There was absolutely nothing in Tolstoy's family background, or in Dostoyevsky's family background, that prepares us for their genius. How then are we to understand Tolstoy and Dostoyevsky in the context of their time? I offer two possibilities.

The first of these is to repeat my conclusion from the fact that the work of Tolstoy and Dostoyevsky, like that of Emily Dickinson and Walt Whitman a continent and an ocean away, does not admit of detailed comparisons with their contemporaries in Europe. The cultural heritage of their respective countries, different though it was, produced a similar effect, as a result of which these four great artists worked more or less independently of the literary trends that predominated in Europe at the time.

In this sense Russia is different from the West, i.e., Western Europe, and has therefore produced literature that is different from that produced in Western Europe. Nevertheless, Russia belongs to Christian Europe, and her Christian heritage offers a way to connect Tolstoy and Dostoyevsky to European culture, if not necessarily to European literature.

Tolstoy and Dostoyevsky both used Biblical epigraphs for their last novels. In doing so, they affirmed the operation of a transcendent order in the lives of their characters. In doing so, they set themselves against the secularizing trends of their times. Since they really do not belong to their own times, they can be assimilated to the earlier anti-secularizing trend in the name of Christianity, the Baroque. It makes sense to think of them as representing something like a latter-day Eastern European Counter-Reformation. Like the great Baroque artists who responded to the Reformation with ever more elaborate churches and altarpieces, Tolstoy and Dostoyevsky responded to the secularizing trends of their times by writing very long novels of unprecedented intricacy that affirmed a transcendent order.

Notes

1　See an early work on the subject, Lev Shestov, *Dostoevsky, Tolstoy, and Nietzsche* (Athens, Ohio, 1969); this translation conveniently brings together Shestov's two books *Dobro v uchenii gr. Tolstogo i F Nitshe* and *Dostoyevsky i Nitsshe: Filosofiya tragedii.* Also from the Symbolist era is Dmitry Merezhkovsky, *L. Tolstoy i Dostoevsky* (Moscow: Nauka, 2000).

2　Isaiah Berlin, *The Hedgehog and the Fox. An Essay on Tolstoy's View of History* (Princeton: Princeton U. Press, 2013).

3　George Steiner, *Tolstoy or Dostoevsky. An Essay in Contrast* (London/Boston: Faber and Faber, 1959).

4　Caryl Emerson, *All the Same the Words Won't Go Away. Essays on Authors, Heroes, Aesthetics, and Stage Adaptations from the Russian Tradition* (Brookline: Academic Studies Press, 2010), 193.

5　Leon Surette, "Metaphor and Metonymy: Jakobson Reconsidered." *University of Toronto Quarterly*, Vol. 56, No. 4 (Summer, 1987), 551.

6　Ludwig von Bartalanffy, *General Systems Theory: Foundations, Development, Applications* (New York: George Braziller, Inc., 2015).

7　Vera Zubaryova, *Chekhov v XXI veke: Positsionnyj stil' i komediya novogo tipa.* (Idyllwild: Charles Schlacks, Jr., 2015), 17.

8　Roman Jakobson, "Two Aspects of Language and Two Aspects of Aphasic Disturbances," *Selected Writings II* (The Hague-Paris: Mouton, 1971), 256.

9　*Ibid.*, 257.

10　Here is the kind of minor detail that only repeated readings of *War and Peace* allow one to identify. The red purse makes its first appearance when Anna settles herself in her train seat for her return trip from Moscow to St. Petersburg" "She opened and closed her red purse with her small agile hands." (8, 121) The way she fusses with her purse hints at her inner agitation, of course.

11 In the interest of integrating literary studies with the intellectual discourse of our day, I direct the interested reader to Malcolm Gladwell's book *Blink*. In it he discusses the findings of psychologists, who have shown that only very brief observations of people, which are called "thin slices," may lead to valid conclusions about behavior and relationships. Logically, thin slices can have general validity only if the situations are such that the part can stand for the whole—that is to say, if the situations allow for metonymical analysis. These "thin slices" of behavior correspond to what I have called "anticipatory microcosms" that Tolstoy created for his major characters, and for some of the minor ones as well. See Gladwell's chapter "The Theory of Thin Slices: How a Little Bit of Knowledge Goes a Long Way," in *Blink. The Power of Thinking Without Thinking* (Boston: Little Brown and Company, 2005). If we can indeed say that Tolstoy's anticipatory microcosms of behavior correspond to subliminal clues that people unconsciously perceive, then this correspondence provides an explanation for why readers find Tolstoy's work so lifelike.

12 Jakobson, "Two Aspects of Language," 258.

13 One partial exception to this generalization occurs in *Anna Karenina*, when two characters are arguing about Christian art, and one of them mentions Ivanov's "The Appearance of Christ to the People." (9, 51) But Tolstoy makes no effort to connect this or any other painting to the themes and characters of the novel, as Dostoyevsky would have done. Surely the fact that in all of Tolstoy's vast oeuvre there is only one passing reference to a famous painting proves the point that visual images did not stimulate his creative process.

14 Gary L. Browning, "Symbolism: The Train Ride," *A "Labyrinth of Linkages" in Tolstoy's "Anna Karenina"* (Brookline: Academic Studies Press, 2010), 26.

15 Robert Louis Jackson, 'Braking the Moral Barrier: Anna Karenina's Night Train to St. Petersburg," *Close Encounters* (Brookline: Academic Studies Press, 2019), 94.

16 Morson, *Hidden in Plain View*, 228-9.

17 Metonymy establishes connections between like entities. In mathematics this is what an equal sign in an equation does, and *War and Peace* is probably the only nineteenth-century novel that contains an equation. In one of the historical essays, Tolstoy analyzes an imaginary battle in the following way: "Consequently, four were equal to fifteen, and, consequently, $4x = 15y$. Consequently, $x{:}y = 15{:}4$. The equation does not give the value of the unknown, but it gives the relationship between the two unknowns." (7:142)

18 Viktor Shklovsky, "Iskusstvo kak priyom," *O teorii prozy*, 2nd ed. (Moscow, 1929), 14.

19 Viktor Shklovsky, *Mater'yal i stil' v romane L'va Tolstogo, "Voyna i mir"* (Moscow: Federatsiya, 1929), 118

20 See Anna Berman, *Siblings in Tolstoy and Dostoevsky: The Path to Universal Brotherhood.* (Evanston: Northwestern U. Press, 2015).

21 Anna A. Berman, "The Sibling Bond: A Model for Romance and Motherhood in *War and Peace*." *Tolstoy Studies Journal*, Vol. XVIII (2006), 3.

22 *Ibid.*, 10.

23 *Diagnostic and Statistical Manual of Mental Disorders*, 5th ed. (Washington and London: American Psychiatric Publish, 2013), 801.

24 Robert Louis Jackson, "Chance and Design: Anna Karenina's First Meeting with Vronsky," *Close Encounters*, 93.

25 Yury Lotman, *Kul'tura i vzryv* (Moscow: "Gnosis," 1992), 194.

26 Browning, *A "Labryinth of Linkages*," 35.

27 *Ibid.*, 119.

28 Levin is having a common experience during moments of peak physical exertion. Athletes call this experience "being in the zone."

29 *Diagnostic and Statistical Manual of Mental Disorders*, 5th ed. (Washington and London: American Psychiatric Publish, 2013), 4.

30 Anna Berman, "Siblings in *The Brothers Karamazov*." *The Russian Review*, Vol. 68 (April, 2009), 281.

31 *Ibid.*, 282.

32 Robert Louis Jackson, "Alyosha's Speech at the Stone: 'The Whole Picture,'" *A New Word on 'The Brothers Karamazov','*" Robert Louis Jackson, ed. (Evanston: Northwestern U. Press, 2004), 234-54.

33 *Ibid.*, 250.

34 Berman, "Siblings....," 281.

35 Bakhtin, *Problemy poetiki Dostoyevskogo*, 434.

36 With regard to intertextuality in Dostoyevsky, see Nina Perlina, *Varieties of Poetic Utterances: The Poetics of Quotation in "The Brothers Karamazov"* (Lanham University of Press of America, 1985).

37 There are very few random details in *Crime and Punishment*. Dostoyevsky chose Carpenter Lane as the street on which Raskolnikov lives because carpentry was the profession traditionally ascribed to Christ.

38 For more details on these matters, see James M. Curtis, "Spatial Form as the Intrinsic Genre of Dostoevsky's Novels." *Modern Fiction Studies*, Vol. 18, No. 2 (Summer, 1972), 135-54. For more detail on the significance of bridges in *Crime and Punishment*, see an essay that refers to my work, Richard Gill, "The Bridges of St. Petersburg: A Motif in *Crime and Punishment*." *Dostoevsky Studies*, Vol. 3 (1982), 145-55.

39 I am indebted to Robert Belknap for these examples of the way grace is transmitted through a window. See Robert Belknap, *The Structure of "The Brothers Karamazov"* (The Hague: Mouton, 1967).

40 See Bakhtin, *Problemy poetiki Dostoyevskogo*, 391-408.

41 Jakobson, "Two Aspects of Language," 62-3.

42 See Gleb Struve, "*Monologue interieure:* The Origins of the Formula and the First Statement of the Possibilities," *PMLA*, 69 (1954), 1101-11.

43 Although the narrator in the *Childhood, Boyhood,* and *Youth* trilogy has brothers, they are of limited importance.

VI.

Why Are Russian Novels So Long?

The Soviet Union collapsed in 1991, and all the major players in Soviet literary history, both the groups of bureaucrats and the writers, which sometimes overlapped, are now dead. The deaths of Joseph Brodsky in 1996 and of Aleksandr Solzhenitsyn twelve years later in 2008 ended not just the careers of the two most famous dissident writers, but also the narrative of repression and exile in the Soviet era.[1] Intellectual as well as social barriers fell away; the two major barriers were the ones between East and West and between Russia before 1917 and Russia after 1917.

In the twenty-first century we therefore assume as a matter of course that it is instructive to juxtapose works by Russian writers with those by Western writers in order to understand how writers in both regions responded to the upheavals of the twentieth century. A key assumption is that some of the shared social experiences of the twentieth century in Russia as well as in the West found analogous literary expression in works by sensitive writers in both countries.

The passage of time often makes the task of understanding such cultural issues easier, as in the case of Osip Mandelstam, for instance. By 1922, five years had passed since the revolution. Even while Lenin had two more years to live, Mandelstam understood all too well what kinds of men the Bolshevik leaders were and what kind of regime they were creating. He expressed this understanding in

Mandelstam's typically indirect way in his poem "The Age," which begins with this question:

> My age, my beast, who will be able
> To look into your pupils
> And glue together with his blood
> The vertebrae of two centuries?[2]

Mandelstam perceived the great trauma of the revolution as conceptual, not political, because it severed (or at least Lenin *said* that it severed) the living connection between the past and the present—specifically, the connection between the nineteenth and the twentieth centuries that made meaning possible.

For Mandelstam the implicit answer to his question was "I will be able to glue together the vertebrae of the two centuries." More generally, he could have said that he would be able to bring together not just this century with the preceding one but also the twentieth century with the distant past, including the past of classical antiquity. Thus, much of his subsequent work, such as his poems about the great artists ("Bach") and buildings of the past ("Hagia Sophia") contribute to his larger project of establishing the connection between the present and the past that Lenin and the Bolsheviks had so grievously imperiled.

As a practical matter, nothing could have assuaged the pain that Mandelstam's isolation caused him. (But it was nevertheless this pain that gave rise to much of his best work.) Although the Soviet authorities marginalized Mandelstam and made him an outsider, he was not as isolated as he thought in his desire or need to create the wholeness of time by bringing together the past and the present. Indeed, just such a desire/need constitutes an essential feature of Russian literature, and it gave rise to the feature that most people associate with it, which is the long novel. Moreover, since the long novel represents the best and best-known work of some of the twentieth century's greatest prose writers, it forms a common element between Russian and Western literature in the modern era. Discussions of this genre therefore promote the integration of Russian and Western literary history.

We may begin a discussion of long novels in Russia with the well-known masterpieces of the nineteenth century:

Leo Tolstoy,

War and Peace (1863-9) 1, 270 pages[3]
Anna Karenina (1876-7) 859 pages

Fyodor Dostoyevsky,

> *Crime and Punishment* (1866) 500 pages
> *The Idiot* (1868) 736 pages
> *The Brothers Karamazov* (1879-80) 992 pages

These novels have an average length of 879 pages.

It may be noted parenthetically that these five novels, which rank among the greatest ever written, were written in a period of 17 years, by two men who had lost their fathers at an early age. For all their obvious differences, the two longest of these novels, *War and Peace* and *The Brothers Karamazov,* share a common element, one that Mandelstam would have heartily endorsed, because they both may be said to restore the wholeness of time. As we know, at the very beginning of *The Brothers Karamazov* the narrator announces that the events of what he calls "the first novel," specifically the murder of Fyodor Karamazov, took place thirteen years ago "and are still remembered among us." (9, 11) This key statement establishes a connection between the events of the past and present-day narration.

In one way or another, all historical novels establish a connection between the past, in which the events depicted take place, and the present, when readers read about those events. In the 1860s, when *War and Peace* appeared, the emancipation of the serfs had called into question just this connection. Since serfdom had existed for centuries, Russians understandably felt cut off from their past. One could say, then, that part of Tolstoy's purpose in writing his novel was not so much to glorify the good old days, as to establish the mores and personalities of the good old days when the aristocracy dominated Russian society. This impetus is especially clear in the first Moscow scene, the scene of Natasha's name-day.

When the two most important novels ever written in Russian—and two of the most important novels ever written at any time in any language—share a common impetus in this way, we are well advised to inquire as the origins of this impetus in Russian history. It is a long-standing goal of Russian studies to bring together literature and politics, and I propose to do so here without regard for personalities or ideology. Rather, there were, and are, long-term historical forces at work that created the kind of patterns which Mandelstam took such delight in recognizing.

Understanding just what kinds of patterns appear in the interaction between literature and politics in Russia requires another necessarily cumbersome list, one that will be familiar to those who have studied Russian history. This list will be followed by an explanation that will show its relevance for literature.

Years in Power for Russian Leaders

Ivan the Terrible 1533-1583
Mikhail Romanov 1613-1645
Aleksey Mikhaylovich 1645-1676
Peter the Great 1696-1725
Catherine the Great 1762-1796
Aleksandr I 1801-1825
Nicholas I 1825-1855
Aleksandr II 1855-1881
Aleksandr III 1881-1894
Nicholas II 1894-1917
Vladimir Lenin 1918-1924
Joseph Stalin 1927-1953
Leonid Brezhnev 1964-1982
Mikhail Gorbachov 1985-1991
Vladimir Putin 2000-?

Behind the dates of this seemingly bland list lurk multiple disasters, dramas, and power struggles. For example, when Ivan the Terrible died in 1683, the terrible period of chaos and social disorder known in Russia as the Time of Troubles ensued, a period that lasted for thirty years. The Time of Troubles came to an end only with the election of Mikhail Romanov in 1613 as tsar by the National Assembly, an action that began the Romanov dynasty. When Peter the Great died a little over a century later in 1725, a confused period of short reigns began. In 1762 the Russian husband of the German princess (later known as Catherine the Great) died under mysterious circumstances. Catherine probably had him murdered and she ascended the throne for a long reign. Her son followed her but soon died, giving way to Aleksandr I. When Aleksandr I died in 1825, a group of idealistic young officers questioned the succession in a doomed, amateurish coup known as the Decembrist uprising, which led to the long reign of Nicholas I.

Succession in Russia proceeded more or less smoothly, or at least predictably, in the nineteenth and early twentieth centuries. In the context of Russian history, the revolution and civil war of 1917-1918 can be considered an especially virulent succession crisis, in which Lenin and the Bolsheviks questioned the legitimacy of Nicholas II and all that he represented. Needless to say, there was no plan for nominating a successor to Lenin, and, in fact, Lenin on his death bed in 1924 said in his Testament that nobody but him could govern the Soviet Union. He had devoted his life to the creation of the Soviet Union; however, that the Soviet Union would be ungovernable after his death did not concern him.

Predictably, Lenin's death was followed by a debilitating, protracted succession crisis that dominated Communist Party politics for several years until Stalin out-maneuvered Trotsky and had him expelled from the Soviet Union in 1927. And then, of course, when Stalin died in 1953, a time of severe anxiety among the party elite ensued. Nikita Khrushchev held power for less than ten years, giving way to the long tenure of Leonid Brezhnev. When Brezhnev died, a succession of men held power briefly, giving way to Mikhail Gorbachov, who held power just long enough to preside over the dissolution of the Soviet Union. After the short, problematic tenure of Boris Yeltsin, Vladimir Putin took over and with various titles has held power to date.

Presenting these well-known facts about the tenure in power of major Russian leaders in this way establishes a fundamental, recurring pattern that has existed in Russian politics for over five centuries. Summarizing the events hidden in the list above, we can say the following: A chaotic period ends when a strong leader comes to power. That strong leader holds power for a considerable amount of time—often for several decades. Sooner or later, though, the leader dies and in the absence of a succession plan a power struggle follows. People with varying claims to legitimacy seize power, usually for fairly short periods. Then a new strong leader eventually appears, and the pattern begins again.

In short, the pattern in which a long tenure in power of a strong leader is followed by a period of struggles over legitimacy constitutes an essential recurring feature of Russian history, and we may well ask about its origins.

Like so much else in Russian history, the pattern of recurring succession crises derives from the enduring significance of the monastery as the key institution in Russian life. If monastic principles emphasized fasting and the denial of the body's needs, and if icons depicted monastic saints in two-dimensional, dematerialized formats, then it makes sense that Russians would be unable to acknowledge the body, and therefore the mortality, of the leader. In *Stalin's Soviet Monastery* I used the admittedly awkward word "decorporealization" (the Russian is *obesteleniye*) to describe this denial of the body, which has had such far-reaching consequences in Russia.

The enduring legacy of decorporealization explains a vital fact about Russian history. If the Russians cannot acknowledge that their leaders have bodies, then it follows that they also cannot acknowledge that their leaders will die. In the absence of such an acknowledgment, they have no rationale for establishing a succession plan. Since they cannot do that, they also have never been able to say some variant of the formula that ensured the succession of kings in both France and England: "The King is dead; long live the King."

It may well be that Russians have a subconscious sense that it would be sacrilegious to create a written, or at least widely known and accepted, succession plan. (Dostoyevsky's hostility toward written laws and Lenin's refusal to grant the Soviet Union a constitution have great relevance here.) In short, because of this age-old reluctance or inability to establish a succession plan, crises after the death of a leader have occurred more or less predictably and regularly.

The alternation of a strong leader whose tenure in power lasts for several decades and whose death is followed by upheavals and uncertainties has prevailed for so long that it seems an unchangeable, permanent feature of Russian life. This consistency is so striking that it has moved thoughtful Russians such as historian Boris Ilizarov to propose a psychological and perhaps even a genetic explanation. Ilizarov writes in his book about Stalin, "We Russians lack the governmental talent, the social sense, the historical creativity, to break out of the system of endless return to tyranny."[4]

The question that has immediate relevance for his essay is this: What do these succession crises mean for literature? The answer is that it appears that Russian writers, at some level of consciousness, have taken it on themselves to do what their government cannot, or will not, do. Mandelstam was by no means the only writer who proposed to create the wholeness of time by showing the connections between various time periods. This is why Hamlet's famous lines in Act I, Scene 5, of *Hamlet* reverberate endlessly in the minds of Russian artists: "The time is out of joint;/ O curs'd spite/That ever I was born to set it right!" These lines, and Hamlet's dilemma in general, help to explain the fixation on Hamlet in Russia. One of many relevant examples is Yury Zhivago's poem "Hamlet" at the end of *Doctor Zhivago*.

Clearly, then, Mandelstam's dilemma in 1922 was not unique to him and to his age, although at the time it must have seemed so to him. As a case in point, Pushkin's only full-length play, the neo-Shakespearean *Boris Godunov*, which is best known in Modest Mussorgsky's operatic version, deals with a succession crisis, and the ongoing related question of the legitimacy of political power in Russia. The dilemma of the succession crisis and thus of the connection between time periods, occurred with greater severity after 1917 (hence Mandelstam's anguish about it), but it was not unique to that period. It was a dilemma to which Tolstoy and Dostoyevsky, among others, responded by creating their greatest works.

The richness of Russian literature suggests a counter-intuitive principle about the relationships between art and politics that result from the previous discussion and will inform the discussion that follows. As much as we may wish that artists might live in a well-ordered society that offers them creative freedom and financial support, the evidence from different countries and different time periods does not suggest that such a society produces great art. Denmark, for example, is just such a well-ordered society with honest politicians, good schools and efficient public transportation, but it has produced very little great art. On the other hand, Renaissance Florence was an unstable city torn by civil strife, and it produced great art. The great artists of the time, like Michelangelo, could often hear fighting in the streets while they were working on their now famous masterpieces.

The evidence of Renaissance art, of the literature of the American South, as well as the evidence of Russian literature, thus suggests the following principle: Artists are attracted to and stimulated by, social dysfunction, because it gives them something to work with. Or, to put it another way: however undesirable it is in obvious ways, social dysfunction tends to promote creativity. This principle is a more general version of the pattern of family dysfunction and parental loss that provides a key to the creativity of the Russian classics in the nineteenth century. If Russian families abound in personal dysfunction, Russian history abounds in social dysfunction of varying degrees of severity, from five centuries of succession crises to the gulag and beyond.[5]

A key issue in nineteenth-century Russian classics was whether or not literary characters experience personal change. By contrast, the long novel in the twentieth century usually portrays large-scale social change rather than personal change, although the two issues are obviously related. It takes many words to fill up hundreds of pages, and writers use those words to create multiple characters in their social interactions. The exception that proves the rule about the predominance of social change over personal change in twentieth-century literature is the very long novel by the greatest French prose stylist of the twentieth century, Marcel Proust. His multi-volume *In Search of Lost Time* (1913-27) is 4, 215 pages long and has a narrator who takes such intense, granular interest in the habits and day-to-day activities of the inhabitants of his village that if social change does occur, he barely notices it. However, the twentieth-century novelists not named Proust, who were attracted to the long form, often exploited the dramatic possibilities of showing characters caught up in war and revolution and social change of various kinds.[6]

Here is a selective list of seven relevant authors with birth and death dates and their long Russian historical novels written after 1917:

- Konstantin Fedin (1892-1977), *Cities and Years* (1924); 384 pages.

- Mikhail Sholokhov (1905-84), *The Quiet Don* (volumes 1-3, 1928-32; volume 4, 1937-40); 1600 pages.
- Vasily (Iosif) Grossman (1905-64) *Life and Fate* (written in the 1950s; first Russian publication in the 1980s in Switzerland); 783 pages.
- Konstantin Simonov (1915-79); *The Living and the Dead*, a trilogy whose parts were published in 1959, 1962, and 1971. 1, 279 pages.
- Aleksandr Fadeyev (1901-56), *The Young Guard* (1946; 1951); 504 pages.
- Boris Pasternak (1890 -1960), *Doctor Zhivago* (1960); 768 pages.
- Aleksandr Solzhenitsyn (1918-2008), *The Red Wheel* (1990; 2007-9); 4, 650 pages.[7]

The average length of the first six of these novels is 1,162 pages. Without regard to the quality of the writing, this increase in the length of the novels is a cultural phenomenon worth noting in itself. Moreover, this figure of 1, 162 pages does not take into consideration Solzhenitsyn's gargantuan multi-volume *The Red Wheel*, which is 4, 650 pages long. Moreover, *The Red Wheel* was first published in Paris by YMCA Press in an edition with very small print, so the length of the novel in a typical edition would go well over 5,000 pages.

In French, *The Red Wheel* would be called a *roman-fleuve*, a "river-novel," a novel so long that it flows like a river. French writers of the *roman-fleuve* include Proust, of course, as well as Roger Martin du Gard, author of *The Thibaults* (1922-40), and Jules Romans, author of *Les Hommes de Bonne Volonté* (1932-47). In English there is Patrick O'Brian's 20-volume novel Aubrey-Maturin series set in the Royal Navy during the Napoleonic Wars, which began publication in 1969.

However, none of these and other authors of *romans-fleuves* employ what might be called Solzhenitsyn's Proustian concept of the multi-volume historical novel. That is to say, he does not tell the story of a family, as du Gard does, and does not portray the distant past, like O'Brian.[8] Like Proust, Solzhenitsyn has an obsessive need to restore lost time, but on a vastly broader scale than anything that Proust ever imagined. Solzhenitsyn presents various levels of Russian society, including Nicholas II as well as ministers, generals, intellectuals, and revolutionaries. Although he gives appropriate space to Nicholas and Alexandra, unlike most writers of *romans-fleuves*, he has little interest in families, and family interactions. Some of his chapters are standalone pieces that present the thoughts and actions of a single individual who is caught up in the turbulent events of the time. The next chapter may begin without any transition at all, and may present a different, unrelated character.

Like all the writers in this list, Solzhenitsyn began his career in the Soviet period, and they were all formed by it in one way or another. Four of them (Fedin, Sholokhov, Simonov and Fadeyev) became pillars of the mid-century Soviet literary establishment. Fadeyev was General Secretary of the Writers' Union from 1946 until his suicide in 1956; Fedin was First Secretary of the Writers' Union from 1959 to 1971. Sholokhov received the Nobel Prize for Literature in 1965. Simonov won no less than six Stalin Prizes. On the other hand, Solzhenitsyn, Pasternak, and Grossman experienced the full force of the condemnation, not just of the Soviet literary establishment, but also of the Soviet government. Their masterpieces, which were the long novels that made their reputations, could only be published in Russia either toward the end of the Soviet period, or after the collapse of the Soviet Union in 1991.

In addition to the political reasons their work was censored, one can also cite the demographic reasons. Pasternak and Grossman were Jews, and although in the twenties and thirties Jews had been prominent in film (Eisenstein and Vertov), in art (Falk and Sterenberg), as well as in poetry (Mandelstam, of course), they had not been so prominent in prose. (Yury Tynyanov wrote historical novels, and Ilya Ehrenburg spent most of his career in Europe. They are the exceptions that prove the rule about Jewish writers.)

The purpose of this essay is to use these seven authors and related works to create something like a Mandelstamian moment of recognition for the twentieth-century Russian novel, a wholeness of history, that is to say, a wholeness of literary history. It proposes to do so by showing that these seven extraordinarily prolific writers have more in common than an examination of their radically different careers might suggest. An examination of what they have in common, not just with each other but also with comparable writers in the West, continues Mandelstam's project of bringing together the past and the present.

Like the nineteenth century Russian classics discussed previously, six of these men share a key biographical experience. Unlike Pasternak, a rare Russian writer who had a good childhood, they had impaired relationships with their fathers. Thus, another list:

- Simonov never knew his father, a general who died in 1915 during World War I.
- Fedin ran away from home at an early age because his father, who owned a stationery story, insisted that he go into business with him.
- Sholokhov was an illegitimate child.
- Grossman's parents divorced when he was still a young boy.

- Fadeyev's father Aleksandr died in 1917, when his son Aleksandr was 16.
- Solzhenitsyn was a posthumous son. His father Isay Solzhenitsyn died in 1918 when his mother was pregnant.[9]

In this group of six Russian writers we find the most common types of impaired relationships with fathers—early death, illegitimacy, and lack of support for the son's ambitions—that are related to literary achievement. Detailed biographical studies of other prominent Soviet writers would probably find similar family patterns.[10]

The four loyalist Soviet writers were all born in the pre-revolutionary Russian countryside, and this fact, along with their impaired relationships with their fathers, explains a good deal about their careers.[11] For one thing, it helps to explain their adherence to traditional literary forms; they disdained the artistic experimentations that in Russia were consistently associated with Moscow and St. Petersburg. These were of course just the experimentations that Pasternak the Muscovite and the son of an eminent painter found stimulating. They were the lucky writers whose middle-of-the road tastes matched the comparable tastes of Soviet leaders like Stalin and Khrushchev, who had also grown up in small towns, and who also retained a village mentality throughout their lives.

More generally, their impaired relationships with their fathers inclined them to associate themselves with the rebellious ethos of the revolution. They found in Nicholas II a widely disliked father figure against whom they could rebel as part of a larger movement. Because they all experienced dizzying social change, as is usually the case with boys who have impaired relationships with their fathers, they had biographically driven needs to make sense of their lives. Fortunately for them, these needs merged with the needs of the Soviet authorities to promote literature that made sense of the history that they had all lived through.[12]

Although Bulgakov's *The Master and Margarita* is not a historical novel, when we combine it with Grossman's *Life and Fate*, and Pasternak's *Doctor Zhivago*, we find that these three novels constitute an astonishing sequence of sustained literary achievement. Among other things, they attest to the high level of achievement that was possible in, and partially because of, the oppressive conditions in which they were written.

All three of these novels, each of which is brilliant in its way, consist of different juxtaposed elements. *The Master and Margarita* consists of two sets of chapters, the Woland chapters, and the Master and Margarita chapters. *Life and Fate* has a remarkable variety of writing styles and ranges widely over Germany and the Soviet Union. And, of course, *Doctor Zhivago* combines prose and poetry.

In each of these three cases, then, the writer invites his readers to integrate the work into a whole by juxtaposing these disparate elements.[13]

In *The Master and Margarita*, *Life and Fate*, and *Doctor Zhivago*, an unspoken assumption is that the major male and female characters will pair off into heterosexual relationships. This unspoken assumption, which may seem to Western observers like such a commonplace that it does not need to be noted, matters in Russia. It matters because such pairings which lead to marriage rarely occur for the major characters in the works of Pushkin, Lermontov, Gogol, Goncharov, Turgenev, and Dostoyevsky.

Significant continuity—continuity that further demonstrates the lasting significance of the monastic mentality in Russia—exists between the Russian nineteenth-century classics and in the classics of Socialist Realism, because such pairings are generally absent in Social Realism as well. In a key scene with far-reaching significance, when Pavel Korchagin in Nikolay Ostrovsky's Soviet classic *How the Steel Was Tempered* (first published to great acclaim in 1934) proposes to his girlfriend Taya, he presents marriage as a kind of platonic heterosexual elder/initiate relationship that has nothing to do with love and sex.

> "Will you become my girlfriend-wife?"
> Taya had been listening to him until then with deep agitation. This unexpected word caused her to tremble.
> "I have decided: Our union will continue until you grow into a real person, one of us. When you grow up, you will be free from all obligations."[14]

While this declaration sounds like an acknowledgment of Taya's independence, Pavel, *and Pavel alone*, defines the terms of the relationship. He says, "I have decided." It does not occur to him to ask for her opinion on this matter of vital importance to her, or even to discuss it with her. This is patriarchal authority that serves as preparation, not for an intimate relationships, but for social engagement—which is the point. The heroes of Socialist Realism are usually presented with a social task, and carrying it out is a measure of their commitment to the Cause. By its very nature, any intense relationship between a man and a woman would detract from this commitment, so Soviet censors would not allow it.

But the characters of Socialist Realism had to have some kinds of relationships with people, so characters in Aleksandr Fadeyev's classic *The Young Guard* experience male bonding in the form of an elder-initiate relationship that ultimately derives from the Father Zosima-Alyosha Karamazov relationship in *The Brothers Karamazov.*

The Young Guard portrays a group of teenagers who fought in the resistance movement in World War II in southern Russia, and has an instructive history. The original version appeared in 1946 and promptly received a Stalin Prize. However, the Party soon thought the better of it, and criticized Fadeyev for not showing party leadership, i.e., patriarchal authority. Only after Fadeyev substantially revised the novel to show patriarchal authority did it receive official acceptance.

The Young Guard shares several key elements with *War and Peace.* Both novels portray specific historic events identified by place and time; both novels portray a traumatic invasion by a foreign army that is ultimately repelled; both novels emphasize the role of partisans in doing so. Not surprisingly, then, Fadeyev adopts some of Tolstoy's devices such as water imagery to present the relationship between people and a certain area. Thus, Tolstoy writes that French soldiers appeared…

> And Moscow absorbed them more and more. It was precisely like the result of pouring water onto dry earth; the water and the dry earth both disappear; exactly in the same way the army entered the abundant, empty city; the army was destroyed, and the abundant city was destroyed; and mud was created; fires and looting were created. (6, 400)

Fadeyev uses an analogous extended simile to create the opposite effect:

> Just as ground waters trickle noiselessly and constantly, unnoticed by the human eye under the roots of trees and grasses, along the cracks and capillaries of the earth, under the soil, so under German authority millions of men, women and children of all nationalities who populate our land moved from place to place by paths in the steppes, forests and mountains, by ravines, under the steep banks of rivers, along the streets and side streets of cities and villages, along crowded bazaars and dark nightly ravines.[15]

I cite this simile in full precisely because of its anomalous nature. Hardly anything else like it appears in *The Young Guard*. More frequently, Fadeyev did not write like Tolstoy. In addition there was the obvious difference between his talent and Tolstoy's genius.

In a sense, family connections did not pose a problem for Fadeyev because of his material; he had a group of unrelated young people to work with, so he had no need to give them family characteristics. However, they take an oath, as Stalin did after Lenin's death, and that oath destroys their former identities.

> Only yesterday they were simply school friends, carefree and lively, but since the day when they took the oath, every one of them as it were said goodbye to his former self. It was as though they broke their former carefree connection of friendship, in order to enter into a new, higher connection—a friendship of common thinking, a friendship of organization, a friendship based on blood, which each swore to shed in the name of the emancipation of his native land.[16]

But even this friendship creates only a partial bond. Late in the novel, Ulya, one of the heroic girls, has an inner monologue of the kind usually reserved for men in Tolstoy. A narrative question is this: "Why is the world so organized that people can never give their heart completely to another?" And Ulya thinks, "Because this is impossible...Because you have given your heart to something more than Valya...You have given it to the emancipation of your native land."[17] The displacement of love from an individual to the Cause (and thus implicitly to the Leader who embodies the Cause), is an essential feature of the official Soviet mentality.

More than friendship is at stake here, of course. Matvey Kostiyevich derives a bond of identity first from those who fought in the Civil War, and then from those who are fighting in the then current Great Fatherland War. "We came from them, all the best, the most intelligent, talented, eminent people—we all came from them, from simple people!... I do not have to tell you that I have labored all my life for their sake."[18] His devotion to the Cause creates a living link to History. And, of course, History is configured by the patriarchal authority of Lenin and Stalin. Their authority imposes itself between people, as it were. Any serious personal relationship necessarily creates a barrier between the individual and History.[19] It is therefore possible to formulate a way of distinguishing between officially approved literature and dissident literature that is not overtly ideological. While officially approved literature did not/could not admit the representation of purely private experiences, dissident literature, as represented here by Bulgakov, Grossman, and Pasternak, did. Moreover, such a distinction constitutes another affirmation of the general interpretation of the Soviet Union as a form of revolutionary monasticism in which Stalin as a sadistic elder imposed vows of poverty, chastity, and obedience on hapless Soviet citizens.

This discussion raises a key question for the historical novels, namely: How do non-official writers represent the relationship between the individual and historical events? *Doctor Zhivago* and *Life and Fate,* the two dominant masterpieces of mid-century Russian literature, provide instructive answers to this question. They were both written at more or less the same time and provide intriguing comparisons and contrasts.

To begin with the comparisons, we may notice a similarity that derives from context. In the twentieth century, artists who undertook a historical novel had numerous choices, both because the social upheavals of their times to which they wanted to respond were spread out in space and time, and also because of the precedent of collage and collage-like compositions in the visual arts. Thus, both *Life and Fate* and *Doctor Zhivago* exhibit considerable compositional freedom. The time sequence matters very little in *Life and Fate,* so Grossman can juxtapose stories and parts of stories more or less at will.

If the purpose of *Doctor Zhivago* is to make sense of the revolution by show-ing the reactions to it of a single gifted man, the purpose of *Life and Fate* is to make sense of World War II, and specifically the crucial battle of Stalingrad by showing the experiences of different groups of people. *Life and Fate* is a stagger-ingly ambitious work. Strictly speaking, it is not a war novel at all. Rather, it is a wartime novel, a novel that is set in wartime. It combines various elements including letters to give a sense for the way different people coped with the agony of war.

Pasternak has less compositional freedom, since he wishes to show the chrono-logical evolution of Zhivago's life from early childhood to his death (and beyond) but he nevertheless juxtaposes different elements such as Zhivago's journal and, of course, his poetry. He also felt free to dispense with explanations and transi-tions in the story of Zhivago's life, as when he begins a chapter like this: "The weather had been vile for three days. It was the second autumn of the war."[20] Even more strikingly, "The Forest War" begins like this: "Yury Andreyevich was in his second year of captivity with the partisans."[21] We never find out when and how the partisans took him captive. To establish the historical coherence of the Russian classics, it is helpful to notice the affinities between the nineteenth and twentieth centuries in this respect. In general terms, then, we can say that *Life and Fate* is to *War and Peace* as *Doctor Zhivago* is to *Crime and Punishment.* Stylistic and thematic affinities exist between each of these two pairs of novels.

These discussions of these pairs of novels suggest a twentieth-century coun-terpart to the numerous comparisons of Tolstoy and Dostoyevsky. Although Grossman and Pasternak have basically only one novel to their credit, they can serve to organize the history of the twentieth-century novel in Russia as Tolstoy and Dostoyevsky organize the nineteenth-century history of the novel in Russia.

It is of course a given that all the Russian writers who undertake a historical novel have a sense that Tolstoy is looming over their shoulders. This must have been all the more true for Grossman, if only because patterns repeat themselves so often in Russian history, thereby dictating the topics of Russian historical novels. Thus, *Life and Fate* and *War and Peace* both depict an invasion of Russia, and emphasize a crucial battle. The Battle of Borodino in *War and Peace* corresponds well enough to the Battle of Stalingrad in *Life and Fate*.[22]

But significant differences also exist between *War and Peace* and *Life and Fate*. For instance, the action in Grossman's novel lasts only about three weeks, as opposed to the decade or so covered in Tolstoy's novel. Of course, Grossman had an intense awareness of his relationship with his awe-inspiring precursor, and of his need to swerve from him.

If the great game of Russian criticism is to compare Tolstoy and Dostoyevsky, and the analogies between Grossman and Tolstoy, and between Pasternak and Dostoyevsky, which I have proposed here, have any validity, then a major task of the critic in the twenty-first century is to propose an analogous comparison between Grossman and Pasternak. In the Jakobsonian terms that I have proposed in a previous essay, Grossman is clearly a metonymical writer, and Pasternak is a metaphorical writer. Metonymical writers like Tolstoy and Grossman present analogies rather than symbols. Thus, Jakobson says, there is an analogy between Anna Karenina and her purse. Her purse is not a symbol of anything, and in fact there are very few symbols in *War and Peace*. In Tolstoy's work things are usually what they are, and nothing else, although they are often related to other things. This is even truer in *Life and Fate*, which has hardly any symbols at all. As Tolstoy had done before him, Grossman juxtaposes place with place, event with event. His juxtapositions take on greater meaning because the events occur more or less simultaneously, as opposed to the measured sequence of events in *War and Peace*.

Grossman deals with his anxiety of influence from Tolstoy directly by having his characters discuss him in ways that anticipate the ways in which Solzhenitsyn's characters will discuss him in his work of the 1960s. Grossman allows one character, a general, to praise Tolstoy, but for the wrong reasons: "Leo Tolstoy wrote *War and Peace*. People have been reading it for a hundred years and will be reading it for another hundred years. Why? Because he participated, he fought himself, and knew who to write about."[23] Someone immediately corrects the general's erroneous statement that Tolstoy fought in the War of 1812. Later, three characters, Malyarov, Strum, and Sokolov, discuss Dostoyevsky as a reactionary writer, and wonder whether any nineteenth-century literature is acceptable in the Soviet era. Malyarov comes to Tolstoy's defense. He implicitly associates

Tolstoy and Stalinism when he says, "Tolstoy poeticized the idea of a people's war, and the government has now headed up a just people's war."[24] Yet Grossman makes Tolstoy's heritage ambiguous when a member of the Cheka reacts against him: "Tolstoy announced that there are no guilty people in the world. But we Chekists put forward a higher thesis—there are no innocent people in the world, no one who cannot be brought to trial."[25] In short, Grossman does not exactly undercut Tolstoy, but lessens his stature by making his heritage ambiguous.

Grossman does something in *Life and Fate* that Tolstoy also does in *War and Peace*. He takes advantage of the compositional looseness that admits non-fictional essays into a fictional work as Tolstoy did in *War and Peace,* and includes in *Life and Fate* some essays on topics related to the themes of the novel. Thus, in a passage possibly inspired by Hamlet's awareness that the time is out of joint, Grossman muses on an essential topic in a historical novel, the nature of time. "Time flows into a man and into a kingdom, makes a nest in them, and then times leaves, disappears, but the man and the kingdom remain…The kingdom remained, but its time has left…the man exists but his time has disappeared. Where is it?"[26] And then having written in a Tolstoyan vein, he implicitly distinguishes his situation from that of Tolstoy, who was a count, after all. Grossman makes what is surely an autobiographical digression: "The most difficult thing is to be a stepson of time. There is nothing harder than the lot of the stepson who does not live in his own time."[27]

Despite the accomplishments of earlier Russian–Jewish writers like Mandelstam and Babel, Grossman had an acute awareness that he was an outsider, as was every other Jew. He was someone who was not fully legitimate in the family of Russian literature. In a bold move, then, he includes an essay on anti-Semitism, which begins like this: "Anti-Semitism manifests itself in a variety of ways—it is in mocking disdainful ill will and in murderous pogroms." He continues, "You will encounter anti-Semitism both at the market and at a meeting of the Academy of Sciences, in the soul of an old man and in children's games in the courtyard."[28]

Chekhov, a non-aristocrat who faced a long line of aristocratic precursors, had a similar sense of himself as an outsider, and this shared sense of outsider identity may have made Grossman feel a personal and artistic affinity with Chekhov. In effect, he enlists Chekhov in his struggle with Tolstoy.

After Malyarov's discussion about the way Tolstoy "poeticized" the idea of a people's war, Sokolov speaks up for Chekhov: "Chekhov is the best of all; both the previous era and our own recognize him."[29] When others disagree with this, as Russians are apt to do in such conversations, a rare unambiguous comment about him follows, "'Do not put down Chekhov,' said Marya Ivanovna; 'I like him the best of all [our] writers.'"[30]

There are passages in *Life and Fate* in which one senses the presence of Chekhov, and beyond Chekhov, Turgenev. Some early scenes in *Life and Fate* that show the camaraderie of men in a dugout at the battle of Stalingrad recall similar scenes showing men with guns in Turgenev's *Notes of a Hunter*. Other scenes are more purely Chekhovian, as in the beautifully written scene in which Getmanov says goodbye to his wife when he leaves to go to the Battle of Stalingrad. The scene, which ends a chapter, recalls the ending of Chekhov's great short story "The Lady with a Lapdog":

> And in this new, final farewell, when the damp and cold street air came in through the half-open door, merging with the warmth of the house, when the rough, worn skin of his coat touched the fragrant silk of her nightgown, they both felt that their life, which had seemed like a single life, had suddenly split apart, and anguish burned their hearts.[31]

Very much in the spirit of Chekhov's unsentimental, tough-minded art, Grossman here acknowledges the pain that these people experience without sermonizing about it.

Even more extreme is the heart-wrenching long scene in which a woman, Lyudmila Nikolayevna, visits the crudely marked grave of her son Tolya, a victim of the war. She is overwhelmed with grief, a grief so intense that it seems to have the ability to bring him back to life.

> Everything living—his mother, Nadya, Victor's eyes, the battle summaries. everything ceased to exist.
> The living had become the nonliving. What was living in the whole world was Tolya. But what quiet stood all around. Does he know that she has come...[32]

Grossman's Chekhovian restraint appears in what he does not say here. He says nothing about patriotism, or about the heroism of dying for the great cause of defending the Motherland. Tolya is dead, and nothing else in all the world matters to his mother.

In having his characters discuss Chekhov and in incorporating his style in this way, Grossman uses him against Tolstoy. The relationship between Grossman and Chekhov thus corresponds to what Bloom calls a "tessera," a relationship between ephebe and precursor that involves completion and antithesis. In tessera, Bloom explains, "A poet antithetically 'completes' his precursor, by so reading the parent-poem as to retain its terms but to mean them in another sense, as though the precursor had failed to go far enough."[33] What Grossman does, more than any Russian writer before or since, is to go far enough.

Grossman acknowledges no spatial or thematic boundaries to his imagination. He even presents the two Adolfs, Hitler and Eichmann, in addition to Stalin, as characters. Miraculously, he treats all three of these evil geniuses in the same even-handed way. It is nothing less than astonishing that a Jewish writer in the 1950s could write a quiet scene in which Hitler takes a walk in a forest alone. "His aloneness in the forest, which initially calmed him, seemed frightful to him. Alone, without bodyguards, without his usual adjutants, he seemed to himself like a boy in a fairy tale, who had entered a dark, enchanted forest."[34] (This forest may be one of the few metaphors in *Life and Fate*.)

Grossman takes us not just inside the mind of Hitler, but also inside what the mind of Hitler created—the death camps. Of all the astonishing scenes in *Life and Fate*, none is more astonishing than the sustained scene that shows the experience of a mother Sofya Osipovna and her young son David in the Holocaust, a topic that no other great twentieth-century Russian writer addressed. The narration takes us with them as their train arrives at the death camp (presumably Auschwitz), as they are sorted, as they enter the lobby, as they undress, and finally enter the gas chamber itself. And then the end comes.

> "I became a mother, "she thought.
> That was her last thought.
> But in her heart there was still life; it contracted, it hurt, it felt sorry for you, the living and the dead people, there was a rush of nausea; Sofya Osipovna squeezed David to herself, a doll, and became dead, a doll.[35]

Perhaps only Varlam Shalamov's *Kolyma Stories* can match the sustained horror of this 12-page passage, of which I cited only a few lines here. Unlike the death agony of Prince Andrey in *War and Peace*, which leads to transcendence, the death of Sofya Osipovna and her son David is just that—death, and nothing else.

Pasternak's *Doctor Zhivago* begins with death, and the treatment of death clearly demonstrates the difference between Pasternak the intensive metaphorical writer and Grossman the extensive metonymical writer. *Doctor Zhivago* begins like this:

> They walked and walked and sang "Eternal Memory," and when they stopped it seemed that in the rhythm that was established, feet, horses, the blowing of

the wind continued to sing. Passersby let the procession through, counted the crowns, and crossed themselves. Curious people entered the process and ask "Who is being buried?" They were answered, "Zhivago." "Oh that's it. Then it makes sense." "But not him. Her." "It doesn't matter. May the kingdom of heaven be hers. It's a rich funeral."[36]

(The response to just the last name does not specify gender.)

On the second page we are told that "It was the eve of Intercession Day."[37] These quotations do not simply contain factual information, as they would in Grossman. These quotations represent the great themes of the novel in embryonic form. Later in the novel, a character named Nikolay Nikolayevich Vedenyapin, who takes young Yura Zhivago under his wing, says, "Life is symbolic because it is meaningful."[38] That is the attitude that informs *Doctor Zhivago*, beginning with the names.

For metaphorical writers such as Dostoyevsky and Pasternak, names have great significance. Thus, Yury Zhivago bears the name of Yury Dolgoruky, the legendary founder of Moscow. Yury is a Russian variant of Georgy, the patron saint of Moscow, who is St. George the Dragon Slayer and thus someone who takes on the human dragons that proliferated in Russia after 1917. Russia's highest military honor is of course the Cross of St. George.

And then there is the matter of his last name. At the funeral, someone asks who is being buried, and the answer is "Zhivago." This carefully chosen name is the accusative case in the Old Church Slavonic spelling of the Russian word *zhivoy*, which is 'living." Thus, the decoded question and answer goes like this: "Who is being buried?" "The living." This brief exchange determines a great theme of the novel, and not coincidentally one of the great themes of Russian literature, death and resurrection. Zhivago will die, but will experience a kind of resurrection through his poems.

Zhivago himself provides two explicit statements of the interrelatedness of death and resurrection. In a rare speech, he says to a patient, "You are worried about whether you will be resurrected, but you have already been resurrected when you were born, and you did not notice this."[39] Then later, when Zhivago has typhus, he has a vision of writing a poem called "Confusion" (*"Smyateniye"*). The passage concludes with four sentences, one of which contains a play on words that could only have been written by someone accustomed to writing poetry:

Hell and decay and dissolution and death [*ad i raspad i razlozheniye i smert'*] are glad to touch [him], and, however, together with them spring, and the Magdalene and life are glad to touch [him]. And—one must wake up. One must experience resurrection.[40]

This intimate interrelationship between death and resurrection informs some of the key passages in *Doctor Zhivago*. It appears in, of all unlikely places, the description of the morgue where Zhivago as a medical student is learning to dissect cadavers.

The presence of a secret was felt in everything, beginning with the unknown fate of all these laid-out bodies and ending with the very secret of life and death, which disposed itself here in the basement as though it were at home or in its quarters. Drowning out everything else, the voice of that secret pursued Yury, distracting him during dissection.[41]

Zhivago the young medical student is not yet Zhivago the poet, so the secret of life "distracts" him. He does not yet know how to turn it into great poetry.

To return to the beginning of the novel and the question, "Who is being buried?" the factual answer is "Yury Zhivago's mother." In symbolic terms the feminine archetype associated with tenderness and compassion is being buried, and thus foreshadows the aggressive suppression of the female archetype by the Soviet regime.[42]

The specific date of Zhivago's mother's funeral is the eve of Intercession Day, October 13. That date also matters, because in Russian folk tradition it marked the end of autumn and the beginning of winter. After that date peasants did not take cattle out to pasture, for example. The word *pokrov*, the equivalent of Intercession, literally means "veil," or "covering," and in peasant lore it referred to the way the snow would fall and cover the earth. (On the night of the funeral a snowstorm that is both literal and symbolic wakes up young Yura Zhivago.) The symbolic reference is to the way Soviet leaders would freeze up Russia, creating what Vasily Aksionov would call in the title of a novel, *Generations of Winter*. Finally, Intercession Day refers to Mary's traditional role of interceding for suffering humanity, and it is this intercession that will be so grievously lacking in Soviet life, because the feminine archetype has been buried.

Like Grossman's characters, Pasternak's characters discuss Tolstoy and Dostoyevsky. Here, for example, is a conversation between two men, Vedenyapin and Vyvlochnov:

"But Lev Nikolayevich says that the more a man gives himself over to beauty, the more he distances himself from the good."

"But you think the opposite? Beauty will save the world, mysteries and the like, Rozanov and Dostoyevsky?"[43]

It is appropriate that the men leave this issue unresolved, because in *Doctor Zhivago* Pasternak reaches out to both writers. He takes an image from each of them and uses it to organize some key elements of his novel.

The following passage in *Doctor Zhivago* has exceptional, pivotal importance:

> They were driving along Kamerherr Lane. Yura noticed a black melted opening in the icy frosting of one of the windows.
>
> Through that opening the light of a candle shone through, penetrating to the street almost with the consciousness of a glance, as though the flame were looking at the travelers and expecting something.
>
> "A candle burned on the table. A candle burned." Yura whispered to himself the beginning of something vague and unformed in the hope that the continuation would come of itself, without being forced. It did not come.[44]

This passage is a key to the symbolic structure of the novel. We find the clue to this exceptionally dense knot of imagery in a scene that occurs two pages previously. In this scene Pasha and Lara are talking. She says to him, "Now you can see. Light a candle and turn off the electricity." A key narrative comment follows:

> Lara liked to have conversations in the semi-darkness of lighted candles...The room filled with soft light. A black opening began to melt in the ice of the window pane at the level of the candle.[45]

When we juxtapose these two passages, we realize that the candle that Lara asked Pasha to light is the candle that Yury sees from the street below. It is this candle, symbolic of Lara's luminous spirit, that reaches out to him, "as though it were expecting something." Although in this scene Lara tells Pasha that she has to marry him, the candle anticipates the love between Lara and Yury, the love that will be the most important experience of their lives, and the love that will be inextricable from the poetry that she will inspire him to write. After he dies at the end of the novel, Lara will recall that moment and the candle, intuitively understanding its fateful meaning.

> Could she think that the dead man lying on the table saw that opening in passing from the street and paid attention to the candle? What from this flame seen from

the outside—"A candle burned on the table, a candle burned"—entered his life, his predestination?[46]

Our understanding of this knot of imagery remains incomplete, however, without knowledge of its source in *Crime and Punishment,* and this knowledge helps us to understand Pasternak's anxiety of influence from Dostoyevsky. As is the case with Grossman and Tolstoy, Pasternak has a tessera relationship with Dostoyevsky. He takes something that Dostoyevsky did and extends it, as though Dostoyevsky had not taken it far enough.

In the passage in *Crime and Punishment* in which Raskolnikov goes for a walk in St. Petersburg and stops on a bridge, he sees the following:

> One distant attic window on the left bank, flashing as though on fire in the last rays of the setting sun, at the darkening water in the canal, and the water seemed to attract his attention, (5, 167)

A previous discussion has established that in this passage, Raskolnikov is looking at Sonya's window, and the scene clearly anticipates the one in which Zhivago sees a candle in Lara's window. Significantly, both men are in liminal, or transitional, spaces. Raskolnikov is standing on a bridge, and Zhivago is riding in a carriage. In both cases, the men's locations in their respective cities have symbolic significance. Raskolnikov is on Resurrection Bridge. Zhivago is in Moscow in Kamerherr Lane, a short street whose most significant landmark was then, and still is, the Moscow Art Theater. Unlike the Bolshoy Theater, which was built for aristocrats, the Moscow Art Theater was built for Moscow's emerging middle class, and was the site of the dramatic triumphs of Russia's premiere middle-class genius, Anton Chekhov. Seeing the candle in Lara and Pasha's room while on Kamerherr Lane marks the beginning of Yury's artistic evolution.

Lara, candles, and light form a rich associative cluster throughout *Doctor Zhivago.* Ultimately, this cluster achieves a transcendent intensity in the following passage, which deserves to be quoted at length.

> Ever since childhood, Yury Andreyevich had loved the evening forest illuminated by the slanting fire of the sun. In such minutes it was as though he was letting these pillars of light through himself. As though a gift of the living spirit entered his breast like a stream, cut through his whole being and came out from under his shoulders like a pair of wings. That youthful primal image, which is formed in everyone for all of life, and then serves forever and seems to him like an inner force was awakened in him, and forced nature, the forest, the sunset and

everything visible to be transformed into a primal and all-embracing image of the girl. "Lara!" Clearing his eyes, he half-whispered and mentally addressed his whole life, all of God's earth, all the space spread out before him, illuminated by the sun.[47]

Pasternak keeps *Doctor Zhivago* from turning into an allegory by grounding his characters in their physical, mortal experience. This is what he does with Lara.

Just as Pasternak develops Zhivago differently from his origins in Raskolnikov, so he also develops Lara Antipova differently from her origins in Sonya Marmeladova. The two women are connected in that Sonya is a prostitute, and Lara feels like a prostitute when she returns home after Komarovsky takes her virginity in circumstances that are never described. (Komarovsky has more than a passing resemblance to Svidrigaylov in *Crime and Punishment*.) Lara distances herself from her awful experience by thinking of herself in the third person.

> If mama finds out, she'll kill her. She'll kill her and commit suicide. "How did this happen? How could it have happened?" It is too late now. You had to have thought about this earlier. Now she is—as it is called—now she is a fallen woman.[48]

It is a measure of the depth of Pasternak's character development that he makes this "fallen woman" much more important than Sonya. Lara becomes an archetypal woman who embodies light and grace and transmits them to Zhivago.

But the association of Lara and light, and all that light implies, is incomplete in the partial line "A candle burned." The full line is, "It blew and blew; a candle burned on a table." ("*Melo, melo; svecha gorela na stole.*") The opposition is between the wind and the candle, and the wind may blow out the candle at any moment. This line is a symbolic statement of the contentious relationship between artists and the Soviet authorities who had the capacity to snuff out creativity in Russia at any moment.

However, just as the association of Lara and light goes back to a source, and the explication of what Pasternak did with that source shows his tessera relationship with a great precursor, the image of the wind also goes back to another source with which Pasternak had a tessera relationship. (Pasternak's larger significance for the history of Russian literature may be said to derive from his ability to create tesseras, or creative variations, on key moments in classical works.) If the image of light comes from Dostoyevsky, the image of the wind comes from Tolstoy. Thus, in this single line Pasternak both implicitly acknowledges his debt to his two great precursors, and defines his swerve from them.

Zhivago comments, "Just think, the roof has been torn off all of Russia, and you and all your people find yourselves under the open sky." This allegorical image of the destructive winds of change goes back to a fateful, decisive scene in *Anna Karenina* between Karenina and Vronsky in a provincial train station. Like the Resurrection Bridge in St. Petersburg and Kamerherr Lane in Moscow, the train station is a liminal, transitional space that anticipates the future. Tolstoy and Dostoyevsky both had an intuitive sense for the psychological implications of public spaces, and Pasternak benefitted greatly as a writer from this aspect of their work.

Karenina is on the train because she is returning to St. Petersburg from Moscow, where in a fine irony she has helped to patch up a rift between her brother Stiva and his wife because of his infidelity. It was during her stay in Moscow that she and Vronsky met. Unbeknownst to her, Vronsky followed her and got on the same train with her. When the train stops on the way to St. Petersburg, she leaves her railroad car, which here symbolizes her stifling marriage, to get a breath of fresh air. She is surprised to see Vronsky, and asks why he is travelling. Then:

> "Why am I travelling?" he repeated, looking directly into her eyes. "You know I am travelling in order to be where you are," he said, "I cannot do anything else." At that moment, as though having overcome obstacles, the wind blew the snow from the roof of the railroad car, some iron sheet that had been torn off clanged, and ahead the thick whistle of the locomotive mournfully and darkly rang out. The whole horror of the snowstorm now seemed still more beautiful to her. He had said the same thing that her soul had desired, but that her reason had feared. She did not answer anything, and he saw the struggle on her face. (8, 121-2)

This fateful incident is one of several instances of the pathetic fallacy in Tolstoy. Here he makes a metonymical connection between the microcosm of Karenina's and Vronsky's feelings and the macrocosm of the train station, and is doing something very much like what Dostoyevsky did in *Crime and Punishment*. The incident in which Raskolnikov sees the light reflected in Sonya's window also presents an embryonic form of the connection between them. If the light on Sonya's window symbolizes grace, the wind that blows the snow off the roof of the railroad car symbolizes the force of the passion that will ultimately result in her death beneath the wheels of a railroad car.

These remarks clarify what Pasternak did in *Doctor Zhivago*. He assimilated the wind that symbolizes the deadly force of Karenina's and Vronsky's passion for each other to the revolution.[49] Not long after the comment about the roof being blown off of Russia, Zhivago offers the following interpretation of the revolution: "One could say: Each person has experienced two revolutions, one of one's own, a personal one, and the other is general."[50]

In the novel, the general revolution affects the personal revolution in the form of wind. Pasternak develops the image of the wind as the destructive force of the revolution throughout the novel. At a holiday gathering at the Gromekos, for example, people talk all night about the revolution. Then they open the curtains. "'It looks like there was a thunderstorm while we were throwing words around [*pustoslovili*],' someone said."[51] The implication is that words mean little in the face of the impersonal force of the wind/revolution.

Just on the eve of the revolution, the Zhivagos have a problem with a smoky stove, and Yury opens the inset window (the *fortochka,* the small inset window typical in Russia), with allegorical results.

> Fresh air poured into the inset window. The flapping window curtain curled up. Several papers flew off the desk. The wind slammed a distant door, and circling along all the corners, started chasing after the remains of the smoke, like a cat chasing a mouse.[52]

While the revolution blew a gust of fresh air into the stuffy Russian empire of Nicholas II, it also slammed doors, cutting off the Soviet Union from the West, and preyed on hapless Russians who could not get out of Russia. As always, Pasternak presents his allegories with a light touch, so that readers such as Soviet censors could read them without sensing the larger implications. Naturally, then, after the Zhivagos have made all their preparations for their trip to the Urals, "On the eve of the departure, a snow storm came up."[53]

It is when Yury is in the Urals that he lives with Lara, and to understand the spiritual implications of their relationship, we need to make another digression to broaden the discussion. A key difference between Pasternak and Grossman, the significance of their Jewish heritage, is one that is best presented indirectly. Generally speaking, twentieth-century literature boasts very few overtly religious writers, such as T.S. Eliot and Flannery O'Connor. In Russia currently, there is Olga Sedakova, one of the great Christian poets of our time.

This does not say that religion no longer affected literature, because it did, and pervasively so. However, religion went underground, and not only in the Soviet Union. I have used the term "churchiness," a translation of the Russian word *tserkovnost',* to refer to the effect of religious beliefs and practices, regardless of the personal piety, or lack thereof, on the part of specific writers.[54]

The preceding comments may serve as an introduction to the issue of Pasternak's Jewish heritage, and how it affected the way he wrote. The distinction of introducing the topic of Jewish "churchiness" in the poetry of Pasternak and Mandelstam belongs to Mikhail Epstein (although he does not call it that). In the tradition of critics who have found systemic patterns in the relationship between Tolstoy and Dostoyevsky, [55] Epstein discusses the relationship between another key pair of writers, Pasternak and Mandelstam, by associating Pasternak with Hasidic mysticism, and Mandelstam with Talmudic thought. He finds evidence of the Jewish element in the creative unconscious of both writers by noticing that they are in dialog with the Russian language. Epstein writes "The speech of Pasternak and Mandelstam moves, as it were, against the current of language itself."[56]

Epstein's essay has the great virtue of discussing Pasternak and Mandelstam as Jewish poets, not just as Jews. Since Pasternak lived a longer and more public life than Mandelstam, discussing his Jewish identity and how his Judaism manifested itself in his writing in a responsible, non-polemical manner presents formidable difficulties. The historical record of Pasternak's life does not tell us as much as we would like on this subject, both because Pasternak was a complex man and also because he learned early on the value of circumspection as a survival technique in a hostile world. Then too, a responsible, non-polemical discussion of Pasternak's writing necessarily respects the unconscious nature of creativity.

Still, the concept that Pasternak had a Hasidic sensibility—which is not at all the same as saying that he "believed in" Hasidic ideas—explains a great deal about *Doctor Zhivago*. Although I cannot do justice here to the complexities of Hasidic thought, which was begun in the eighteenth century by Baal Shem Tov, suffice it to say here that it emphasizes finding God, or evidence of God's presence, in the natural world.

In this delicate matter it makes more sense to offer suggestions rather than conclusions. Thus, it is suggestive that we read in one of Pasternak's first published poems, which he wrote in 1912 when he was 22, the following lines about a "sleepy orchard":

> The worlds that have bloomed hang
> Even with me, with my candle.
> And I pass into this night

As into an unheard of faith.[57]

In this poem we find a very early version of the association of candle, nature, and faith that will recur throughout his work for the next four decades. It seems reasonable to interpret the essential association in Pasternak's work as an idiosyncratic, estheticized version of Hasidic thought. Although candles have religious significance for both Jews and Orthodox Christians, Orthodox Christians associate them with the interior space of churches and home altars, whereas in Pasternak's works, candles are either outside, as in this poem from 1912, or they shine through to the outside.

For an artist as complex as Pasternak, who lived in a time when any statement of interest in religion or spirituality was fraught with danger, we cannot say that he had a definite religious credo. Rather, with Pasternak we may take the reference in this poem to an "unheard of faith" as a useful clue. Even to ask "What did Pasternak believe?" is to do violence to his work by making it more explicit, more conscious, than it was or ever could be. Rather, it is fair to say that he had a sensibility that was some amalgam of Judaism, Christianity, and modern poetry, and that he expressed his discovery of this "unheard of faith," a discovery that psychologists would call his individualism, in this remarkable poem.

The question of how much Pasternak knew about the Hasidic faith, and how whatever he knew was transmitted to him, is, and will probably remain, problematic. Nevertheless, at least one of his poems has a source in a Hasidic text. And it is not just any poem, either. The poem in question is "Being famous is not pretty," which he wrote at a moment of personal crisis during the Soviet government's intense press campaign against him. This line amounts to a slight variation of a phrase that occurs in a Hasidic story told by the "Spola grandfather": "To be famous is not a good thing."[58] Moreover, Pasternak's poem reads like a version of various Hasidic stories, in which learned rabbis teach the virtue of modesty. Pasternak's line "One must live without self-assertion"[59] could be a summary of Hasidic teaching.

With regard to Pasternak's poetry, Epstein speaks of "His inclination to fracture the world into tiny particles in order to reveal the sanctity in them."[60] Notably, Gary Saul Morson comes to a similar conclusion without reference to Judaism at all. He writes, "In a world where intellectuals presume materialism, Pasternak offers vitalism, a mystical sense of life as inexplicable in terms of this world." [61] When we read *Doctor Zhivago* carefully, we find numerous examples of the way the natural world reveals its sanctity, or inexplicability, as Morson would have it, to him. If in his poem Pasternak passes "into an unheard of faith," a faith that he finds in the orchard, Zhivago does something very much like this when he is living with Lara in the Urals.

A narrative comment tells us that at that time Yury and Lara were not like other lovers. "For them, however, and this was their exceptionalism, moments when like an emanation of eternity an emanation of passion flew into their doomed human existence; there were moments of revelation and recognition of every-thing new and what was new in themselves and life."[62] This attitude is consistent with what a certain Rabbi Barukh says in a Hasidic story entitled, "Everything is Wonder." In response to a question about God as the "Creator of remedies," he says, "God does not want to be praised as the Lord of supernatural miracles. And so here, through the mention of remedies, Nature is introduced and put first. But the truth is that everything is a miracle and wonder."[63] Although Hasidic stories are usually ahistorical, Pasternak wants to make the image of the revolution as wind into a gentle historical force that lifts them beyond themselves by creating a transcendent connection. It is not enough to say that Lara creates this connection to Yury, but rather that their connection is so strong that it creates something like a spiritual force field, very much in the spirit of Hasidic mysticism.

Late one night after Lara and her daughter have gone to sleep, Yury achieves a state of mystical transport in an extraordinary passage.

> A blessed silence full of happiness and sweetly breathing life surrounded Yury Andreyevich. The light of the lamp fell onto the white sheet of the paper in calm yellowness and floated on the surface of the ink in the inkwell like a golden gleam. Outside the window the frosty winter night had a bluish tint…
> The luxury of the frosty night was unconveyable. There was peace in the doctor's soul. He returned to the bright, warmly heated room and set about his writing.[64]

It is characteristic of states of mystical transport that the world falls away, and visual characteristics separate themselves from physical objects. This is what happens in this passage, when light has a 'yellowness" (*zheltizna*) and the night emanated a "bluish tinge" (*golubela*). When things lose their materiality, then language becomes inadequate, since language is usually tied to things. This is the point of the sentence, "The luxury of the frosty night was unconveyable." Mystical transport such as this lifts him out of time and space. Thus, a certain tension exists between the historical specificity of the novel (we know when he was born and when he died), and his mystical states. It may well be that the appeal of Hasidic thought for Pasternak is precisely that it is ahistorical. Although much remains to be said about the relevance of Pasternak's Hasidic legacy, with respect to his poetry as well as to his prose, these specific comments must suffice for now.

In the context of Russian literature as a whole, Pasternak's presentation of the transcendent experience of nature in *Doctor Zhivago* remains unique for a very specific reason. Russians who are devout Orthodox Christians may have moments of transcendence during worship, but they occur within the highly structured environment of a church, and that church itself is often located within a monastery. This fact of Orthodox worship explains why, for example, the most devout great Russian, Dostoyevsky, had little interest in nature, and rarely wrote about it.

A point that is often overlooked is that Zhivago is able to have this mystical experience because he has firewood, food, and the companionship of the woman he loves. Without these factors Varlam Shalamov in Kolyma, to the north and east of where Zhivago was, experienced the frozen north as hell on earth, and represented it as such in his devastating short stories. Pasternak and Shalamov thus created characters that experience Russia's wide-open spaces, the destination of Gogol's troika, in diametrically opposed ways.

If we wish to interpret *Doctor Zhivago* in a more general way, we can do so by noticing that Pasternak shared with Stalin a love of Dostoyevsky. Stalin esteemed Dostoyevsky more than any other Russian writer, and Dostoyevsky in *Crime and Punishment* gave Stalin the overarching theme of his career. In that great novel Dostoyevsky drew on the age-old Russian folkway of passion-suffering, according to which people who accept suffering are thereby imitating Christ, and become passion-sufferers (*strastoterptsy*, in Russian).[65] In causing suffering to the pawnbroker whom he murders, Raskolnikov brings suffering on himself, which he eventually accepts, and thus becomes a passion-sufferer. It was what the Russians would call their fate to have in Stalin a sadistic leader determined to make people suffer, and also to have the folkway of passion-suffering, which enabled at least some of them to make sense of, and therefore endure, this suffering.

In the Stalin era, the ultimate crime was individualism, and Yury Zhivago and Lara are both individualists, as their desire for each other, and for their mutual desire to live together in private space, indicates. This crime therefore qualifies them to be passion-sufferers: Lara in the gulag, and Yury in his Christological poems at the end of the novel.[66]

The immense historical significance of *Doctor Zhivago* derives from the fact that it simultaneously constitutes both a culmination and a beginning. One can say that *Doctor Zhivago* represents the culmination of one of the world's great literary sequences, from Pushkin to Pasternak. By drawing on the themes and images of Tolstoy and Dostoyevsky, making them essential elements of the work, Pasternak gave new meaning to these writers who might otherwise have seemed mired in the rhetoric of Soviet authorities. As T.S. Eliot understood so well, tradition retains its meaning only when great writers renew it, and Pasternak certainly did that.

If, in terms of the literary history of literature, *Doctor Zhivago* represents a culmination, in terms of the social history of literature, it also represents a new beginning. The literary campaign against Pasternak that the Soviet authorities unleashed when he was awarded the Nobel Prize in 1958, and the difficulties that he encountered when they denied him access to his royalties for *Doctor Zhivago* that had accumulated in the West, anticipate the subsequent campaigns against Solzhenitsyn and Brodsky, which culminated in their Nobel Prizes. The Soviet authorities' actions against artists hit a low point in 1974, on the occasion of the infamous Bulldozer Show, so called when they used bulldozers to plow under works that dissident artists displayed in a park. With the great advantage of hindsight, knowing that the Soviet Union will collapse in 1991, we can recognize these and other actions as expressions of the way Leonid Brezhnev, Yury Andropov, and other Soviet authorities were flailing about in the aftermath of Stalin's death.

The horrific experiences that Stalin and Hitler created had a lasting effect on mid-twentieth century Russian literature. Briefly, it may be said that, just as the concentration camps stripped life down to its essentials, the concentration camps also stripped literature down to its essentials. There is no symbolism to speak of in Grossman, as there is none in Valam Shalamov, and comparatively little in Solzhenitsyn, who are the three great literary witnesses to Russian suffering in the twentieth century. To be sure, some suggestion of passion-suffering and some symbolism appears in Solzhenitsyn's *The First Circle*, but virtually none of either appears in *Cancer Ward*, or in several later volumes of *The Red Wheel*, except in the "screen" sections.

The absence of symbolism is the effect of the horrors of life on the battlefield and in the concentration camps. A character named Dudorov makes just this point in a conversation with Yury Zhivago's childhood friend Misha Gordon at the very end of *Doctor Zhivago*, when the two men are surrounded by the horrors of World War II. He says, "Now everything metaphorical has become literal."[67] The work of Grossman, Shalamov, and Solzhenitsyn demonstrates the truth of this observation.

As a final comment on this topic, another aspect of Pasternak's pivotal significance in mid-century literary history is that he knew Shalamov, who asked him for an evaluation of his poetry. And then of course Shalamov knew Solzhenitsyn, and thus the Pasternak-Shalamov-Solzhenitsyn link stretches for some 85 years, from 1922, when Pasternak published *Sister My Life,* to 2007, when the publication of *The Red Wheel* was completed.

If we ask whether there are any works in the West that are comparable to these long Russian novels, the answer is an emphatic yes. In France, Proust's *In Search of Lost Time* invites comparison with Solzhenitsyn's *The Red Wheel.* These very long, multi-volume novels by great prose stylists could be said to be mirror images of each other. If Proust gives us minute-by-minute versions of a boy's stream of consciousness in a small French village, where nothing very important ever happens, Solzhenitsyn gives day-by-day versions of life all over Russia as stupendously important events occur, all of which culminate in the collapse of a great society. Yet what unites these radically opposed writers—perhaps the two novelists of the twentieth century who are most different—is their common desire to retrieve what Proust called "lost time". If Proust obsessively chronicles personal time as the humdrum life of his village unfolds around him, Solzhenitsyn obsessively chronicles historical time as the traumatic collapse of Russia played out in the lives of his hundreds of characters. Although they had different writing styles that served different needs, the basic impulses—the need to rescue lost time—that compelled them to write, and write, and write, were remarkably similar.

Regarding multi-volume twentieth-century novels in English, we realize that some major works by major authors create an instructive pattern within the extremes created by Proust on one hand and Solzhenitsyn on the other. We can begin this discussion with John Galsworthy (1867-1933), an exceptionally prolific and popular Nobel Prize Winner, author of *The Forsyte Saga* (1906-21), which includes:

> *The Man of Property* (1906) 364 pages
> *In Chancery* (1920) 320 pages
> *To Let* (1921) 336 pages

Although his general subject is the Chekhovian one of the decline of the upper middle classes, he is more interested in marital and financial issues than social change. His series is basically a family saga.

More relevant for Russian literature are the trilogies by two of the most important American writers in the twentieth century, John Dos Passos and William Faulkner. Dos Passos' metonymical work, spread out in space and time, inevitably reminds someone familiar with Russian literature of Tolstoy, while

Faulkner's metaphorical work, filled with cultural allusions, brings to mind Dostoyevsky, who was in fact a major influence on him. Dos Passos and Faulkner both wrote important trilogies of novels.

John Dos Passos (1897-1977), *USA Trilogy:*

- *The 42nd Parallel* (1930) 352 pages
- *1919* (1932) 400 pages
- *The Big Money* (1936) 468 pages

William Faulkner (1897-1962), *The Snopes Trilogy*:

- *The Hamlet* (1940) 409 pages
- *The Town* (1957) 448 pages
- *The Mansion (1959)* 371 pages

Both of these trilogies by major American writers describe social change in their society, and, more specifically, social decline. Once that has been said, though, the differences between them are more important than the similarities. Dos Passos deals with the macrocosm of social change, while Faulkner deals with the microcosm of social change. These key differences derive as much from their life experiences as anything else. Dos Passos was a Harvard graduate who spent considerable time in New York and was a world traveler. Faulkner, on the other hand, had little interest in formal education, and left Oxford, Mississippi, where he spent almost all of his life, only to go to Hollywood so that he could work on movie scripts and make some spending money. Although Faulkner won a Nobel Prize, and Dos Passos did not, Dos Passos has far greater relevance for Russian literature in general and for Solzhenitsyn in particular.

Of all the American writers such as John Reed who visited Russia during the Soviet period, Dos Passos is by far the most important, and the one whose work was most affected by his cultural experiences there. For a while it seemed that Dos Passos might serve as a model for Soviet writers. His 1928 trip to Russia consisted of two very different parts. He first went to the south of Russia, and then to the Caucasus to have the kind of wilderness experience that many Americans experience in the West. When back in Moscow, he studied Russian by day and attended the theater by night. He was more of an American individualist than he ever knew and had an unshakable belief in his ability to understand his environment simply by looking around him. He even said of his theater experiences, "Not knowing the language is hardly a barrier at all. You can look at the stage all the better for not following the lines."[68] His biographer Virginia Spencer Carr says that, in his encounters with Russians, "He meant to read their faces and the way they carried themselves."[69] Although we do not know which plays he saw, we can, almost a century later, make sense of his enthusiastic reaction. Since he could not understand the dialog, he missed the overt propaganda and stilted style of the plays, so he thought they were better than they were.

In general, Dos Passos' reactions to Russia were determined by the fact that he was also more of an esthete than he knew. Although he was a typical liberal of the twenties and thirties and said that he wanted to assess what people at the time called "the Soviet experiment," he made little if any effort to gain insight into Soviet politics from this stay in Moscow. What mattered, though, was his fateful encounter with filmmaker Sergey Eisenstein, with whom he discussed the theory of montage.[70] It was a fateful encounter, because Eisenstein had long been interested in the relationship between literature and film.[71]

Dos Passos was an intuitive, rather than a reflective, artist, and he never seems to have articulated even to himself the problem that Eisenstein solved for him. Dos Passos was probably Walt Whitman's most gifted admirer in the twentieth century. Like Whitman, he heard America singing and wanted to record what he heard in its raw immediacy. He wrote in the introduction to his story *Three Soldiers* that, "The mind of a generation is in its speech. A writer makes aspects of that speech enduring by putting them into print."[72] Or, more generally, "We must deal with the raw structure of history now."[73] If Whitman wrote long poems that incorporated his quasi-cosmic sense of America, Dos Passos wrote long novels with a similar quasi-cosmic reach. As a novelist, then, he risked being overwhelmed by "the raw structure of history" in the form of the flow of language all around him. Since neither he nor anybody else could ever capture all of it, any more than Proust could capture all the minutiae of daily life in his village, he had to settle for what he called "aspects" of it.

This is how Eisenstein performed a career-saving service for him, and it is significant that Dos Passos entered the mature period of his career only after his encounters with Eisenstein and return from Russia. After talking to Eisenstein, and seeing what Eisenstein had done by juxtaposing images without creating connections between them in films like *Potemkin,* he realized that he could do something similar. He realized that he could make similar juxtapositions and thereby bring together the microcosm of American colloquial speech with the macrocosm of American society. This is surely what he meant when he wrote, 'A writer who writes straight is the architect of history."[74] Like Eisenstein, Dos

Passos proposed to take elements of history and, by juxtaposing them, create a coherent structure.

Possibly thinking of Ezra Pound's dictum that poetry is "news that stays news," and surely affected by James Joyce's use of stream of consciousness, Dos Passos introduced montages of headlines of the day in what he called "Newsreels." Here, for example, is the beginning of "Newsreel XLIV" in *The Big Money*:

Yankee Doodle that Melodee
COLONEL HOUSE ARRIVES FROM EUROPE
APPARENTLY A VERY SICK MAN

Yankee Doodle that melodee
TO CONQUER SPACE AND SEE DISTANCES[75]

These Newsreels have the effect of Joycean stream of consciousness passages but are taken from the outside world. They balance the immediacy of the fictional chapters that depict the experiences of his characters such as Charley Anderson and others.

Dos Passos' liberal sympathies and the obvious value of his writing brought him to the attention of Soviet critics, and their comments about his work constitute an instructive study of early Soviet criticism. In Deming Brown's valuable book *Soviet Attitudes Toward American Writing* (published in 1962) there is an illuminating survey of Soviet criticism of Dos Passos. A reading of Soviet criticism of Dos Passos from the 1930s provides an opportunity to formulate a post-Soviet perception of this material. The subtext of Soviet criticism, and not just the criticism of Dos Passos, was often that the Soviet Union had achieved a final solution of what they could only interpret as a zero-sum game of cultural rivalry between Russia and the West.

What Soviet critics do not say about the work of Dos Passos is as instructive as what they do say. They do not say anything at all about Dos Passos' use of film technique and the impact of Eisenstein on his work. This is all the more remarkable since Dos Passos had recently been in Moscow, and surely at least a few people knew that he had met with Eisenstein. Also, there was a tremendous amount of publicity about Eisenstein's use of montage techniques in *Potemkin*, which had premiered to great acclaim in 1927. Two explanations suggest themselves for this curious conceptual lacuna. One is that Soviet critics were still mesmerized by the achievements of the Russian classics, and Tolstoy above all, of course. None of those writers showed any effect of film, so it made sense to maintain the special status of literature by keeping it separate from their other arts. One Soviet critic wrote, "He [Dos Passos] has been compelled to mechanically combine several methods of creative work, various modes and genres. I repeat, combine mechanically, not dialectically, not organically."[76]

And then there was the influence of critic Vissarion Belinsky, whose writings were taken as the gold standard of criticism. Belinsky's nineteenth-century mentality forced him to emphasize the cognitive significance of literature, whose value—he believed—derived from the fact that they gave information about "Reality." If the key criterion for literature was its relation to "Reality," then Dos Passos posed challenges of interpretation for them.

On one hand, the Russians were so taken by Dos Passos that they translated *Manhattan Transfer* in 1927, reissued it in 1930, and translated *The 42nd Parallel* in 1931, within a year of its appearance in America.[77] General access to these books provoked considerable ambiguity. Soviet critics could not deny that Dos Passos' books contained snippets of "Reality" in its newspaper headlines in the service of a critique of American capitalism. On the other hand, their cultural rivalry with the West compelled them to contrast what Dos Passos had actually written with what Soviet authors might write in the future, which would be a more complete version of "Reality". Addressing Dos Passos, one critic wrote, "Our problem is not to see the world like an ant, crawling from particle to particle, but to comprehend the real makeup of the world, in order to change it."[78] Although Dos Passos' methods had their Soviet defenders,[79] his stylistic innovations and his expressed doubts about the Soviet Union brought discussion of his work to an abrupt halt at the end of 1936, and his name virtually never again appeared in print until many years later.[80]

Of course, Dos Passos matters for Russian culture not just because of Eisenstein's decisive influence. He matters, and matters greatly, because of the circuit Eisenstein to Dos Passos to Solzhenitsyn, which is a key to Russian-American cultural relationships in the twentieth century. We now know that Solzhenitsyn read Dos Passos' *1919*, in, of all places, Lubyanka prison![81] Even in that awful place, he had what Mandelstam would have called a moment of recognition. He sensed that Dos Passos had addressed the same issues in American history that he wanted to address in what even then he was thinking of as a large-scale work on Russian history. When reading Dos Passos, Solzhenitsyn realized that he had found a way to juxtapose the microcosm of his characters with the macrocosm of historical events. Thus, in *August of 1914*, the first volume of the series, he introduces both historical documents, and his versions of Dos Passos' newsreels, "along newspapers," as he calls them. The first one begins:

A LIVING CORPSE is he who does not know the magical effects of Lazital…
A stimulant for MALE NEURASTHENIA…
Coconut hammocks for ladies…
Click-Click London perfumes. S-Bouquets
…the ethical idealism in social affairs, in which the Slavic soul is so rich, but
the enlightened West is impoverished…(54)[82]

Solzhenitsyn's indebtedness to Dos Passos is obvious and was widely recognized when *August of 1914* was first published in English. Michael Scammell, Solzhenitsyn's biographer, notes this indebtedness, and continues, "Solzhenitsyn's approach differed from Dos Passos's 'seeing eye' technique, however, in that his attempts to reproduce the cinematic effect were more exhaustive and literal."[83] It is noteworthy, however, that Scammell, like most reviewers of *August of 1914,* confined his remarks to these verbal montages that create an obvious link between Dos Passos and Solzhenitsyn. Hardly anyone commented on these writers' shared connection to Eisenstein, and on the fact that they were doing with words what Eisenstein did with images. This difference meant that Dos Passos and Solzhenitsyn were taking other people's words published in other places and incorporating them into their own works, whereas Eisenstein created montages from images that he himself had shot.

Moreover, Scammell, and other critics as well, miss the larger affinity of purpose between Dos Passos and Solzhenitsyn, and it was this larger purpose that proved decisive for Solzhenitsyn. Although we cannot know this for sure, it is reasonable to infer that Dos Passos confirmed Solzhenitsyn's sense of the rightness of the staggeringly audacious project that he had undertaken. Understanding the affinity of purpose between Dos Passos and Solzhenitsyn requires a brief digression on Dos Passos' understanding of America.

A decisive event for Dos Passos and many other American liberals was the execution in 1927 of Nicola Sacco and Bartolomeo Vanzetti for murdering two men during a robbery, despite legal irregularities and accusations of anti-immigrant bias. Their executions evoked protests and riots all over the world, and traumatized liberals like Dos Passos. In a thoughtful essay, "Dos Passos, Society, and the Individual," critic Alfred Kazin pointed out that at the end of the Camera Eye section on Sacco and Vanzetti in *USA*, there is a comment "all right we are two nations."[84] Kazin goes so far as to summarize Dos Passos' glum conclusions about America in these words: "The modern equation cancels out to zero, everything comes undone, the heroes are always broken."[85] Or as Dos Passos put it in a letter to F. Scott Fitzgerald written in 1936, "We're living in one of the damnedest tragic moments in history."[86] Thus, Dos Passos, filled with pessimism about the future of America, depicted "tragic moments" in history, and filled his novels with "broken heroes."

And Solzhenitsyn also did this in *The Red Wheel*. It is not too much to say that even as Solzhenitsyn was sitting in his cell in Lubyanka, filled with anxiety about his future, reading Dos Passos clarified his understanding of what he proposed to do. He found in Dos Passos a kindred spirit, another writer who had also witnessed—and chronicled—a tragic moment in the history of his country, a moment made tragic by the splitting of his country into us and them.

Solzhenitsyn's first but by no means his last, broken hero (to use Kazin's phrase) is General Samsonov. Samsonov commits suicide in *August of 1914* after the horrific battle of Tannenberg, when the blithe incompetence of irresponsible generals caused the Russian army to sustain the greatest loss in military history.

In the subsequent volumes of *The Red Wheel,* it becomes more and more obvious that Solzhenitsyn's great theme is the great tragedy that befell Russia between 1914 and 1917. This period constitutes lost historical time because Lenin and the Bolsheviks did their considerable best to suppress everything in this period that did not show the inevitable march to the apocalyptic moment of the revolution.[87] For Proust, time was lost because no one, not even someone as verbal as he was, could put the flow of existence into words fast enough. For Solzhenitsyn, though, time was lost because ruthless men like Lenin and Stalin carried out deliberate campaigns of widespread incessant violence and either suppressed the evidence of their actions or proclaimed self-serving justifications for them. In no other country had a writer ever confronted a time that was so out of joint. I think this is a key explanation for the enormous length of *The Red Wheel*. Solzhenitsyn shows in exhaustive detail the collapse of Russian society day by day, even hour by hour. The four major divisions of *The Red Wheel,* or "knots," as Solzhenitsyn called them are:

- *August of 1914*. Two volumes.
- *October of 1916*. Two volumes
- *March of 1917*. Four volumes
- *April of 1917*. Two volumes

Solzhenitsyn gives the key month of March 1917, when Nicholas II abdicated the throne, no less than four volumes. Here are the numbers of pages for each of the four volumes in the standard Russian edition:

- Volume I. 774
- Volume II. 800
- Volume III. 776
- Volume IV. 736

This amounts to a total of 3,056 pages. If we divide this number by the 31 days of March, we get 197 pages per day, or 8 pages per hour. This is minute-by-minute history!

To return to the American context and its relevance to Russian literature for a moment, we can say that as a true heir to Whitman's vast reach, Dos Passos wanted to take in all of America. He wanted to hear all of America singing. Faulkner, on the other hand, had no interest in all of America, or indeed any part of the country outside of Mississippi. It is not more true of any other writer that he wanted to "see the world in a grain of sand," to cite Blake's phrase. But such was the power of his imagination that his imaginary grain of sand, Yaknapatawpha County, of which he proclaimed himself proprietor, gave him abundant material for a career that culminated in his being awarded a Nobel Prize.

If we follow T.S. Eliot's directive to see literature steadily and see it whole, then we can say that Faulkner's trilogy of novels that chronicle Flem Snopes' rise from tenant farmer to president of a bank constitutes a vital if indirect link between Chekhov and Solzhenitsyn. Snopes is a darker version of Yermolay Lopakhin, the former peasant boy in *The Cherry Orchard* who buys the estate on which he had grown up. Lopakhin and Snopes both take possession of the manor house in the town where they grew up. Unlike Lopakhin, however, Snopes seethes with hostility and resentment.

Faulkner was a great admirer of Chekhov, and often recommended him to his fellow writers, so a connection probably exists between Lopakhin and Snopes. In fact, it is not too much to say that *The Cherry Orchard* probably gave Faulkner the idea for his whole trilogy. In it, Faulkner created a fictional microcosmic version of events in the South. Solzhenitsyn would later create a historical macrocosmic version of comparable, but much more disastrous, events in Russia. There are affinities between Russia and the American South, such as the shared legacy of slavery in an agricultural region torn by civil war and social injustice. If Solzhenitsyn had ever had a chance to read Faulkner, he would have said that Flem Snopes was a Southern version of Joseph Stalin. He would have said that Faulkner had done on a small scale what he, Solzhenitsyn, had done on a large scale. Both multi-volume novels show the slow, seemingly inevitable triumph of amoral manipulation as society collapses and an evil genius takes over.

Another set of affinities remains to be discussed. An American writer James Jones, and a Russian writer, Konstantin Simonov, were almost exact contemporaries, and have so many similarities that they invite numerous comparisons. However, they surely had never heard of each other, so there is no possibility of influence. Both Jones and Simonov received widespread recognition in their own countries.

James Jones (1921-77):

- *From Here to Eternity*, 1951; 816 pages.
- *The Thin Red Line*, 1962; 475 pages.
- *Whistle* (completed by Willie Morris), 1978; 496 pages.

Konstantin Simonov (1915-79):

- *The Living and the Dead* trilogy published in 1959, 1962, 1971, total of 1, 279 pages

Both of these trilogies about World War II came out at about the same time. Their collected novels occupy comparable places in the esteem of their fellow countrymen, esteem that in no small part derives from the enduring popularity of the movies made from them.

Although Jones and Simonov both wrote about the experiences of common soldiers in World War II, they created quite different novels. Although surely some of these differences are to be explained as personal and idiosyncratic, the larger, substantive differences—the ones that interest us here—derive from the differences between their societies, and from their societies' different experiences of the war. Whereas Jones' soldiers in *The Thin Red Line* are fighting on the distant island of Guadalcanal, Simonov's soldiers are defending their homeland, which has been invaded.

Jones and Simonov are both born storytellers. Each writer has a story to tell, although each tells it differently from the other. As is usual in war novels, their stories deal with male experiences, and male comradeship. The differences in the stories derive from the larger differences in the historical experience of each country. Jones had what Americans would recognize as impeccable credentials for writing about World War II as he really did fight on Guadalcanal, just as his protagonists in *The Thin Red Line* do. His work also fits into the American tradition of creating individualistic characters, a tradition that goes at least as far back as Mark Twain's *Huck Finn*. Commentators have noticed that he writes about the tensions between personal concerns mandated by America's individualistic heritage on one hand and the sense of duty imposed by the war on the other. The knee-jerk reaction of hard-core individualists was to reject the war. Thus, Robert E. Lee Prewitt, one of the principal characters in *From Here to Eternity* defiantly says, "And if the rest of them dehorn each other, kill each other, blow the whole damned world to hell, its [sic] none of my business."[88] The war gave great immediacy to the age-old conflict between individualism and duty, which became a commonplace in mid-century American culture. This conflict appears in the phrase "a separate peace," which is associated with Ernest Hemingway's *A Farewell to Arms*. Rick Blaine (played by Humphrey Bogart), articulates it in the classic movie *Casablanca*. (Rick has a change of heart in the last scene of the movie, of course.)

Before examining Jones' treatment of character in more detail, it is worth noticing that he has some anxiety of influence from two illustrious predecessors. As one might expect, Simonov and Jones deal differently with Tolstoy's heritage. For example, in *The Thin Red Line*, one of the soldiers, John Doll, is wounded. "He knew where he was, but was he alone? What had happened to the others?"[89] Those who know *War and Peace* well will recognize these lines as a reworking of the famous scene when Nicholas Rostov is knocked off his horse at the battle of Austerlitz.

Jones also takes over the looseness of Tolstoy's compositional technique that allowed him to include historical essays in *War and Peace*, and includes some essays of his own. Here, for example, is an excerpt from Jones's essay on Fatigue.

> There is, in the Army, a little known but very important activity, appropriately called Fatigue. Fatigue, in the Army, is the very necessary cleaning and repairing of the aftermath of living. Any man who has ever owned a gun has known Fatigue…A recruit never finds out about Fatigue until some time after he has held up his right hand and then it is too late.[90]

Unlike Tolstoy, Jones has no theory of history to expound in his essays. He is so caught up in the immediate experiences of his characters that he has no sense of, or interest in, history at all. Rather, he feels such an urgent need to tell people "What It Was Like" that he includes essays such as this one.

Not surprisingly, Jones' major anxiety of influence comes from an American writer, Dos Passos. Dos Passos and Jones are fascinated by the same kinds of characters, who are often working-class men who cope as best as they can with circumstances not of their own making. They often have difficulty in finding a place for themselves. Thus, Charley Anderson has to figure out his place in American society when he gets off the boat at the beginning of Dos Passos' *1919*. It is as though Jones in *From Here to Eternity* is dealing with the next generation of American men. Dos Passos' Charley Anderson comes home after a war; Jones' Prewitt is already a long way from his home in Kentucky.

In this group of novels, Jones' *From Here to Eternity*, which is now best known in the movie version, is an outlier, since it takes place in Pearl Harbor, before the Japanese attack in 1941. As a result, Jones' soldiers can display their range of interests in sports and popular culture—interests that had hardly any equivalent in Russia at the time. In any case, since Simonov's *The Living and the Dead* begins with the trauma of the German invasion of June 22, 1941, Simonov's characters have no time for thoughts of leisure activities.

Like Jones, Simonov tells us more about his society than he realizes. The Russian equivalent of the American individualists' conflicts with authority is the dealings with bureaucracy of Sintsov, one of his principal characters. Caught up in the chaos that followed the German invasion, Sintsov quite understandably loses his identification papers, and the consequences of this loss take up something like 30 pages. Although Russia is reeling from the trauma of the invasion, and the German troops are approaching the outskirts of Moscow, nothing matters more to Sintsov and the various officials that he deals with than getting a new set of papers. Everybody involved understands and accepts the overwhelming importance of bureaucratic procedures in Russia even in a time of extreme national emergency.

The interrelated forces of bureaucracy and censorship combined to perpetuate nineteenth-century propriety in the works that were published in the Soviet Union. Thus, at one point in *the Living and the Dead*, Simonov blandly tells us, "He cursed with frightful words."[91] Simonov does not tell us what any of these frightful words were, unlike Jones. Jones managed to overcome censorship in America, which—unlike the Communist Party in the Soviet Union—lost its battle to maintain linguistic propriety. As a result, Jones filled his novels with profanity. He created completely believable dialog for his soldiers, as Simonov did not and could not.

Like Jones, Simonov resembles Tolstoy in his use of authorial commentary. However, Simonov uses it much more often, and to much greater effect. War is so gripping and frightening that most war novelists stay close to their characters. Even when dealing with an event as emotionally charged as the German invasion, Simonov shows his essential humanity by including humane comments.

Although the Holocaust had hardly begun in the early summer of 1941, and later Russian writers proved unable and/or unwilling to discuss it, Simonov acknowledges the Nazi persecution of the Jews. Thus, he describes the Jewish refugees from the *stetls* of western Belarus:

> Thousands of people rode on unimaginable carts, buggies, and wagons; old men with sidelocks and beards, in top hats from the last century rode; exhausted Jewish women who had aged before their time rode; small dark-faced children with frightened eyes—six, eight, or ten per cart—rode. Still more people walked alongside the carts.[92]

Simonov not unreasonably assimilates these Jewish refugees to the larger groups of Russians who were trying to report for duty: "This was one of the darkest tragedies of those days—the tragedy of people who died under bombings on the roads and fell captive without getting to their command posts."[93]

The other deeply problematic issue for Simonov, and one that he has also justifications for minimizing, was the role of Stalin. Because his principal characters are soldiers, Simonov has to acknowledge in one way or another Stalin's purge of the Soviet officer corps of 1937. He gives one of his officers, a man named Fyodor Serpullin, in whose regiment Sintsov serves, a back story about Stalin's purge. In some lectures at the military academy, Serpullin was naïve enough to tell his students that Hitler was creating a formidable fighting force in the Wehrmacht. Naturally, he was arrested for this, but not, apparently, tortured. Naturally, he was given ten years, of which he served four, presumably in the gulag, but Simonov discreetly passes over this detail in silence. He was let out early, and returned to Moscow the day the Germans invaded. Although Simonov acknowledges that the purge of the officer corps took place, he assesses it through Serpullin's consciousness.

> But for all these four years he never once blamed Soviet power for what had been done to him. He considered it a monstrous misunderstanding, a mistake, a stupid thing. But for him communism was and remained a holy and unstained cause.[94]

Here we notice how a clever writer could adapt Tolstoyan stream of consciousness for his own purposes. On one hand he does acknowledge that an unjust purge of at least one officer occurred, by having Serpullin insist that it was a "mistake." However, he avoids addressing the crucial issues such as the scale of the purge, Stalin's guilt for causing it, and—most urgently in 1941—the way the officer purge left Russia unprepared for the Nazi invasion. Simonov discreetly ignores all these issues.

In the same vein, Simonov does a disingenuous verbal dance around the issue of how people felt about Stalin. He says, for example, that: "People loved him in different ways: unreservedly and with reservations; admiring him and fearing him; sometimes they did not love him."[95] Posing the life-or-death issue of loving or not loving Stalin in this way gives the impression that it was a random choice such as a consumer preference, one that people exercised independently of Stalin's policies. Obviously, Simonov had no hope of ever explaining why people "didn't love" Stalin.

Simonov also gives Sintsov a Tolstoyan interior monolog. After listening to one of Stalin's speeches about the war, Sintsov thinks, "Would I give up my life for Stalin, if they simply came to me and said, die, so that he could live? Yes, I would give it up, more readily today than ever!"[96] Russian men's love of the Leader is a special case of the vital but little-understood role of Russia's monastic legacy (as I explained in *Stalin's Soviet Monastery*). In any case, Simonov is never more Tolstoyan than when he has Sintsov express his willingness to die for his leader; although he does not cite it, the key source for a scene in which a soldier expresses his willingness, indeed his eagerness, to die for his leader occurs in *War and Peace*. In Book Three of *War and Peace,* Nikolay Rostov attends a review of the Russian troops by Tsar Aleksandr I. Tolstoy presents the Tsar first and then Rostov, in the following way:

> The handsome young Tsar Aleksandr, in the uniform of the Horse Guards, wearing a three-cornered hat with its peaks front and back, with his pleasant face and resonant though not loud voice, attracted the full force of attention.
>
> Rostov stood not far from the trumpeters, and with his keen sight had recognized the Tsar from a distance and followed his approach. When he approached to within twenty paces, and Nikolay could clearly examine in all details the emperor's handsome, happy young face; *he experienced a feeling of tenderness and ecstasy the likes of which he had never known before. Everything—every feature of the Tsar's face and every movement seemed enchanting to him.* (My emphasis)
>
> After stopping across from the Pavlograd Regiment, the Tsar said something in French to the Austrian emperor and smiled.
>
> Upon seeing that smile, Rostov himself began involuntarily to smile and had an extremely strong feeling of love for his Tsar. He wanted to show his love for the Tsar somehow.
>
> …How happy Rostov would have been if he could at that moment have died for his Tsar! (4, 322-3)

Rostov's experience of seeing the leader from afar, feeling love for him, and expressing happiness at the thought of dying for him became commonplaces in Soviet society.

We find a startling, detailed confirmation of Tolstoy's prescience in a diary entry by the writer Korney Chukovsky from April 22, 1935. To appreciate the full impact of what Chukovsky wrote, we must keep in mind that he was a thoroughly decent man who wrote charming children's verse. No Stalinist, he was often harassed by official critics. And then at a writers' conference, the following happened:

> Suddenly Kaganovich, Voroshilov, Andreyev, Zhdanov, and Stalin appear. What happened in the hall! And HE stood there, a little tired, thoughtful, and magnificent. One felt that he was enormously accustomed to power and force and at the same time had something feminine, soft. I looked around: Everyone had tender, spirited, laughing faces that were in love. Seeing him—simply seeing him—was happiness for all of us. Mrs. Demchenko kept talking to him. And we all envied her; we were jealous—she was fortunate! His every gesture was perceived with reverence. I had never considered myself capable of such feelings. While he was being applauded, he took out his watch (a silver one) and showed it to the audience with a delightful smile—we all started whispering. "His watch, his watch, he showed his watch." Even when we were leaving and standing at the coat racks, we recalled that watch.[97]

It is a very curious and noteworthy fact, one that deserves general recognition, that Russians such as Simonov and Chukovsky assimilated the rhetoric of romantic love as a way of expressing their loyalty to their leader.[98]

Like Tolstoy's Rostov, Simonov's Sintsov is willing, indeed eager, to give up his life for his Leader, in an updated version of Glinka's opera *A Life for the Tsar*. Rostov sees Aleksandr I at a distance; Sintsov listens to Stalin on the radio. Here, as elsewhere in Russian culture, the Leader is and remains distant and unapproachable. No Russian man could imagine becoming friends with the Leader. Perhaps it is because men's romantic love for their leader could not lead to a relationship of any kind, even to friendship, Rostov and Sintsov fantasize about death as its logical expression and conclusion.

Sintsov also has a certain affinity with Tolstoy's Pierre Bezukhov. Both men are occasionally out of place and do not fit in, as when Sintsov loses his identity papers. Both are taken prisoner by the enemy, and both feel intense joy when they get free. This passage may well convey the feelings of a twentieth-century Pierre:

But now all this, that flashed before his eyes made him rejoice and brought happiness. Everything was happiness: the truck that they were riding in, the familiar blond locks of Koryshov, which poked out of the cab of the front truck, the blue pines, the yellow birches, the glades and fields, the puffs of smoke from chimneys, the people, the anti-aircraft guns, the Soviet planes in the sky, the snatches of song that came back from the front truck.[99]

Without the living, vivifying presence of the Russian classics, no American mid-century war novelist ever wrote anything like this.

Simonov has another connection to the nineteenth century, one that he probably shares with other Soviet writers, and one that cannot easily be shown without excessively long quotations. One way to articulate this somewhat delicate matter is to say that Simonov's *The Living and the Dead* often feels over-written. Overall, the proportion of battle scenes to dialog and commentary is low. Simonov has such facility with words that he lets conversations go on and on. Despite the urgency of the situation, the novel has a leisurely feel to it, and thus recalls the prose of Leskov. As a matter of fact, much of Soviet literature, which did not experience the bracing effects of modernist irony, retains the slow pace of nineteenth-century narration.

Finally, one must say that Simonov's authorial comments show him to be a deeply humane man. To be sure, he cannot acknowledge Stalinism for what it was—probably for reasons of his own as well as the censorship. Although neither he nor any other war novelist is, or was, a pacifist, he had a humane understanding of the costs of war. For Simonov, this is not just a matter of body counts, but also the psychological damage that war does. An authorial comment says, "No, it is possible to learn to fight, but it is impossible to get accustomed to war."[100] And after Sintsov witnesses the burial of a tank crew:

> They say that such things harden the soul. That's true, of course. But as they harden it, at the same time they also wound it. And a man lives and fights on with a soul that is simultaneously hardened and wounded. These are two sides of one and the same coin, and no matter what people say, there is no getting away from that.[101]

To sum up, Simonov offers a classic example of a writer who brings to bear—at what level of consciousness we will never know—the richness of the Russian classics to help make sense of a traumatic historical event.

In conclusion, despite the break in Russian history that allegedly occurred in 1917, a study of long novels in Russia suggests two general conclusions about the links between the Soviet period and the imperial period that Mandelstam would have appreciated. The first is social, and the second is conceptual.

The dominant art forms of nineteenth-century Europe, the novel in literature and the symphony and the opera in music, were both long forms. They were created for people who had the leisure to devote several hours to experiencing them. In America, the automobile and the movie theater combined to produce experiences of personal mobility and light entertainment that had no counterpart in the Soviet Union.

By dominating public space with their ubiquitous statues and signs, the Soviet authorities made public space off-putting for many Russians, who all the more eagerly sought refuge in whatever private space they could acquire for themselves. If they wanted to go out to the theater, for example, they had to take public transportation, which was often unreliable, and in the winter they had to brave the cold. Staying at home and reading seemed like a more attractive option. Although it might be difficult to document this conclusion, it seems reasonable to suppose that Russian novelists found a larger number of receptive readers than their American contemporaries.

It also seems reasonable to suppose that Mandelstam was not alone in wanting to connect the vertebrae of the centuries. Even Russians who had no nostalgia for imperial Russia could, and surely did, enjoy reading about the non-political experiences of people in the nineteenth century.

The vitality of any given art form derives from the connection between the artists and the social receptiveness to the art form in question. The vitality of the long novel in Russia is a key fact about Russian culture, and thus provides a productive way to discuss the evergreen topic of the relationship between art and society.

Notes

1 Note that the issues raised by repression in the Putin era of Russian history lie outside the scope of the present study.
2 Osip Mandel'shtam, *Stikhotvoreniya,* 163. The search for the wholeness of time is, of course, one of Mandelstam's great themes and also appears in, among other poems, "The Man Who Found a Horseshoe." See *ibid*, 165-70.
3 Obviously, the number of pages of the edition of these various novels will depend on the format of the edition, whether it has illustrations and so forth. Here and below I cite the number of pages in standard editions, which will serve well enough for the purposes of comparison.

4 Boris Ilizarov, *Iosif Stalin,* (Moscow: AST, 2015), 351.

5 Andrey Tarkovsky's 1966 film *Andrey Rublyov* strikingly juxtaposes terrible human suffering with brilliant art in a way that makes a case for the principle that social dysfunction stimulates creativity.

6 Roger Martin du Gard, whose work is generally associated with the term *roman-fleuve,* is the author of *The Thibaults,* a family saga that follows the fortunes of two brothers. It has limited relevance to the novels discussed in this chapter, which emphasize the experiences of people caught up in war and social change.

7 *The Red Wheel.* For more on this matter, see the final essay in this book.as a cultural phenomenon deserves a more detailed discussion than I can give it here. Suffice it to say that its extreme length results from the combination of two things. First, there was the predominance of literature in the Soviet period, when movie and television programs offered little that was entertaining. Also, it was dangerous to read samizdat literature. It was always safe to lose oneself in the nineteenth-century classics, so people did that. This was the general attitude that motivated Solzhenitsyn to take up his huge task to begin with. The other factor that facilitated the creation of this gargantuan novel was the combination of the computer and the ideal environment for writing—including of course the freedom from censorship—that Solzhenitsyn enjoyed in his hideaway in Vermont. Yet there is a poignant quality about *The Red Wheel,* which mostly appeared in the twenty-first century, when the computer that had facilitated its creation was also creating a marked decline in the interest in, and leisure for, reading, especially long novels. As a result, Solzhenitsyn put his heart and soul and genius into telling in excruciating detail the story of the collapse of Russian society that the Soviet authorities had suppressed for so many years, only to find a limited readership for his magnum opus. Aside from earnest graduate students who are writing dissertations on Solzhenitsyn, I suspect that very few people have ever read, or ever will read, all of *The Red Wheel.*

8 The dates suggest that the *romans-fleuves* of de Gard and Romans originated in a desire to take stock of Europe after the devastation of World War I. If so, this desire makes these authors in a sense Solzhenitsyn's predecessors.

9 Two other famous posthumous sons are Isaac Newton and Bill Clinton.

10 Vladimir Mayakovsky is an example. His father Vladimir Mayakovsky died in 1906, when the future poet was 13. (In comparison, the fathers of Gogol and Turgenev died when their sons were 16.) Knowing that Mayakovsky suffered parental loss at this key age helps us understand his frenetically rebellious behavior and association with the Futurist movement in later life. His experience of parental loss may well be related to the manic-depressive syndrome that caused him to commit suicide in 1930 at the age of 37.

11 Much of the official Soviet hostility to innovative modern art is to be explained as a matter of the attitudes of Soviet authorities who never outgrew their small-town roots (See *Stalin's Soviet Monastery*). For example, on December 1, 1962, Nikita

Khrushchev expressed outrage at the sight of abstract paintings when he was touring an exhibit of modern art. What other response to modern art could one have expected from an impetuous, semi-literate man who had grown up in the Ukrainian countryside?

12 In *Stalin's Soviet Monastery,* I show that biologist Trofim Lysenko, a Stalin favorite who became infamous for his false claims of record wheat yields, also acted as he did out of biographically driven needs. He associated the overthrow of the tsarist regime with the overthrow of the scientific method, which involved keeping meticulous records and replicating his results. See *Stalin's Soviet Monastery*, 191.

13 The use of two different elements in *Doctor Zhivago* and *Andrey Rublyov* invites comparisons. *Doctor Zhivago* shows the experiences of an artist in difficult times, and then ends with examples of the work which that artist produced in his responses to his times. *Andrey Rublyov* also shows the experiences of the artist in difficult times, and then ends with examples of the artist's work. Moreover, in both works the endings differ from what has come before. In the end, *Doctor Zhivago* switches from prose to poetry, just as, in the end, *Andrey Rublyov* switches from black and white to color. This similarity is so striking in two works created during the same time period that I suspect that we are dealing here with Pasternak's influence on Tarkovsky.

14 Nikolay Ostrovsky, *Kak zakalalyas' stal'* (M. Pravda, 1982), 194.

15 Aleksandr Fadeyev, *Molodaya Gvardiya* (N.p.: Izdatel'stvo TsK BLKSM "Molodaya Gvardiya," 1971), 213.

16 *Ibid.*, 319.

17 *Ibid.*, 391.

18 *Ibid.*, 268.

19 Note that this separation of the individual from history and social engagement is precisely the point of Hemingway's *A Farewell to Arms*, whose principal character has made "a separate peace." That is why nothing like it could ever be published in the Soviet Union.

20 Boris Pasternak, *Doktor Zhivago* (Moscow: AST, 2010), 81.

21 *Ibid.*, 322.

22 On Grossman and *Life and Fate*, see Maxim D. Shrayer, "Grossman's Resistance," in *Holocaust Resistance in Europe and America: New Aspects and Dilemmas*. Victoria Khitere and Abigail S. Gruber, eds. (Cambridge: Cambridge Scholars Publishing, 2017), 134-63.

23 Vasily Grossman, *Zhizn' i sud'ba.* (Kishinyov: Literatura Artistike, 1989), 209.

24 *Ibid.*, 250.

25 *Ibid.*, 570.

26 *Ibid.*, 42.

27 *Ibid.*

28 *Ibid.*, 438.

29 *Ibid.*, 250.

30 *Ibid.*

31 *Ibid.*, 99.

32 *Ibid.*, 132.

33 Bloom, *The Anxiety of Influence*, 14.

34 *Zhizn' i sud'ba*, 592.

35 *Ibid.*, 500.

36 Boris Pasternak, *Doktor Zhivago*, 20.

37 *Ibid.*, 21.

38 *Ibid.*, 44.

39 *Ibid.*, 60.

40 *Ibid.*, 148.

41 *Ibid.*, 58.

42 The death of the maiden known as "The Chosen One" in the Stravinsky-Roerich-Nijinsky ballet *Holy Spring*, known in English as *The Rite of Spring*, was a prescient expression of the coming death of the female archetype in Russia. I discussed this aspect of the ballet in *Stalin's Soviet Monastery*, 55-7.

43 Pasternak, *Doktor Zhivago*, 44.

44 *Ibid.*, 68.

45 *Ibid.*, 66.

46 *Ibid.*, 334.

47 *Ibid.*, 235.

48 *Ibid.*

49 Of course, Pasternak knew well the opening lines of Blok's "The Twelve," which also image the revolution as a winter wind.

Black evening.

White snow.

Wind, wind!

A man can hardly stand on his feet.

(Aleksandr Blok, *Stikhotvoreniya i poemy* (Moscow: EKSMO, 2009), 444).

The key difference between Blok's and Pasternak's use of the wind as an image for the revolution is that in Blok the wind remains an impersonal force, whereas Pasternak takes over Tolstoy's image of the wind as representing the passion that a man and a woman have for each other.

50 Pasternak, *Doktor Zhivago*, 109.

51 *Ibid.*, 132.

52 *Ibid.*, 136.

53 *Ibid.*, 151.

54 Churchiness has relevance for writers in countries other than Russia. In stories like "A Clean, Well-Lighted Place" Ernest Hemingway expresses something like Protestant churchiness, although he was himself anything but pious.

55 It is an intriguing characteristic of Russian literary history that some of its most important writers are often discussed in pairs: Pushkin and Lermontov, Tolstoy and Dostoyevsky, Blok and Bely, Pasternak and Mandelstam, and Akhmatova and Tsvetayeva, Sedakova and Shvarts. In geography, the key pairing of Moscow and St. Petersburg offers the possibility of extending these pairings. Thus, one can put Akhmatova and Mandelstam together to form a St. Petersburg school of poetry, and put Tsvetayeva and Pasternak together to form a Moscow school of poetry. In the same vein, one can include painters and the poets and thereby organize a cultural history of Russia. Thus, to the Moscow writers Boris Pasternak and Marina Tsvetayeva, one can add the Moscow painter Natalya Goncharova. To the Muscovite trio Pasternak-Tsvetayeva-Goncharova, one can add a comparable St. Petersburg trio: Anna Akhmatova, Osip Mandelstam, and Zinaida Serebryakova. A detailed discussion of these six artists would show that they all incorporated into their work attitudes associated with the cities in which they lived and worked.

56 Mikhail Epshteyn, "Khasid i talmudist. Sravnitel'nyi opyt o Pasternake i Mandel'shtame." *Zvezda*, Vol. 4 (2000), 82-98.

57 *Boris Pasternak* (Yekaterinburg: U-Faktoriya, 2003), 9. It seems significant that when both Mandelstam and Pasternak write early poems about finding faith and identity, they had recourse to fruit imagery. The first poem of Mandelstam's first anthology, *Stone*, begins: "The careful and dull sound/Of a fruit torn from a tree" (Mandel'shtam, *Stikhotvoreniya*, 29).

58 Martin Buber, *Tales of the Hasidim* (New York: Schocken Books, 1975), 133.

59 *Boris Pasternak*, 390.

60 *Ibid.*

61 Gary Saul Moron, "Crimes Against Culture." *New Criterion*, May 1, 2017, 18.

62 *Ibid.*, 268.

63 Buber, *Tales of the Hasidim*, 93.

64 *Ibid.*, 294.

65 On passion-suffering in Russia, see Daniel Rancour-Laferriere, *The Slave Soul of Russia. Moral Masochism and the Soul of Suffering* (New York: NYU Press, 1996).

66 See John Givens. "'Emphatically Human, Deliberately Provincial': The Christ of Boris Pasternak." *The Image of Christ in Russian Literature: Dostoevsky, Tolstoy, Bulgakov, Pasternak* (Cornell University Press, 2018), 177–204.

67 Pasternak, *Doktor Zhivago*, 345.

68 Quoted in Virginia Spencer Carr, *Dos Passos. A Life* (Garden City: Doubleday and Company, 1984), 245.

69 *Ibid.*, 237.

70 *Ibid.*, 243.

71 See, for example, Viktor Shklovsky, "Kino i literatura," *Eyzenshteyn* (Moscow: Iskusstvo, 1973), 146-9.

72 John Dos Passos, "Introduction," *Three Soldiers* (New York: The Modern Library, 2002), xvii.

73 *Ibid.*, xix.

74 *Ibid.*, xvii.

75 John Dos Passos, *The Big Money* (New York: The New American Library, 1963), 35.

76 Deming Brown, *Soviet Attitudes toward American Writing* (Princeton: Princeton U. Press, 1962), 93.

77 *Ibid.*, 85.

78 *Ibid.*, 90.

79 See *ibid.*, 93-4.

80 *Ibid.*, 105.

81 *Solzhenitsyn. A Biography by Michael Scammell* (New York London: W. W. Norton, 1984), 162.

82 Page numbers after quotations from *August 1914* refer to the following edition: Aleksandr Solzhenitsyn, *Sobraniye sochinenii, VII, Krasnoye koleso. Povestvovaniye v otmerennykh srokakh. Uzel I. Avgust chetynadtsatogo*, I (Moscow: Vremya, 2017).

83 *Ibid.*, 789.

84 Alfred Kazin, "Dos Passos, Society, and the Individual," in *Dos Passos. A Collection of Critical Essays.* Andrew Hacker, ed. (Englewood Cliffs: Prentice-Hall, 1974), 112.

85 *Ibid.*, 104.

86 Quoted in Blanche H. Gelfant, "John Dos Passos: The Synoptic Novel," in *ibid.*, 39.

87 I have discussed the Russian perception of the revolution of 1917 as the Apocalypse in *Stalin's Soviet Monastery,* xiii.

88 James Jones, *From Here to Eternity* (New York: Charles Scribner's Sons, 1951), 211.

89 James Jones, *The Thin Red Line* (New York: Charles Scribner's Sons, 1962), 236.

90 Jones, *From Here to Eternity*, 77-8.

91 Konstantin Simonov, *Zhivye i mertvye* (Moscow: Eksmo, 2013), 63.

92 *Ibid.*, 33.

93 *Ibid.*, 33-34.

94 *Ibid.*, 130.

95 *Ibid.*, 86.

96 *Ibid.*

97 Korney Chukovsky, *Dnevnik 1930-1969.* (M. Sovremennyi pisatel', 1994), 141.

98 The ambiguity of the "beautiful lady" in Blok's "Verses about the Beautiful Lady" is a key missing link that connects the passage in *War and Peace* to the overheated rhetoric of statements expressing love for the Leader in the Soviet period. In Russian "lady"; "Russia"; and "revolution" are all feminine nouns. In post-reform Russia it was easy to conflate these meanings. And then when the cults of Lenin and Stalin matured, the two men became the incarnations of the revolution, and thus appropriate love objects for both men and women.

99 Simonov, *Ibid.*, 245.

100 *Ibid.,* 525.
101 *Ibid.,* 588.

VII.

A Proposed Periodization of Russian Literature, 1825-1918

As Vladimir Linkov points out, "The problem of periodization is not popular in our time; people have not simply a skeptical, but even an ironic, hostile attitude toward it."[1] However, he goes on, "Periodization, unless it has a formal character, is an indicator of an understanding of the literary process."[2] What he means by referring to the "formal character" of periodization is the widespread belief that literary periods necessarily begin and end in years that end in 0.

It is therefore instructive to cite a classic Russian example of periodization, which has a formal character. I reproduce here a table that Natalya Vorobyova posted online.[3]

Table I. Russian Literature of the Nineteenth Century

Years	Literary Direction
1800-1830s	Collision of Various Styles
1830s	Romanticism and Realism
1840s-1850s	Idealism
1860s	Realism, Romantic Poets
1870s	Realism, *Narodnik* Writers

Years	Literary Direction
1880s	Critical Realism
1890s	Critical Realism, Proletarian Literature

A noteworthy feature of this scheme is the way it carries over terms and concepts from Soviet histories of Russian literature. It incorporates such features of Soviet criticism as an unquestioning belief on the validity of terms ending in –ism, and a comparable belief that literary periods can be neatly divided into decades.

When it comes to discussions of writers, the implicit reasoning is that all good writers are democratic; therefore even such politically conservative writers as Tolstoy, Dostoyevsky, and Leskov qualify as "democratic." Moreover, this is a scheme whose simplicity derives from its practice of exclusion. Thus, the 1890s qualifies as a period of proletarian literature because the only writer whom Vorobyova mentions is Maksim Gorky. Shockingly, she finds it unnecessary to mention Anton Chekhov, Ivan Bunin, and Valery Bryusov. The intellectual deficiencies and historical gaps in this scheme make it easy to criticize. However, these issues direct a thoughtful investigator's attention to developing ways to present a more thorough, more rigorous periodization.

The detailed periodization that I present here prevents literary history from becoming what Tynyanov aptly called "a history of generals," which Tynyanov with tongue in cheek described like this: "Lomonosov begat Derzhavin; Derzhavin began Zhukovsky; Zhukovsky began Pushkin; Pushkin began Lermontov."[4] In such a history, chronology is all, and the only thing that matters is sequence.

As I treat the matter here, defining the beginnings and ends of literary periods has the effect of defining literary generations, and it is generations that give coherence to a given era. (Sorting out these generations will require numerous sub-headings.) To quote the always perspicacious Tynyanov again, "An author's individualism is not a static scheme; the literary personality is dynamic, like the literary era, with which and in which it moves."[5] Thoughtful Russian scholars rethought the concept of a literary era, and its dynamics, after the Soviet Union collapsed in 1991. Mention must be made here of the exemplary *History of Russian Literature*, by Andrew Kahn, Mark Lipovetsky, Irina Reyfman, and Stephanie Sandler.[6] The advantage of a multi-authored volume—something that has numerous precedents in Russian scholarly practice—is that it ensures full coverage of genres and time periods.

For the sake of clarity I present here my proposed periodization of Russian literature from 1825 to 1918. A full clarification and justification will follow.

Table II. A Proposed Periodization of Russian Literature, 1825-1918

The Golden Age of Aristocratic Poetry, 1825-41
A Period of Beginnings, 1841-56
The Golden Age of Aristocratic Prose, 1856-81
The Age of Chekhov, 1881-1904
The Silver Age, 1894-1910
The Acmeist and Futurist Generations, 1910-18

Anyone who wishes to understand Russian literature from the 1890s on will do well to keep in mind the key principle that literary generations do not necessarily march in sequence as discrete entities. In 1910, for example, the major Symbolist, Acmeist and Futurist poets were all active, and a comprehensive periodization will take that into account.

If another Chomskian analogy be allowed, literary history has both a surface structure and a deep structure. Because of its biographical orientation, the periodization proposed here is limited to the surface structure of the subject. It does not analyze the relationships between works or styles; those issues belong to deep structure. It also does not analyze inter-generational issues such as the long-term effects of Pushkin's legacy. However, for the sake of completeness, Tynyanov's principles for analyzing the deep structure of literary history may be cited here as inspiration for a future project.

Tynyanov states his key principle of the deep structure of literary history and uses some key Formalist terms when he writes, "But if the sense of *interaction* of factors disappears...the fact of art is erased; it is automatized."[7] (Tynyanov's emphasis) In order to have interaction there must be two or more factors in play, and thus this principle shows Tynyanov's commitment to conceptual pluralism. Tynyanov was too restrained to use a word like "shock," but what he is talking about here is what art critic Robert Hughes called "the shock of the new" as a principle of modern art.[8] A shock, or in Tynyanov's milder terminology, a sense of interaction, results from genuine innovation, which produces a sense of the difference between the present, when the genuinely new work appears, and the readers' memories of works that appeared in the past. Clearly, the study of the deep structure of literary history requires detailed analyses, which is why the present essay can only address surface structure, primarily in terms of biography.

As the title of this chapter indicates, it addresses a little less than a century of Russian literature, and it proceeds in two ways. It establishes the time limits for the beginnings and ends of the various periods, and in the spirit of Tynyanov's deep historical sense, asks two questions about them: Which writers were writing during these periods? And how do they and their works form coherences of various kinds with each other?

In this chapter I propose to treat the issue of literary generations in Russia in a new way, by loosening the usual connections with poiltical history, and strengthening the connections with social history. As Astrid Erll points out in an informative essay, the use of generations as a historical concept goes back to the work of German sociologist Karl Manheim.[9] Generations are formed, she suggests, because they share what is called in German a *Zeitheimat*, which she defines as "a certain period of time which was formative for the group, in which its members feel rooted, which has shaped them, to which they travel back in their memories."[10] This is a very useful experiential definition of literary generations and thus of historical periods. The complexity of history is such that historical periods, as defined in this way, rarely if ever begin or end in years that end in 0.

Clearly, the nature and definition of literary periods is a broad subject. Here, as in previous chapters, I rely on research by American scholars and propose to apply it to Russia. In this respect the key publication is *Generations. The History of America's Future 1584-2069,* by William Strauss and Neil Howe. Very persuasively, and in the tradition of American individualism, Strauss and Howe begin by identifying the historical actors who were born in a particular generation-defining era; they then trace the activities of these people over the lifespan of that generation. They claim, controversially, that four identifiable kinds of generations have predominated in American history, and that the alternation of these generations forms a long-term historical pattern.

In analyzing the generations of Russian literary history, I will apply an adapted version of Strauss and Howe's method as well as some principles first articulated by the Spanish writer Julian Marías in his book *Generations. A Historical Method.* Marías flatly asserts, "Without generations, history is incomprehensible."[11] I would adapt this programmatic formulation to say that without generations, literary history lacks coherence. Literary history without generations is merely a succession of authors and masterpieces in which chronology alone dominates.

I do associate myself with Marías's milder statement that, "The theory of generations reveals itself procedurally, that is, it has to be applied to historical reality in order to become fully realized as a theory."[12] The issue of the length of generations is a prime example of the way the theory of generations, when applied to historical reality, reveals itself procedurally. Marías says that a generation lasts 15 years; Strauss and Howe say that it lasts 22 years. For the purposes of what generational theorists call "generational succession," will adopt the latter figure, keeping in mind the advantages of flexibility in including key figures. The question of which writers to include in a given generation and which to leave out is obviously of major importance. My balance of representativeness versus inclusiveness may provoke discussion of this issue, for which there may be no solution that enjoys general consensus.

Thus, in this chapter I offer a proposed periodization of Russian literature that retains Strauss and Howe's use of biographical groupings as a key to generational identity, yet also allows for the variations that inevitably occur in history. In Russian political history, the death of a leader, such as the death of Stalin in 1953, sometimes marks a sharp division between one era and another, and has far-reaching implications for cultural history as a whole. The chronic instability of the Russian political system, characterized as it is by long reigns of strong leaders followed by periods of crisis, gives exceptional importance to such divisions, or inflection points. Solzhenitsyn had a term for these inflection points; he called them "knots" in history.

In the interest of promoting social history, I wish to point out that the death of a major writer as well as the death of a major leader can also create a cultural knot, and also function as a marker of generational succession in literary history. However, one reason why chronology alone serves as an inadequate guide to a literary period as a coherent era is that a period can, and often does, come to an end while some of its major representatives are still alive. As Marías puts it, "Generations do not come and go in a single file, but are overlapped, joined, and interlaced."[13]

A classic example of the overlapping of literary generations is the career of Pyotr Vyazemsky, one of the longest-lived of all Russian writers. Vyazemsky died in 1878 at the age of 84. Vyazemsky had been good friends with Pushkin, and could have read *Anna Karenina* before he died! Then there is Tolstoy, who died at the height of the Silver Age in 1910 at the age of 82. Moreover, two major representatives of the Silver Age lived into the age of Socialist Realism. Andrey Bely died in 1934 at the age of 54, and Mikhail Kuzmin died in 1936 at the age of 64.

As a striking example of the way periods and styles in Russian literature overlap, let us take three very different writers—Pyotr Vyazemsky, Vyacheslav Ivanov, and Aleksandr Solzhenitsyn. The lives of Vyazemsky and Ivanov overlapped, as did the lives of Ivanov and Solzhenitsyn. Vyazemsky was born in 1792, and Solzhenitsyn died in 2008. That is a span of 216 years in the lives of only three writers!

Given overlaps such as these, in this proposed periodization of modern Russian literature I find it metodologically useful to distinguish between biographical and literary coherence. It is convenient to organize biographical coherence as a matter of the dates of birth. Writers who were born in the same period face the same historical and cultural situations as they move through life. When they publish in a certain time period, the shared features of their work create the tenor of an era.

Literary coherence, however, is another matter. In establishing literary coherence, one must often decide which deaths define the end of an era. The exemplary case is the death of Pushkin in 1837. Naturally, Russians tend to think that that traumatic event defined the end of an era. For reasons stated below, I believe that it makes much more sense to say that the death of Lermontov in 1841, and then the publication of *Dead Souls* in the next year, defined the end of an era.

Since the following discussion of periodization in Russian literature primarily uses the dates of birth and death to demonstrate the coherence of literary periods with one another, it does not deal with family dynamics, as previous chapters have done. While birth order and parental loss play vital roles in forming the mentality of writers, these personal matters do not meaningfully affect generational identity. Except in discussing the exceptional importance of the inflection point between Turgenev and Chekhov, and thus at the end of the aristocratic era in Russian literature, this chapter will not deal in literary analysis.

Twentieth-century Russia offers an especially vivid illustration of the principle that generations overlap. In 1913, the extraordinary last year of peace, the year of *The Rite of Spring*, *Victory over the Sun*, and of the Romanov Centennial, the Symbolists, the Acmeists, and the Futurists were all writing. One cannot therefore calculate the relative ages of these generations in any meaningful way. However, if we begin with the Golden Age of Aristocratic Poetry, beginning in 1825, and end with The Symbolist Generation in 1910, that grouping includes five periods for a total of 85 years. That number produces an average cultural age of each generation of 17 years, which is a little short, and is to be explained by the significant overlap between the Age of Chekhov and the Symbolist Generation.

Social Class and Russian Literary History

In nineteenth-century Russia, as in Europe in general, social class mattered, and it mattered enormously. It is one of the numerous deficiencies of Soviet historians that despite their professed belief in Marxism and the class struggle they could not adequately address the overriding significance of social class for the Russian classics. Yet this lacuna is not solely a matter of the abundant inadequacies of Marxism; the well-informed, open-minded authors of the *Oxford History of Russian Literature* also do not include social class as a factor in literary development either. Nevertheless, the fact that Tolstoy, Dostoyevsky and Turgenev were hereditary aristocrats is fraught with implications. They may, or may not, have been Realists. The validity of that term has been disputed; what has not been disputed, and cannot be disputed, is that they were aristocrats. Similarly, Goncharov, Leskov, and Chekhov were not aristocrats, and that fact is also fraught with important stylistic and thematic implications. Writers who were not aristocrats thought and wrote differently from writers who were aristocrats.

When one construes social class not as a moral category, but rather as a defining biographical marker like other biographical markers such as birth order or sexual orientation, one reads both aristocratic writers and non-aristocratic writers in a different, more informed way. Social class matters in literary history because, among other things, class differences translate into stylistic differences. Thus, a great deal of Chekhov's importance for Russian literature, and an explanation for some of his innovations, derives from his non-aristocratic origins. Turgenev, Chekhov's major literary precursor, wrote like an aristocrat; Chekhov, the son of a bankrupt store owner, did not. Although Tolstoy did not die until 1910, it is the assassination of Tsar Aleksandr II in 1881 that marks the end of the aristocratic era in Russian literature, as a subsequent discussion will show in more detail.

The two outliers in the age of aristocratic prose, Ivan Goncharov and Nikolay Leskov, deserve a separate comment. They both came from the merchant class, and as such they represent two possible responses to the aristocratic dominance of literature at the time. Goncharov's *Oblomov*, about an aristocrat who won't get out of bed, and would probably have been diagnosed with agoraphobia, the fear of public spaces, if the term had been used at the time, does not exactly criticize the aristocrats. The novel does, however, express an awareness of their inadequacies as a social class. The acclaim with which it was received, and the speed with which Oblomovism became a byword for aristocratic indifference to the world indicates a certain social awareness of the problem that aristocrats posed for Russian society. One could consider Oblomov's withdrawal from the world an extreme form of secularized monasticism, thus as one response to the threat of the open spaces along which Gogol's troika makes its way.

Leskov is another matter altogether. In his works such as *The Sealed Angel* aristocrats either do not matter at all, or play secondary roles. Although he would not have put it like this, what Leskov really cared about was the Russian language. (His delight in vernacular Russian invites comparisons with Mark Twain's comparable delight in vernacular English.) If one were to take a sentence at random from Tolstoy, and a sentence at random from Leskov, it would be readily apparent which sentence belonged to whieh author. It would also be readily apparent which author was an aristocrat, and which one was not. As a writer who created characters who speak quirky, substandard Russian, Leskov the stylist clearly anticipates Solzhenitsyn.[14]

The Great Age of Russian Literature

Let us begin, then, at the beginning of the great era of modern Russian literature. Here is my grouping of the relevant poets, with their dates of birth and death, and their ages at death.

Table III. The Golden Age of Aristocratic Poetry, 1825-42

Poet	Year of Birth	Year of Death	Age at Death
Denis Davydov	1784	1839	55
Konstantin Batyushkov	1787	1855	58
Pyotr Vyazemsky	1792	1878	84
Aleksandr Griboyedov	1795	1826	31
Wilhelm Kűchelbecker	1797	1846	49
Anton Delvig	1798	1831	33
Aleksandr Pushkin	1799	1837	37

Poet	Year of Birth	Year of Death	Age at Death
Yevgeny Baratynsky	1800	1844	44
Aleksandr Odoyevsky	1802	1839	37
Fyodor Tyutchev	1803	1873	70
Nikolay Yazykov	1803	1846	43
Nikolay Gogol	1809	1852	43
Mikhail Lermontov	1814	1841	27

As presented here, this generation spans 30 years, from 1784 to 1814. However, if we remove the two outliers, we get a span of only 15 years. Davydov and Lermontov, poets with guns, deserve inclusion for both historical and literary reasons.

As poets, it was the historical task of this generation to assimilate the Russian heritage of Lomonosov and Derzhavin to the French heritage of Enlightenment literature. It is appropriate to associate them with Romanticism, since they are the contemporaries of Victor Hugo, who was born in 1802. They entered the stream of literary history a generation later than William Wordsworth in England and Friedrich Hölderlin in Germany, who were both born in 1770.

In deciding on a year for the beginning of a literary era, birth dates will obviously serve no useful purpose. It takes a while even for literary geniuses to come to artistic maturity. The year 1825 has such exceptional poiltical significance that it clearly marks a knot, or inflection point. It was of course in 1825 that Aleksandr I died, and the ill-fated Decembrist uprising occurred. But a death, even the death of a tsar and an abortive coup, does not necessarily mark an inflection point. What matters about 1825 is the confluence of dramatic political events with an exceptionally important literary event, the publication of the first chapter of *Yevgeny Onegin*, the first work of enduring importance in Russian literature.

The statist orientation of Soviet critics has made it difficult to think productively about the long-term effects of the Decembrist Uprising. Immediately after the event, Pushkin was affected because he was close to some of the participants.

More generally, though, the event had minimal literary effect on the major figures. A case could be made for Lermontov, but even there the evidence, I would argue, is sketchy.

As the well-informed authors of the Oxford *History of Russian Literature* acknowledge, "No fixed date marks the end of Romanticism."[15] However, Donald Rayfield in his thoughtful, perceptive essay "The Golden Age of Russian Poetry" understands the Golden Age more as a socio-political phenomenon than a literary one.

> For our purposes, the Golden Age begin in 1813, with the surge of creative optimism that followed Russia's defeat of Napoleon, reaching its climax in 1825 at the end of Alexander I's reign and persists until about 1845, when Nicholas I's censorship and the triumph of prose genres over verse marks the Age's demise.[16]

I prefer to think of literary history in personal, rather than purely political terms, so with regard to the end of this generation as a literary grouping, I believe it appropriate to extend its life for a mere four years, from 1837 to 1841. Doing so makes it possible to include a major era-defining death, the death of Lermontov.

Consider the advantage of extending the period to 1841. By 1841, it was not just Pushkin and Lermontov who were dead. By 1841, Griboyedov, Delvig, Davydov, and Odoyevsky were also dead. That makes six of the original thirteen poets who were dead. Of those who remained alive, Baratynsky had only three more years to live; Kűchelbecker had only five. Thus, by 1841, well over half of the original group was either dead or no longer actively writing. In Russia, as in Europe, the members of this poetic generation died young. Pushkin's contemporary John Keats (1795-1821), the ultimate example, died at the age of 26.

And then there is the matter of Gogol and his unique genius. He was so idiosyncratic, so caught up in his extravagant wordplay, that he was hardly affected by the uprising. As a gay Ukrainian man, he was out of place in St. Petersburg, so it makes sense that he, a prose writer and dramatist, is also out of place in this literary generation of poets. Still, he did call *Dead Souls* a "poem," perhaps as an acknowledgment of the dominance of poetry at the time. *Dead Souls* was published in 1842, and marks the transition from poetry to prose, which will dominate the next half-century of Russian literature. Gogol never wrote any significant fiction after *Dead Souls*, so the end of his career almost coincides with the death of Lermontov in 1841.

That leaves Tyutchev and Vyazemsky, the only members of this literary generation who survived into old age. Tyutchev died in 1873 at the age of 70. He was an outlier not just because he spent so much of his life in Germany. Rayfield goes so far as to say, "Tiutchev does not belong to the Golden Age—he is too much a timeless poet to belong to the nineteenth century."[17] Rayfield's statement poses a key question for literary history in general, namely the relationship between specific qualities of a writer's work and the era. This intriguing question cannot be resolved here. Vyazemsky died in 1878 at the age of 84. He and Tyutchev both had long, successful careers in the imperial bureaucracy, Tyutchev in the diplomatic corps, and Vyazemsky in the censor's office, of all things. In the interest of establishing coherence between the imperial and the Soviet periods of Russian literature, I might point out that the careers of Tyutchev and Vyazemsky anticipate those of the Konstantins, Fedin and Simonov. Apparently, all four writers were also able administrators, and rose to the highest levels of the governmental organizations in which they served.

Vyazemsky's long life merits our attention because he represents a case study in the continuity of Russian culture. He was born into an old aristocratic family, and inherited a fortune at an early age. He never lacked for money, so he was that rarest of things, a rich poet! Like Tolstoy, he wrote what he wanted to write, when he wanted to write it, without any financial considerations at all. He had success both as a poet and also as an administrator. Nevertheless, his life was marked by bouts of depression as well as grief brought on by the early death of several of his children.[18]

The short period of 15 years between 1841 and 1856 is an anomalous one in Russian literary history in that it was a period of beginnings, of first publications of short works for the geniuses of the 1860s, rather than mature works. One has the sense that Russian literature was preparing itself for the huge burst of energy that was about to be unleashed. To emphasize the continuity between this period and The Golden Age of Aristocratic Prose, I list the major writers of that period here:

A Period of Beginnings, 1841-56

Table IV. The Golden Age of Aristocratic Prose, 1856-81

Writer	Date of Birth	Date of Death	Age at Death
Ivan Goncharov	1812	1891	79

Writer	Date of Birth	Date of Death	Age at Death
Ivan Turgenev	1818	1883	65
Afanasy Fet	1820	1892	72
Fyodor Dostoyevsky	1821	1881	60
Nikolay Nekrasov	1821	1877	56
Mikhail Saltykov-Shchedrin	1826	1889	63
Leo Tolstoy	1828	1910	82
Nikolay Leskov	1831	1895	64

The birth years for this tightly grouped selection of writers cover a period of only 19 years. They lived an averate of 67.6 years, just over Turgenev's 65 years. Tolstoy is the exception in this respect, as he is in so many things.

In transitional periods, national literatures need people who have the artistic ability to recognize talent and the organizational skills to nourish it. In the 1840s, that person was the poet-editor-organizer Nikolay Nekrasov, the first of several such key figures. To further establish the coherence of Russian literature over the centuries, it is worth noting that in transitional periods two other men have appeared and played vital roles as organizers. Nekrasov's successor in this role was another aristocrat who was not born in St. Petersburg, but who left his stamp on its culture. This was Sergey Dyagilev, or Diaghilev, as his name is usually transliterated, the legendary impresario of the Ballets Russes. In turn, Diaghilev's successor in this vital role (in different circumstances, to be sure) was someone very much like Nekrasov, the poet Aleksandr Tvardovsky, who served as editor of *The New World* for a number of years, and who promoted Solzhenitsyn's career at the time when it was dangerous to do so.

The Formalist critics pointed out that in the 1840s Russian literature lacked the coherence necessary to produce the sustained story line of a novel (Goncharov's *An Ordinary Story*, published in 1847, is the exception that proves the rule), so it resorted to collections of stories. The obvious example is *A Hero of Our Time,* which is a collection of stories narrated by Pechorin. Similarly, *Dead Souls* does not have a unified plot, but is a series of episodes as Chichikov travels around the countryside and deceives one landowner after another. In the spirit of the time,

Nekrasov edited a series of collections of both poetry and prose, or almanacs, as they were called at the time. The best-known of these was *The Physiology of St. Petersburg*, from 1845.

In 1843 something momentous for the future of Russian literature happened. In that year Nekrasov met Vissarion Belinsky. It has been well said that Belinsky loved literature, but threatened to smother it in his embrace. I showed in *Stalin's Soviet Monastery* that by asserting the authority of the critic over the artist, Belinsky in his famous "Letter to Gogol" (1847) anticipated the principles that Soviet authorities would later use to suppress literary innovation. Belinsky's forceful personality had aggressive, authoritarian elements that Soviet critics would exploit as a way of suppressing creativity. He died in 1848, so he did not outlive the decade. In a very Russian way, he combined a belligerent intolerance of dissent with a genuine love of literature. He was the right man for an era in which Russian literature lacked an identity; his regular historical surveys gave it the beginnings of one.

If Belinsky and Nekrasov had done nothing else, they would have an honored place in the history of Russian literature because they facilitated the beginnings of the careers of both Dostoyevsky and Tolstoy. The publication of "Poor Folk" in 1846 made Dostoyevsky temporarily famous, and the effusive Belinsky declared him a genius. For his part, Tolstoy sent the manuscript of his first published work "Childhood," the first work in his trilogy "Childhood. Boyhood. Youth" to Nekrasov in July of 1852. Tolstoy published one short story after another until the early 1860s until he began work on *War and Peace.*

Although Tolstoy and Dostoyevsky knew that they wanted to be writers from an early age, Turgenev did not. He studied Latin and Greek and for a while thought he might pursue a scholarly career. One striking feature of his life is his wide circle of acquaintances. He met Pushkin and Lermontov briefly at the very ends of their careers, and later in life became friends with Henry James. Turgenev wrote poetry and drama until he finally began work on the sketches that would become *Notes of a Hunter*, which came out between 1847 and 1851. After the death of Nicholas I in 1855 the censorship eased up, and in 1856 he was able to publish his first novel *Rudin*, thereby bringing the period of preparation to an end.

If we combine the first three periods of aristocratic literature and take them as a whole, we find that they lasted for a total of only 56 years, from 1825 to 1881, and thus for about two generations. However, the Golden Age of Aristocratic Prose has a key inflection point, the emancipation of the serfs in 1861, which may be usefully understood as part of the worldwide upheavals that occurred in the 1860s and that had far-reaching repercussions.

The tumultuous decade of the 1860s witnessed the American Civil War as well as other important events. In 1866 there was a revolution in Spain; in 1868 the Tokugawa Regime in Japan collapsed, and was followed by the Meiji Restoration, which began the modern era of Japanese history. The Suez Canal opened in 1869 and vastly enlarged the possibilities for world trade. In their different ways, then, these events created the pre-conditions for what we call the modern world. It is most appropriate that Charles Baudelaire published his influential ideas about modernity in *The Painter of Modern Life* in 1863.

To return to Russia, the emancipation of the serfs released tremendous creative energy in all the arts in the1860s. It was in this decade that Tolstoy and Dostoyevsky wrote two of their masterpieces, *War and Peace* and *Crime and Punishment*. In 1863, fourteen painters including Ilya Repin and Ivan Kramskoy left the Academy and ultimately formed the group known as the Wanderers, who dominated Russian painting until the 1890s. In 1867, critic Vladimir Stasov gave the name "The Mighty Bunch" to the group of composers, including Modest Musorgsky and Nikolay Rimsky-Korsakov, who would dominate Russian music in a comparable way for decades.

If we consider the overall cultural geography of Russia, the first three periods of Russian literature as I have defined them here continue the St. Petersburg era of Russian culture as a whole. Peter the Great required some of the nobles to live in St. Petersburg, and it was there that the imperial bureaucracy was centered, of course. For much of the quarter century of the Golden Age, Goncharov, Nekrasov, and Dostoyevsky lived in St. Petersburg. Turgenev traveled a lot, but he visited the capital from time to time. And of course the aging Pyotr Vyazemsky still lived in St. Petersburg. Only Tolstoy kept his distance from the capital, living in baronial splendor on his estate.

The works produced in this period have of course formed an essential part of the curriculum in Russian schools for generations, and rightly so. This is not the place for further textual analysis of these masterpieces, so the following discussion will concentrate on the personal and cultural dynamics that produced them and thus on the social history of the period.

The Significance of Nikolay Chernyshevsky

A key figure in the dynamics of the period was Nikolay Chernyshevsky (1828-89), both for what he did at the time, and for the way Lenin and the Bolsheviks later canonized his work. Chernyshevsky was not an aristocrat, and it is in defining his social position that the quasi-feudal social organization of Russia makes the inadequacy of European terminology inadequate. Chernyshevsky was not somebody that the French would have recognized as a bourgeois, nor was he a proletarian. What he was, was a *popovich*, or priest's son. (Orthodox clergy in the lower ranks are allowed to marry.) It is the great virtue of historian Laurie Manchester that she has drawn our attention to the great social significance of the *popovichi*, a social grouping united by shared life experiences, rather than social class in the usual meaning of the word. Manchester about writes of them that, "They identified themselves as 'new men' ready to lead Russian and entitled to do so because they were superior to Russia's only other educated group, the nobility, who so viciously attacked them."[19] As I showed in *Stalin's Soviet Monastery,* the *popovichi* indirectly bequeathed their sense of themselves a separate elite destined to rule Russia to the Communist Party; a key element in their legacy came from the fact that Stalin spent the formative years of his adolescence with *popovichi*, and took over their attitudes.[20]

To understand Chernyshevsky's role in the dynamics of the Golden Age, we must begin with the relationship between Nekrasov and Chernyshevsky. Although Nekrasov was only seven years older than Chernyshevsky, he became a father figure to the young man, rather as Georgy Plekhanov would later become a father figure to Vladimir Lenin.

If we can say nothing else about Chernyshevsky, then we must say that he was true to his convictions, spending something like 20 years in prison and exile. In defining his larger historical significance for Russia, it is useful to distinguish between the historical Chernyshevsky and what Lenin made of Chernyshevsky. Neither Lenin nor any other revolutionary leader would have, or could have, accepted Chernyshevsky's ardent feminism, for example.

Early in his dissertation *The Aesthetic Relations of Art to Reality*, Chernyshevsky uses an indicative phrase, "the respect for real life."[21] By "real life" he meant life outside the monastery, and all that the monastery implied for Russian life, and life after serfdom. In such new (new for Russia anyway) conditions the new Russians whom he believed he represented had little social precedent to fall back on. On their behalf Chernyshevsky wrote a programmatic novel and used the question that was on their mind as the title: *What Is to Be Done?*[22] What his characters do is to make their way in the world by taking up small-scale capitalism (dress-making), and in this respect it is indicative that one of the characters is an American.

Writers usually don't understand the larger implications of what they write, and Chernyshevsky certainly did not. There is an instructive opposition, of which Chernyshevsky was certainly not aware, between two of his male characters, Lopukhov and Rakhmetov. On one hand Lopukhov advocates "striving for utility"; on the other hand Rakhmetov engages in such ascetic practices as sleeping on nails. Obviously, Rakhmetov does not strive for utility; he has no interest in it. Sleeping on nails serves no useful purpose. What it does, however, is something that will become of paramount importance in the Soviet era, namely bringing ascetic practices out of the monastery and engaging in them as a response to a long-standing imperative from Russian history. Thus, Rakhmetov is, as it were, the mirror image of the art for art's sake that Chernyshevsky associated with aristocrats and that he so despised. Rakhmetov practices asceticism for asceticism's sake. Neither he nor anybody else can articulate a useful purpose for it. As admirers of Chernyshevsky, Lenin and the Bolsheviks could no more practice utility than Lopukhov could, which is why they created an exceptionally inefficient economy. And in the gulag people involuntarily followed Rakhmetov's example, and practiced asceticism for the sake of asceticism.

Aside from Chernyshevsky's long-term significance, he played a key role in the literary dynamics of the 1860s. It has been said that he wrote *What Is to Be Done?* in response to *Fathers and Sons.* He was dissatisfied with Turgenev's portrayal of Bazarov, believing with some justice that an aristocrat couldn't adequately a "new man." That was the beginning of the dynamic that continued when Dostoyevsky read *What Is to Be Done?* and was outraged. Utilitarianism and the striving for good flew in the face of everything that he believed, and Part I of "Notes from the Underground" arose as a polemic with Chernyshevsky. Dostoyevsky's reaction against utilitarianism continued in *Crime and Punishment.*

The Literary History of Literature

Turning now from the social history of literature to the literary history of literature, we notice that Dostoyevsky had a serious, long-term engagement with a far greater writer than Chernyshevsky, Gogol. Dostoyevsky worked through most of his anxiety of influence from Gogol, in the person of Porfiry Petrovich, in *Crime and Punishment.* This achievement may explain why he was able to break out of St. Petersburg in his next novel, *The Idiot*. In the second half of that novel, Dostoyevsky moves from St. Petersburg, which had obsessed him for his entire literary career until that moment, to the provinces. His remaining novels—*The Devils, A Raw Youth* and *The Brothers Karamazov*—are all set in the provinces.

The break in Dostoyevsky's work begins in the middle of *The Idiot*. Part Three of that novel begins like this:

> People constantly complain that we have no practical people, that we have many political people, for example; also lots of generals; as many administrators as you need, at the moment you can find whatever kind you want—but there are no practical people. At least everybody complains that there aren't any. (6, 367)

Obviously, Chernyshevsky and his "new people" were still on Dostoyevsky's mind. It may well be that Dostoyevsky begins the part of his career set in the provinces with reference to "practical people" because he sensed that Chernyshevsky had a provincial sensibility.

The Idiot began publication in 1868, just as *War and Peace* was completing its publication. Tolstoy's masterpiece may have been on Dostoyevsky's mind, because this section of *The Idiot* begins with a new situation for him. In it, Yelizaveta Yepanchina frets about marrying off her daughters, and of course marrying off daughters is on the mind of the various parents in *War and Peace*. To be sure, this is a common topic in nineteenth-century novels, but the novelty of the topic for Dostoyevsky that makes the suggestion of the influence of *War and Peace* a reasonable one. Perhaps it is because the topic is new to Dostoyevsky, he makes Yepanchina a comic figure not unlike Anna Andreyevna Skvoznik-Dmukhanovskaya, the Mayor's wife in Gogol's *The Inspector General*. "'In the first place, why won't they get married?' she constantly asked herself. 'To torture their mother. They see the goal of their life in that, and that of course is because there are these new ideas, this damned woman question!'" (6, 371)

We can best understand the significance of *The Brothers Karamazov* in Dostoyevsky's evolution by referring to what psychologist Dean Keith Simonton has called the "swan-song effect."[23] Simonton studied the last works of 172 classical composers and found that they had used their last works to sum up their careers. In classical music, Beethoven's Ninth Symphony, his longest symphony and the only one that uses a chorus, is an exceptionally clear example of a swan song. And surely *The Brothers Karamazov* is Dostoyevsky's swan song. It is his longest novel, and the trial scene at the end, which runs to 125 pages, is Dostoyevsky's longest sustained scene.

In cultural and social terms, the key moment in *The Brothers Karamazov* is the one in which Father Zosima tells Alyosha that he must leave the monastery. We may interpret this instruction as Dostoyevsky's acknowledgment of the necessity to which Chernyshevsky had responded in the previous decade, the necessity for Russians to learn how to live in the world, to figure out what was to be done.

If Dostoyevsky's *oeuvre* breaks into two parts, the first part set in St. Petersburg, and the second part set in the provinces, Tolstoy's *oeuvre* in the Golden Age at least breaks into two parts as well. *War and Peace* is set in the past, of course, while *Anna Karenina* is set in the present. Although Tolstoy would probably not have considered Chernyshevsky worth polemicizing with, as Dostoyevsky did, the question of what to do, how to live one's life in post-reform Russia, hangs over and bedevils the characters in *Anna Karenina*. Anna experiences an unbearable tension, caught between her husband and her lover as she is. This tension causes her to become a paranoid schizophrenic, and she commits suicide under the wheels of the symbolic train that is destroying traditional Russia—the same train, as it were, that Tolstoy himself rode to his death in 1910.

The question of what to do, of how to live one's life, also hangs over Konstantin Levin. He decides to join the peasants in harvesting wheat, but although this communal activity temporarily mitigates his feelings of alienation, it has little economic significance, and Levin gives no sign that he intends to repeat it. Levin doesn't know how to undertake anything new any more than Chernyshevsky's Rakhmetov does. If Rakhmetov repeats ascetic practices of the past because he doesn't know what else to do, Levin also runs his estate because he doesn't know what else to do. In a key scene, he confesses to a fellow-landowner, "So we're without a plan and we live like vestal virgins, put here to watch a fire." (9, 262) Thus, both Rakhmetov and Levin, the man of the new order and the man of the old order, both engage in symbolic, non-goal-oriented practices rooted in the past, not the present. Neither of them can find anything useful to do. Only two decades later would Chekhov in Yermolay Lopakhin be able to present an energetic, goal-oriented Russian character. In that regard, Lopakhin remains unique in pre-1917 Russian literature.

Tolstoy and Dostoyevsky Acknowledge Each Other

Although Tolstoy and Dostoyevsky had friends in common, they never met and they did not correspond. (One might suppose that there was no room in Russia large enough to accommodate both of them at the same time!) It is instructive to notice, however, that each writer implicitly acknowledged the other's work. There are some Dostoyevskian passages in *Anna Karenina*, for example, and to make sense of them, we must understand that Tolstoy's uncanny ability to create a large array of characters meant that he was something of psychological chameleon. It is one of the signs of his literary genius that he could take on the personality and mindset of characters who were very different from him. Anna Karenina is a classic example. By a logical extension, then, his literary genius also enabled him to take on the style of a writer very different from him, namely Dostoyevsky.

The extended scene during which Konstantin and Kitty take care of his brother Nikolay as he dies begins with this startling passage, which is unlike anything that Tolstoy had ever written before:

> In a small dirty hotel room, stained along the painted panels of the walls, behind the thin wall of which a conversation was heard, in the air pervaded by the choking smell of human waste, on a bed moved away from the wall lay a body covered by a quilt. One hand of this body was above the quilt; the enormous palm of this hand, like a rake, was fixed to a long thin bobbin, which was thin and even from beginning to end. The head lay on its side on the pillow. Levin saw see the thin sweaty hair on the temples and tight, seemingly transparent forehead. (9, 70)

Tolstoy's characters do not usually enter—much less die in—dirty, smelly hotel rooms. Nikolay Levin is a recognizably Dostoyevskian character, and his hotel room has a recognizably Dostoyevskian look and feel. Although Tolstoy devotes his usual sensitivity to the scene in which Nikolay dies, it has something of the quality of a stylistic exercise.

Although Nikolay Levin suffers greatly toward the end, he does not achieve the transcendence of Tolstoy's other two men whose suffering and death scenes Tolstoy describes—Prince Andrey in *War and Peace* and Ivan Ilyich in "The Death of Ivan Ilyich." When anomalies occur in mature works by great writers, they cry out for explanations. One possible explanation for this anomaly is that this scene is a response to a scene in *The Idiot*, which had come out just before Tolstoy started *Anna Karenina*. In it, Rogozhin shows Prince Myshkin (significantly named Lev Nikolayevich, like Tolstoy) Nastasya Fillipovna's body: "The sleeping person was covered from head to toe, but the limbs were vaguely distinguished; one could see by the bump that a person stretched out was lying there." (6, 686)

Thus, Russia's two greatest novelists implicitly acknowledged each other as much as they ever could; each writer incorporated some elements of the other's style into one of his great novels. This discussion of their mutual acknowledgment brings the Golden Age of Aristocratic Prose to an end because the publication of *Anna Karenina* and *The Brothers Karamazov* preceded a great historic trauma. On March 13, 1881, the surge of energy that had vivified all the Russian arts in the 1860s and 1870s came to a crashing halt when the seventh attempt to assassinate Tsar Aleksandr II succeeded on a street in St. Petersburg. This, the first assassination of a tsar in a public space, predictably produced widespread revulsion and dismay, even among Russians who were not knee-jerk conservatives.

Deaths in the 1880s

However, for our purposes here what matters is that it was not just the tsar who died and brought an era to a close. In fact, the 1880s was a decade of death that resulted in lasting changes in Russian and European culture, and not just because of the assassination of the tsar. Here is a list of the major artistic figures who died between 1880 and 1890:

Table V. Deaths of Major Aristic Figures, 1880-90

1880 George Eliot; Gustave Flaubert; Jacques Offenbach
1881 Fyodor Dostoyevsky; Modest Mussorgsky
1882 Anthony Trollope
1883 Ivan Turgenev
1886 Aleksandr Ostrovsky
1887 Aleksandr Borodin; Ivan Kramskoy
1890 Vincent Van Gogh

Although between them France and England did lose three major writers, a popular composer and a great painter, these losses surely had less significance than the devastating losses suffered by a single country, Russia—once again, at a time of widespread grief caused by the first assassination of a tsar. Within a period of six years, Russia lost two major composers, two major writers, a major painter, and the dominant playwright of the era. Nekrasov, who died in 1877, predeceased Aleksandr II by four years. Saltykov-Shchedrin and Chernyshevsky both died eight years after him, and five years after Turgenev, in 1889. As if all this were not bad enough, in 1884, Tolstoy published his *Confession*, in which he more or less renounced literature and his previous life in general. And then he brought the decade of death in Russia to a close in 1889 with *The Kreutzer Sonata*, in which the deranged protagonist kills his wife. No country can experience the loss of writers like Dostoyevsky, Turgenev, Tolstoy, and Ostrovsky combined with a traumatic assassination in a single five-year period without major changes in its literary culture.

The publishing histories of Fet and Leskov in this period are also indicative. In 1883 and 1885 Fet published the last two volumes of his poetry, with an indicative title: *Evening Lights*. Leskov did not publish any novels at all in the 1880s. Sixteen years lapsed between *A Wretched Family Line* in 1874 and *The Devil's Dolls*, which came out in 1890. An era had truly drawn to an end. Clearly, 1881 and the years immediately afterward, mark a major inflection point in Russian history, and in Russian culture in general. More specifically, this period marks the end of the aristocratic period in Russian literature.

Although a general discussion of the cultural changes in Europe that began in the 1880s and were the counterparts to the changes in Russia greatly exceeds the scope of this book, I do wish to note a comment by Pierre Bourdieu in his book *The Rules of Art*. Bourdieu identifies a crisis that occurred in French literature in the 1880s and that was comparable to the contemporary crisis in Russia. After a discussion of the relations of various Symbolist writers to their predecessors, he continues:

> But the Symbolist reaction is not completely comprehensible unless it is considered in relation to the specific crisis undergone by literary production in the 1880s, a crisis whose effects on the different literary genres are felt to a greater degree the more economically viable they are.[24]

Bourdieu thinks of what he calls "the literary field" in terms of genre, not individuals, so he does not discuss the relevance of the death of Flaubert in 1880 to what he calls "the crisis undergone by literary production in the 1880s." It was also in the 1880s that the key Symbolist poets in France, Stéfane Mallarmé and Paul Valéry, began to publish. Clearly, a new era in European literature had begun,

To return to Russia, we know, of course, that the first period of great literary achievement in Russia, the aristocratic period, lasted only 56 years, from 1825 to 1881, and thus about two generations. Generally speaking, the first generation consisted of poets, and the second generation consisted of novelists.

The Rise of Chekhov

The absence of the geniuses from the Golden Age cleared the way, as it were, for the non-aristocratic era, an era dominated in literature by Chekhov, the son of a bankrupt merchant. The ways in which Chekhov defined himself in opposition to his aristocratic precursors informed each of his four great plays, and is thus a subject that exceeds the scope of this book, as is a discussion of his mastery of the short story.

However, for the sake of the coherence of Russian literary history, and to emphasize the under-appreciated inflection point that Chekhov represents in Russian literature, and indeed in Russian culture as a whole, we may briefly note two works from 1888 that mark his maturation as an artist. In these works, written at the end of the decade of death, Chekhov defined himself, and his age, in opposition to the aristocratic culture that had preceded him.

The first of these works is his short play *The Proposal*, from 1888, whose wit and verve masks its serious intent. The title of the play refers to the intention of a certain Ivan Lomov to propose to Natasha Chubukova, the daughter of a landowner. This is the surface structure, and only the very naïve think that that is all there is to this play. There is also a deep structure, and Lomov's name, which comes from the verb *lomat'*, "to break," gives us a way into it. In its deep structure, the play is an allegory about the entry of a non-aristocrat who is breaking into the previously inaccessible space of aristocratic society, symbolized here by the manor house, of course. (Lomov signals the awkwardness and insecurity that this audacious act causes him by wearing a tuxedo when he comes to propose.)

And to whom does Lomov wish to propose? To Natalya, of course. For all practical and symbolic purposes there is only one Natalya in Russian literature, and that is Natalya Rostova, from *War and Peace*. In asking for the hand of this Natalya, Natalya Chubukova, Chekhov's surrogate Lomov is symbolically seeking the heart of Russian literature.

However, Chekhov's prime precursor, whom he engaged in some early stories that would be funny if they were not so serious, was not Tolstoy, but Turgenev. The encounter with Turgenev was for Chekhov what the encounter with Gogol was for Dostoyevsky—a long-term, career-defining experience.[25] For example, each of Chekhov's four great plays uses the specific version of the arrival motif—the arrival at an estate in the summer—that is Turgenev first used his play 1850 play *A Month in the Country*.

Chekhov took on Turgenev in an early stage of his career. Whether consciously or unconsciously—we'll never know for sure—Chekhov positioned his plotless story "The Steppe" in opposition to the style of Turgenev's *Notes of a Hunter*. His story "Bezhin Meadow" begins with a classic example of the nature descriptions for which Turgenev is justly renowned:

> It was a beautiful July day, one of those days that occur only when the weather has established itself for a long time. From very early in the morning the sky is clear; the dawn does not come on like a fire; it develops with a gentle reddening. The sun is not fiery, not heated, as it is during a dry spell, not dark-reddish, as before a storm, but bright and radiant in a welcoming way. It peacefully comes out under a narrow and long cloud; it will freshly gleam forth and sink into its purple fog.[26]

The style here is consistent with the style of Turgenev's poem "Spring Morning." The use of evocative colors and the reference to the silent forest suggest an observer looking at a visual display, and Turgenev's nature descriptions surely owe something to the landscape paintings that he had seen in Paris. Although there certainly are people, and interesting ones, in Turgenev's Russian landscapes, nature in them remains primarily a visual display, a silent backdrop to human activities. These silent, colorful landscapes form the next step in the literary treatment of the landscape across which Gogol's troika speeds.

If in "The Proposal" Chekhov took on Tolstoy, in his first long story "The Steppe," Chekhov took on Turgenev. Like "The Proposal," "The Steppe" has both a deep structure, which deals with the past, and a surface structure, which anticipated the future. It is convenient to begin with the deep structure. "The Steppe" is many things, and one of them is an example of how of how somebody who was not an aristocrat would write about nature.

In opposition to so many Russian classics, Chekhov's "The Steppe" begins, not with an arrival, but with a departure. Two men, a priest and a merchant, are taking a little boy, Yegor/Yegorushka away from his home village for the first time to enroll him in a *Gymnasium* in a distant city. Although Chekhov did not write programmatic works, one can say that the treatment of nature was consistent with Bazarov's famous statement in *Fathers and Sons*: "Nature is not a temple, but a workshop, and man is a worker in it." Chekhov's version of the steppe is not exactly a workshop, but it is not a temple, either. It teems with life.

> Ancient murrelets flew over the road with a merry cry; in the grass gophers called back and forth; somewhere far off to the left peewits cried. A flock of partridges, frightened by the cart, fluttered and with their soft "trrr" took flight for the hills. Grasshoppers, crickets, violin beetles, and mole crickets drew out in their grass their squeaky monotonous music.[27]

In this passage, and throughout the story, the steppe hums and buzzes, as a Turgenev landscape never does. One could compile a substantial list of the birds, animals, and insects that Chekhov identifies as inhabitants of the steppe.

While not symbolic or allegorical, "The Steppe" has exceptional historical importance. It presents in beautifully written prose a key process in the social evolution of late nineteenth-century Russia: the departure of boys and men from their home villages for the city in search of education and of employment opportunities. (Although women had fewer opportunities for education, the Bestuzhev Courses for Women had begun in St. Petersburg in 1878.) In "The Steppe," the two men and a boy go out into the world traversed by Gogol's troika not for some unidentified symbolic destination, but as part of the breakup of traditional society under the impact of industrialization and the attendant changes in the Russian economy.

In 1888, the year of "The Proposal" and "The Steppe," Chekhov had sixteen years remaining until his premature death in 1904. During these years, the years of his mastery, he would go on to write four great plays and classic short stories like "The Lady with Lap Dog." In the twentieth century his plays were performed with a frequency second only to those of Shakespeare, whom he took on as a precursor in the play within the play in *The Seagull*. His work had a decisive influence on literature and drama in the West, especially in England. The fascination with Chekhov in the English-speaking world reached an apogee in the spectacularly successful British series *Downton Abbey* (2010-15). Both the general situation of *Downton Abbey*—a manor house under threat—and its characters—aristocrats with personal agendas and servants aspiring to social mobility—derive from Chekhov's *The Cherry Orchard*.

Chekhov's cohort consisted of his friends who fall into two groups, the writers and the artists in other fields. The writers were Maksim Gorky and Ivan Bunin. They both enjoyed Chekhov's friendship, and his influence is readily discernible in their work. For example, Gorky's 1904 play *Summer Folk (Dachniki),* is a pastiche of the themes and characters in Chekhov's plays. And of course Gorky and Bunin invite comparisons in the any discussion of the social history of Russian literature because their careers represented the two possible extremes for twentieth-century Russian writers. Although they both emigrated soon after the revolution, Gorky made visits to the Soviet Union before finally returning there to much acclaim in 1932. Bunin made it clear that he would never go back, and thus these two writers represent the bifurcation of Russian literature for most of the twentieth century. Bunin won the Nobel Prize in 1933, the first Russian writer to do so, and of course the Soviet authorities proclaimed Gorky the gold standard of Socialist Realism.

Despite the importance of Gorky and Bunin for his legacy, Chekhov's closest friends were not other writers, but artists in different fields who were outsiders like him in a rapidly diversifying Russia. These remarkable men included Isaac Levitan, Russia's first major Jewish painter, as well as two other major painters, Konstantin Korovin and Valentin Serov. Chekhov was also good friends with Fyodor Schechtel, a major architect who came from a Russified German family, and who is known as the father of Art Nouveau in Russia. Schechtel, whom Chekhov met through his brother Nikolay, drew the illustrations for Chekhov's first volume of short stories, *Variegated Stories (1888)*. After Chekhov died, Schechtel later built a library and an elegant townhouse for a local merchant in Chekhov's hometown of Taganrog in memory of his brilliant friend.

Here is the list of Chekhov and his literary and artistic cohort.

Table VI. The Age of Chekhov, 1881-1904

Artist	Date of Birth	Date of Death	Age at Death
Fyodor Schechtel	1859	1926	67
Anton Chekhov	1860	1904	44
Isaac Levitan	1860	1900	40
Konstantin Korovin	1861	1939	78
Valentin Serov	1865	1911	46
Maksim Gorky	1868	1936	68
Ivan Bunin	1870	1953	83

Thus, we have seven close friends—three writers, an architect, and three painters—all born within eleven years of each other. Their temporal and personal closeness create a microcosm of Russian culture in this period.

On 17 October, 1896, Chekhov's *The Seagull* had its premiere in St. Petersburg. It met with a cold reception, and a devastated Chekhov took the midnight train back to Moscow, swearing that he would never write for the theater again. We now understand that this awful experience for Chekhov marked a key inflection point of the period, the dissociation of Moscow culture from St. Petersburg culture in the Silver Age. As anybody who has any interest in modern theater knows, Konstantin Stanislavsky and Vasily Nemirovich-Danchenko had the sensitivity to understand what Chekhov had done with *The Seagull*, and they presented it in all its understated eloquence in a spectacular, epoch-making premiere at the Moscow Art Theater a little over two years later, on 16 December, 1898.

The Moscow Art Theater, both as an institution and as a building, may serve as a microcosm of Moscow culture in the Silver Age as well as a reminder of the importance of the performing arts in early twentieth-century Russia. Without the pomp and circumstance of the capital, and also without its bureaucracy and concentration of aristocrats, Moscow was primarily a city of businessmen, and some of them wished to achieve a measure of self-definition by supporting the arts. The first of these was the art patron Pavel Tretyakov, who commissioned the portraits by which Tolstoy, Dostoyevsky, and Turgenev and other great Russian artists are now best known. His collection formed the basis of the world-renowned Tretyakov Gallery. Two other Moscow businessmen, Mikhail Morozov and Sergey Shchukin, also collected art and even played a certain role in the development of modern art when they bought works from Pablo Picasso and Henri Matisse at a time when collectors in Parris were reluctant to do so. [28]

But Tretyakov was not the only Moscow businessman who was interested in the arts. Other families such as the Ryabushinskys and the Morozovs had also made money in business and wished to spend some of it on the arts. One Morozov, Savva Morozov, was interested in the theater, and lavishly subsidized the Moscow Art Theater, so that Stanislavsky had more time for rehearsals that any previous Russian director had ever had. That mattered, because the innovations of Chekhov's plays, which relied on atmosphere rather than plot, made them fiendishly difficult to stage properly, at least until the modern theater assimilated their innovations.

The Moscow Art Theater mattered as a building as well. It was designed by Chekhov's friend Fyodor Schechtel. Thanks to Morozov's generosity, Schechtel was able to carry out a project of total design for the theater, very much as Frank Lloyd Wright would do a few years later in Oak Park. He designed, not just the building, but also details down to the doorknobs and ushers' costumes. The theater, a major cultural landmark in Moscow, still stands on Kammerherr Lane, very much as Schechtel designed it. His elegant sketch of a seagull still serves as the theater's trademark and appears on its programs.

A major factor in the success of *The Seagull* was the performance of Vera Komisarzhevskaya as Nina Zarechnaya. She had intuitive sense for Chekhov's women characters and delighted him with her readings of them. And, like the building of the Moscow Art Theater, Komisarzhevskaya stands for something larger. In the Silver Age something that we can recognize as celebrity culture appeared in Russia, primarily because of the fame of four women, two from Moscow and two from St. Petersburg. The differences between these two pairs of women speak to the larger differences between Moscow culture and St. Petersburg culture.

Four Women Celebrities in the Silver Age

Moscow

- Mariya Yermolova (1853-1928)
- Vera Komisarzhevskaya (1864-1910)

St. Petersburg

- Olga Preobrazhenskaya (1871-1962)
- Matilda Ksheshinskaya (1872-1971)

Mariya Yermolova at the Maly Theater, and Vera Komisarzhevskaya at the Art Theater, were not so much rivals as representatives of two different concepts of theater. Yermolova, who was known for her meticulous preparation for her roles, was a star in a traditional system that rewarded stars. Komisarzhevskaya, eleven years younger than Yermolova, belonged to a different generation. She was an exceptionally talented actress in an ensemble system that included other great actresses such as Chekhov's wife Olga Knipper. Despite these differences, both Yermolova and Komisarzhevskaya have theaters named after them in Moscow today—the first theaters in Russia to be named after actresses.

The Moscow Art Theater was not just the Moscow Art Theater. Its full name was, in Russian, the *khudozhestvenno-dostupnyi teatr,* the "art-accessible theater." Unlike the Maly Theater, it had a populist quality, and proposed to put on plays that were accessible, that ordinary, i.e., non-aristocratic, people could understand, like Gorky's *The Lower Depths.* This was not a theater for the masses, but for the intelligentsia, as opposed to the aristocrats, who had subscriptions to the Bolshoy Theater. This is why Mandelstam once wrote, "The Art Theater is a child of the Russian intelligentsia, flesh of its flesh, bone of its bone."[29]

Mandelstam's comment explains why there was never anything like the Art Theater in St. Petersburg. In St. Petersburg during the Silver Age the Marinsky

Theater dominated, as it still does today. No theater in aristocratic St. Petersburg pretended, or wanted to pretend, to be "accessible." The Marinsky Theater, with its special box for the imperial family, was the home of opera and ballet, the favorite entertainments of the aristocracy. Its great ballerinas, like Olga Preobrazhenskaya and Matilda Ksheshinskaya, were major stars in an elitist art form and performed in an elitist theater. It shows the exceptional status of women celebrities during the Silver Age that Ksheshinskaya in St. Petersburg and Yermolova in Moscow accumulated enough money from their performances to build, and live alone in, elegant Art Nouveau townhouses.

The Silver Age, 1894-1910

The Silver Age in St. Petersburg illustrates the statement by Marías that generations intersect and overlap because it begins during the age of Chekhov, and some of its major figures lived on into the age of Socialist Realism. The long joint careers of Dmitry Merezhkovsky and Zinaida Gippius lasted about half a century; they began in the 1890s, and ended only in the 1940s. The cohort of Symbolism thus overlaps with those of the other literary "isms" of the twentieth century: Futurism, Acmeism, and Socialist Realism. The era teems with different styles and the personalities that went with them, so I offer here a series of proposals for sorting out these difficult matters.

The untidiness of the Silver Age also comes from its exceptional geographic and demographic diversity. The Silver Age was the first era when Moscow and St. Petersburg experienced cultural efflorescences at the same time; moreover, these contemporary efflorescences showed the long-standing differences between the two capitals. After Peter the Great moved the capital from Moscow to St. Petersburg in 1712, the power and resources of that city attracted writers and artists from other areas.

When we speak of the Silver Age, we think of Aleksandr Blok and the other St. Petersburg writers, and that association gives us a clue for sorting out this exceptionally complex period. I also wish to note that given the plethora of Russian writers who appeared in the twentieth century, and the maelstrom of often destructive events that engulfed them, any discussion of periodization, specifically including this one, can only be offered as tentative, as a proposal intended to stimulate further discussion. The principal purpose in this endeavor is to define dates that create a coherent period. Hence, this list of the principal writers of the period:

Table VII. The Silver Age

Name	Year of Birth	Year of Death	Age at Death
Innokenty Annensky	1855	1909	54
Dmitry Merezhkovsky	1865	1941	76
Vyacheslav Ivanov	1866	1949	83
Konstantin Balmont	1867	1942	75
Zinaida Gippius	1869	1945	76
Dmitry Filosofov	1872	1940	68
Mikhail Kuzmin	1872	1936	64
Valery Bryusov	1873	1924	51
Maksimilian Voloshin	1877	1932	55
Aleksey Remizov	1877	1957	80
Aleksandr Blok	1880	1921	41
Andrey Bely	1880	1934	54
Sergey Gorodetsky	1883	1967	83
Igor Severyanin	1887	1941	54

This list of birth years goes from 1855 to 1887, or 32 years. However, if we remove the outliers, Annensky and Severyanin, we have a very manageable period from 1865 to 1883, or 18 years.

By general agreement, the literary history of the Silver Age began in 1894, with the publication of Valery Bryusov's *Russian Symbolists,* which gave a name to the age. The purpose of the name was to make a statement, distinguishing the Russian symbolists from the French Symbolists who served as Bryusov's principal inspiration. However, deciding when the Silver Age ended is not a simple matter.

The literary history of early twentieth-century Russia is so dense that no general agreement exists on this point. For my part, I am persuaded by Blok's comments in the preface to his play *Retribution* (1919):

> The year 1910 is the death of Komisarzhevskaya, the death of Vrubel and the death of Tolstoy. With Komisarzhevskaya the lyrical note on the stage died; with Vrubel died the enormous personal world of the artist, insane stubbornness, insatiable searching—all the way to insanity. With Tolstoy died human tenderness—wise humanity.
>
> Further, the year 1910 is the crisis of Symbolism, about which very many people wrote and spoke at the time in the camp of the Symbolists as well in the opposite one. In that year tendencies that took a hostile position to Symbolism and to each other arose: Acmeism, Egofuturism, and the first beginnings of Futurism.[30]

Blok had in mind such events as the first publications of poems by Osip Mandelstam and Marina Tsvetayeva, the publication of Velemir Khlebnikov's astonishing "Incantation by Laughter" as well as of the defiant Futurist manifesto *A Trap for Judges*—all of which occurred in 1910. Voloshin also published his first anthology in poetry in 1910, which was also the year Kuzmin published his essay "On Beautiful Clarity," which in effect served as a program for Acmeism. In the same year the Triangle Group published its anthology *The Studio of the Impressionists*. Although this is a book about literature, given the importance of the visual arts in the period, it is worth noting here that the Jack of Diamonds group of painters held its first exhibit in 1910. Given all these initiatives that lead to important developments in the future, it is therefore reasonable to conclude that the Silver Age lasted for 16 years, from 1894 to 1910.

The Social History of the Silver Age

A hallmark of the fascinating, convoluted social history of the Silver Age was the emphasis on interiority. These writers were often immersed in, not to say overwhelmed by, their states of mind, which they recorded in their diaries as assiduously as Tolstoy and his wife recorded theirs. Vera Shvarsalon, for example, got caught up in the extremely convoluted interrelationships of the Vyacheslav Ivanov-Lidiya Zinovyeva-Annibal household. No doubt like other people whom she knew, she both experienced her feelings and stood apart from them at the same time. In one diary entry from 1908 she wrote, "My inner experiences and suffering are so confused, undefined, and monotonous."[31]

No single individual illustrates the significance and the dilemmas of the tangled relationships of Silver Age aesthetes better than Lyubov Mendeleyeva, an actress who was the daughter of the chemist Dmitry Mendeleyev and who entered literary history as Blok's Beautiful Lady. Unfortunately for her, Blok's version of Russia's monastic heritage meant that he proposed to worship her from afar, as monks used to worship the Mother of God in icons, and also visit prostitutes for sex.

Like so many other great Russian writers, Blok had experienced parental loss at an early age. His father died when he was very young, and his mother soon remarried. These early experiences left Blok more insecure than he seemed to his admirers who were in awe of his talent. He became good friends with Andrey Bely—the two writers admired each other's work—and as things happened in those times, Bely fell in love with Mendeleyeva. Unfortunately, he was no better prepared for a relationship than Blok; he had grown up in a household in which his parents quarreled constantly. His very impaired relationship with his father prepared him for literary success. Mendeleyeva thus found herself caught between two gifted men whose childhoods did not prepare them to sustain an adult relationship; even a confident, self-assured woman would have had cause for great anxiety. Mendeleyeva herself says in her memoirs that she was incapable of coping with her situation: "I didn't understand anything about love to the point of idiocy."[32] It was as though Mendeleyeva and the St. Petersburg esthetes had brought the disorienting, boundless space through which Gogol's troika hurtled into their comfortable apartments and townhouses. They turned the disorienting absence of spatial boundaries into an equally disorienting absence of social and artistic boundaries.

As one studies their lives and works, one has the impression that they had committed themselves to take seriously Oscar Wilde's quip, "I put my talent into my writing and my genius into my life." They proposed to bring about a *rapprochement,* a word with multiple applications in the period, between art and philosophy, and between art and religion. One way of summing up what they wanted is to say that they wanted the beauty and ritual of Orthodox Christianity without the patriarchal authority and asceticism.

Given the way the walls of the monastery divided space into the sacred and the profane, Russians have always encountered difficulties when they propose to bring about *rapprochements* in Russian society. Although they were not political activists, their interest in *rapprochements* put them at odds with the authorities, whose monastic sensibilities made them suspicious of any attempts to unify Russian society, which they understood as consisting of separate parts.

Naturally, then, they had their doubts about suspicious about the Religious-Philosophical Meetings between 1901 and 1903, and the Religious-Philosophical Society between 1907 and 1909. In her memoirs, Zinaida Gippius records that Konstantin Pobedonotsev, the Procurator of the Holy Synod, a true believer whose attitudes and career anticipate those of Yury Andropov, who served as a head of the KGB for a long time, gave a nihilistic version of the open spaces that post-reform Russians had to navigate. Russia, he said, was an "icy desert" (*lednyaya pustynya*.)[33]

I have previously mentioned the appearance of women celebrities as something new and noteworthy in Russia's Silver Age. The topic of Jews in modern Russia has comparable interest, and it begins in *Anna Karenina*. In Part VII, Stiva Oblonsky, who is having money problems as usual, needs to see a Jewish lawyer, one Bolgarinov, about a potentially lucrative position, and has to wait two hours to see him. With the quick intuition that he shared with his sister Anna, he has a disorienting sense that social change is in the air. "Whether he, Prince Oblonsky, a descendant of Ryurik, felt awkward because he waited for two hours in the waiting room of a Jew, or because for the first time in his life he wasn't following the example of his forebears, serving the government, but entering a new field, he felt very awkward." (9, 337) Bolgarinov anticipates the Jews whose careers made them prominent in early twentieth-century St. Petersburg. Here I can only discuss three of them.

Jews in St. Petersburg Culture in the Silver Age

- Semyon Vengerov (1855-1920)
- Akim Volynsky (Haim Flexer) (1861 or 3-1926)
- Leon Bakst (Leib-Haim Rosenberg) (1866-1924)

These three men offer case studies of the various ways in which Jews assimilated and became successful in early twentieth-century Russia, and especially in St. Petersburg. The quota system, which limited the number of Jews who could live in the capital and attend its university, had the unintended effect of concentrating the most brilliant, most motivated Jews in a place where their careers would make them prominent.

In Chekhov's "The Proposal," Lomov the outsider wants the hand of Natalya, who stands for Russian literature as a whole. Lomov's real-life equivalent was Semyon Vengerov, a professor of literature at St. Petersburg University, who claimed Pushkin for his own—an audacious act for a Jew. Vengerov is best-known for his Pushkin Seminar, which he taught for many years at the St. Petersburg University. Vengerov's Pushkin Seminar began the modern era of Pushkin studies, and trained some of the best literary minds of the time, scholars who went on to write important books and edit major editions of the classics in the Soviet era. Vengerov's seminar also showed the diversity of the best of St. Petersburg culture at the time. The backgrounds of its students ranged from princes (Dmitry Svyatopolk-Mirsky) to poets (Nikolay Gumilyov) to Jews (Viktor Zhirmunsky and Yury Tynyanov).[34]

Akim Volynsky was another matter altogether. One of the most brilliant men of his era, he could have had an academic career, like Vengerov, but very much in the spirit of the times, he spurned books in favor of ballet. He became close with Zinaida Gippius and wrote extensively on the arts.

Although this book is about literature, I include here a painter, Leon Bakst because he had such a unique career. His career showed that a Jew could succeed even within the turbulent, unstable environment created by the assorted geniuses and near-geniuses of the Ballets Russes, where he designed costumes and sets until his death in 1926.

Lesbians in the Silver Age

Here is a question for a trivia quiz on Russian literature: "Who is the first lesbian character in a Russian novel?" The answer is Sappho Stolz in *Anna Karenina*, whose name deserves a separate comment. Tolstoy hardly ever used telling names such as this one, which tells us who she is. Dostoyevsky, on the other hand often used them (Raskolnikov, Myshkin), and Tolstoy's use of this blatantly obvious telling name is another indication of the impact that Dostoyevsky's work had on him.

Stolz appears at a society gathering that Anna attends. Tolstoy, always the master of social nuance, describes her and then gives us Anna's perception of her:

> Sappho Stoltz was a blonde with dark eyes. She entered with small, energetic little steps on high-heeled shoes, and firmly shook hands with the ladies like a man. Anna had never met this new celebrity and was struck by her beauty and by the extreme to which her outfit was taken and by the boldness of her manners. (9, 351)

This passage is a masterpiece of indirect characterization, and I include it here as testimony to the prophetic quality of *Anna Karenina*, which anticipated the various examples of sexual experimentation in the Silver Age.

The first Russian lesbian writer was Poliksena Solovyova (1867-1924), who used the pseudonym Allegro. Solovyova belonged to one of Russia's most distinguished families. Her father Sergey Solovyov was an eminent historian, and served as rector of Moscow University. Her brother Vladimir was the most influential philosopher of the Silver Age. Solovyova, who was surely the first Russian woman who wore pants in public, had a successful career as a writer and publisher of children's book. She had a stable, life-long relationship with her partner, Natalya Manaseina (1869-1930).

And then there was the fascinating case of Vera Hedroiz (1870-1932), who had a distinguished career as a surgeon. She organized field hospitals and published scholarly papers. A life-long lesbian, she interests us here because she was also a poet, and belonged to the Guild of Poets. In 1913 she published *The Path (Veg)*, an anthology of her poems.

The first major lesbian character in Russian literature seems to be the unnamed narrator in "Thirty Three Monsters" (1906) by Lidiya Zinovyeva-Annibal. The story is written in first-person narration, in a very truncated form, which allows the narrator to suggest much while saying little.[35] Zinovyeva-Annibal was married to Vyacheslav Ivanov, whose personal life had mind-boggling complexity, so she was presumably bisexual.

The same applies to Marina Tsvetayeva, who had a lesbian affair with Sofiya Parnok (1885-1933) in the years 1914-5, even though Tsvetayeva herself was married and had a small daughter at the time. What matters for the literary history of literature is that Tsvetayeva devoted a cycle of poems to Parnok, "Girlfriend."[36] Although Tsvetayeva was one of the most complex of all the great Russian writers, her sexual history was not uncommon. A number of married women at the time had lesbian affairs and/or flirtations, often as part of a *ménage á trois,* to be discussed below.

Gay Men in the Silver Age

Although various men in Russian high society such as the editor and extremely conservative court official Prince Vladimir Meshchersky (1839-1914) had been more or less openly gay, gay artists like Gogol and Tchaikovsky lacked the power that came with court positions, so they remained deep in the closet.

The Silver Age marked the first time when gay men had been major cultural figures, and not just isolated artists who spent a lot of time in Europe. The obvious examples are Sergey Diaghilev and Vatslav Nizhinsky, although Mikhail Kuzmin and Iosif Yurkunas had a longer, more stable relationship. Kuzmin is the first major openly gay writer in Russia; his novel *Wings* (1906), about a young man who accepts his homosexuality, created a sensation when it appeared. When his major collection of poetry *The Trout Breaks the Ice* appeared in 1925-8, it provided a striking example of the way literary generations overlap, and was surely the last major literary statement of the Silver Age.

After the famous first sentence in *Anna Karenina* about happy families all being alike, and unhappy families begin unhappy in their own way, comes the second sentence: "Everything was mixed up in the Oblonskys' house." (8, 7) Although Tolstoy did not write allegories, it is fair to say that that sentence applied to many actual houses in Russia in addition to the fictional Oblonsky house in the novel. Silver Age Russians posed to themselves Chernyshevsky's question "What is to be done?" in personal, rather than social or political terms. They tried out various highly unorthodox domestic configurations.

In the spirit of the cosmopolitanism that predominated in the Silver Age, it is worth noting the similarities between the sexual relationships of St. Petersburg's Silver Age aesthetes and that of their British contemporaries who belonged to the Bloomsbury Group. In both cases these were groups of talented writers and artists who experimented with various sexual relationships. The people who made up the Bloomsbury Group came primarily from the Britain's upper-middle classes, and with a few exceptions like Mandelstam and Kuzmin, the Silver Age aesthetes came from the Russian equivalents of the upper-middle classes.[37]

To develop further the advantages of cross-cultural comparisons with the Silver Age, let us not forget that there was also a Silver Age in Spain.[38] It would be instructive, for example, to compare the distinctive features of the Silver Age in Spain with those of the Silver Age in Russia, and search for commonalities.

Before pursuing this topic further, we must pause to ask "Why St. Petersburg? Why did the artists of Moscow (with the exception of Tsvetayeva) lead more or less orderly lives, by the standards of the times at least, while so many artists of St. Petersburg gave themselves over to unusual their domestic arrangements? One answer is that the Western orientation of St. Petersburg, and its physical separation from the vast stretches of the Russia heartland, produced a *laissez-faire* environment for the personal lives of the aristocrats who moved there. As a matter of fact, there are four Russians who were famous, or infamous, for their sex lives, and they all lived in St. Petersburg. They were:

- Catherine the Great, with her numerous lovers;
- Aleksandr Pushkin, who compiled a Don Juan list of the women that he had slept with;
- Grigory Rasputin, the "mad monk" who used his position of favor with the imperial family to take advantage of society women;
- Anna Akhmatova, a sensuous woman who wrote sensuous poetry.

In the hothouse atmosphere of St. Petersburg, the artistic elite, who probably numbered no more than a thousand people in a city with a population of almost two million in 1910, proposed to bring together the heady, unstable mixture of sex, art, and spirituality by creating what the French call *ménages á trois*.[39] Like the topic of Jews in twentieth-century Russia, this topic offers both great interest and great complexity. Moreover, since it involves intimate relationships, satisfactory documentation is often lacking and can only be characterized briefly here.

Ménages á trois in the Silver Age

The first thing to say about *ménages á trois* among twentieth-century writers is that they exhibit some diversity. Some of them consisted of two women and a man; some of them consisted of two men and a woman. Some of them were brief and informal, more like brief, adventurous relationships than households. These threefold relationships in Silver Age St. Petersburg had a nineteenth-century precedent in the Nikolay Nekrasov-Ivan Panayev-Avdotya Panayeva household, which seems to have been the first one in Russia, and which lasted for several decades, as did the Dmitry Merezhkovsky-Zinaida Gippius-Dmitry Filosofov household in the twentieth century. The most stable of these *ménages* seems to have been the NikolayPunin-Anna Akhmatova-Galina Punina household, which was formed in the early twenties and lasted until the late thirties. In 1927 Abram Room's film about a *ménage á trois, Third Meshchanskaya Street,* finally put on the screen what Russians had been doing for several decades.

Table VIII. *Ménages á trois* Among Twentieth-Century Russian Writers

Dmitry Merezhkovsky	Zinaida Gippius	Dmitry Filosofov
Nikolay Minsky	Lyudmila Vilenkina	Zinaida Vengerova
Aleksandr Blok	Lyubov Mendeleyeva	Andrey Bely
Andrey Bely	Nina Petrovskaya	Valery Bryusov
Vyacheslav Ivanov	Lidiya Zinovyeva-Annibal	Margarita Sabashnikova
Arthur Lourie	Vera Glebova-Sudeykina	Anna Akhmatova
Nikolay Punin	Anna Akhmatova	Galina Punina
Mikhail Kuzmin	Vsevolod Knyazev	Olga Glebova-Sudeykina
Mikhail Kuzmin	Iosif Yurkunas	Olga Hildebrand
Vladimir Mayakovsky	Lilya Brik	Osip Brik

As this list shows, the subject of *ménages á trois* deserves a separate treatment, which would surely involve the careful study of letters and diaries that remain in archives in a way that separates gossip from fact. In the absence of such research, we may well wonder how these arrangements were formed, and what agreements the participants made among themselves.

In the published record I have found only one such discussion. Although it did not lead to anything, I cite it here as having unusual historical interest. It comes from the memoirs of Margarita Sabashnikova, the wife of Maksimilian Voloshin, who spent a good deal of time with Vyacheslav Ivanov and his wife Lidiya in their famous apartment, the Tower.

> I soon understood that Vyacheslav loved me. I told Lidiya about this and about my decision to leave. But for her everything had long ago become clear. Lidiya's answer: "You have entered our life, you belong to us. If you leave, something dead will be left...We both can't get along without you." Then the three of us talked. They expressed a strange idea: Two people, merged into one like they are in a state to love a third person. A love like that is the beginning of a new human community, even the beginning of a new church, where Eros is embodied in flesh and blood.[40]

Although Sabashnikova vacillated for a while, she finally decided to remain with her husband and refuse this offer. Sabashnikova refused her chance at what we would now call polyamory, and it had no lasting consequences for anyone, unlike many negotiations and disappointments in the sexual politics of the Silver Age. There were at least two suicides because of disappointing relationships—those of Vyacheslav Knyazev (an incident mentioned in Akhmatova's "Poem Without a Hero") and of Nadezhda Lvova.

Clearly, the social history of the Silver Age is easier to research and discuss than its literary history. Since Soviet scholars couldn't discuss the poetry of the Silver Agers, the Acmeists or the Futurists (with the obvious exception of Mayakovsky's work), scholarship on Russian poetry did not develop as robustly as scholarship on British, American, and French poetry. As a result, only a few organizing principles for a literary history of the Silver Age can be suggested here.

The Literary History of the Silver Age

Catherine Evtuhov has perceptively commented that, "In the platform of voices and confusion of ideas which made up the Silver Age, nothing is perhaps more difficult than to find a connecting thread, a central idea which might tie together various aspects of the period to characterize it as a whole."[41] I concur fully with this statement, and I draw from it the conclusion since finding a "connecting thread" is so difficult that it is not worth doing. Rather, I propose to adopt a procedure from linguistics called minimal pairs. Minimal pairs are units that create meaning through difference. In Russian studies Yury Lotman of Tartu used such oppositions in a variety of ways, as does Caryl Emerson in her *Cambridge Introduction to Russian Liteature*.[42] Thus, it is useful to organize the literary history of the Silver Age not as a series of discussions of discrete individuals, but as a series of oppositions, in which the key figures play off of each other. These oppositions are ones into which other Silver Age writers can be integrated in later, more detailed discussions. Moreover, these oppositions show the irreducible complexity of the period, and remind us that no single writer incorporated all its significant features.

For the Silver Age, surely the key opposition is Aleksandr Blok-Andrey Bely.[43] Here we have the opposition of St. Petersburg and Moscow, of Blok the intuitive artist fascinated by *stikhiinost'*, or elemental force, as opposed to Bely the son of a mathematics professor, who had an intellectual bent, and developed theories of versification. Like true members of the Age of Wagner all over Europe, they were fascinated by music, and used it in various ways. Bely wrote a series of "Symphonies," while Blok converted history to music, and later said that he was infatuated with "the music of the revolution."

Among their richly evocative oppositions is the one between poetry and prose. Bely wrote a series of novels, one of which, *St. Petersburg*, is arguably the most important Russian novel between *Anna Karenina* and *The Master and Margarita*. Until "The Twelve," Blok was a relatively conservative poet, although he did use the *dol'nik*, or accented verse, while some of Belyi's innovative poetry anticipated, and influenced, Mayakovsky.

With the opposition of Zinaida Gippius and Mikhail Kuzmin, we have the same opposition of poetry and prose, the same opposition of a St. Petersburg native and a gifted outsider, as with Blok and Bely. Although people do not usually associate Kuzmin and Chekhov, no one in the period wrote the clear, deceptively simple prose of Chekhov with more assurance than Kuzmin in his still under-appreciated novel *Wings*. Although the literary legacy of both writers shows the variety of genres that is characteristic of the period, some differences do appear. Although Blok and Bely, among others in the Silver Age, were fascinated with music, and used it in a variety of metaphorical ways, only Kuzmin had a genuine musical gift. He studied briefly at the St. Petersburg Conservatory, and was renowned in his time as songwriter and performer.

What music was for Kuzmin, religion was for Gippius. Although she was too much of an individualist to accept Orthodoxy completely, she remained a religious seeker all her life, and the Gippius-Merezhkovsky-Filosofov household has a strongly spiritual quality. Kuzmin, however, lived a secular life, and his work is that of the consummate Silver Age esthete. Then there is the matter of poetic form. Gippius' significant poetic output is conservative in meter and rhyme, while Kuzmin was apparently the first major Russian poet to write free verse, and thus there is an unlikely connection between him and Mayakovsky—two very different poets indeed!

The final opposition in this necessarily schematic discussion is between Valery Bryusov and Vyacheslav Ivanov, between a Muscovite, the writer who began the period and a St. Petersburger, its least understood writer. Here we have what is perhaps the last major opposition of Moscow and St. Petersburg in the pre-revolutionary period. Bryusov, whom the Russians sometimes refer to as "the emperor of Symbolism," possessed an authority over younger writers in Moscow that was comparable to that possessed by Ivanov in St. Petersburg. The literary discussions that Ivanov hosted in his apartment, known as the "Tower" (where

Kuzmin lived for a long time) were attended by virtually all of St. Petersburg's literati, including the newlyweds, Nikolay Gumilyov and Anna Akhmatova.

Bryusov's father did not allow him to read religious books, and thus young Bryusov grew up to be a writer with exclusively secular interests. He is unique in the Silver Age in his disinterest in religion and myth, and this forms a striking contrast between him and Ivanov, who was deeply interested in myth and religion. Unlike Bryusov, Ivanov possessed deep and wide erudition, which makes his work written over the course of his long career very demanding. A full-length biography of Ivanov would greatly enrich our understanding of twentieth-century Russian culture.

The Age of Isms: The Acmeists

The age of Isms, 1910-8, includes overlapping generations. Let us begin with the Acmeists.

Table IX. The Acmeist Generation

Poet	Date of Birth	Date of Death	Age at Death
Nikolay Gumilyov	1886	1921	35
Mikhail Zenkevich	1886	1973	87
Anna Akhmatova	1889	1966	77
Osip Mandelstam	1891	1938	47

The Acmeists, who were all born within five years of each other, were the most star-crossed of all Russian literary generations and groups. Gumilyov was shot, and Mandelstam died in the gulag. Akhmatova was forbidden to publish for decades, in 1946, Andrey Zhdanov denounced her and Mikhail Zoshchenko in a speech that became required reading in Soviet schools. Zenkevich survived because he did translations, wrote conformist poetry, and even joined the party in 1947. Gumilyov ran afoul of the Soviet authorities because he was a militant monarchist, and did not care who knew it. I have argued in *Stalin's Soviet*

Monastery that Mandelstam more or less consciously chose his arrest and death in the gulag.[44]

This is not the place to attempt even a cursory analysis of the rich poetic legacy of Akhmatova and Mandelstam. However, I do wish to point out an attitude that they shared, one that seemingly had nothing to do with politics, but that deeply alienated them from the Soviet establishment. Akhmatova and Mandelstam shared a quasi-mystical awareness of the unity of time, and specifically in the unity of the past and the present. For Akhmatova, the unity of the past and present appears in "A Poem Without a Hero" and other poems such as "Lot's Wife" as the connection between post-1917 Soviet Russia and pre-revolutionary St. Petersburg. Mandelstam, in his enigmatic poem "The Man Who Found a Horseshoe," and elsewhere, made various provocative connections between the ruins of Russian culture and the fragments of the culture of antiquity.

Although Stalin caused Akhmatova much grief, and had Mandelstam arrested, which led to his death in the gulag, the suffering that followed the revolution deepened and broadened the work of both these great poets, who responded eloquently to the plight of their fellow countrymen. Some of their best work, from Mandelstam's short "Let Us Glorify, Brothers, the Twilight of Freedom," to Akhmatova's ambitious and deeply moving "Requiem," resulted from the narrow-mindedness of the violence of the Soviet regime.

The poetry of Akhmatova and Mandelstam expressed this unity of time in a period when Soviet authorities obsessively insisted that 1917 marked a new era in human history, and everything that happened before in 1917 had significance only insofar as it prepared for 1917. In general, the nature of time, and specifically of the relationship between the past and the present, remained problematic throughout Soviet history.

Akhmatova and Mandelstam didn't write poetry as we usually understand the term "write"; they said that poems "came" to them. It appears that they composed the way Mozart is said to have composed; they did what we would nowadays call channeling. It is a fascinating subject, and deserves further investigation.

It rarely happens that two groups of talented writers who were contemporaries differ as much as the Acmeists and the Futurists. Akhmatova and Mandelstam were introverts who preferred private space and private experience. The Futurists, on the other hand, were primarily extroverts who enjoyed boisterous street demonstrations and provocative public performances.[45]

The Futurist Generation

Table X. The Futurist Generation

Poet	Date of Birth	Date of Death	Age at Death
Yelena Guro	1877	1913	36
David Burlyuk	1882	1967	85
Vasily Kamensky	1884	1961	77
Velemir Khlebnikov	1885	1922	37
Aleksey Kruchonykh	1886	1968	82
Benedikt Lifshits	1886	1938	52
Sergey Bobrov	1889	1971	82
Vladimir Mayakovsky	1893	1930	37

Thus, we have a tight grouping of 15 years, from 1877 to 1893 for the Futurist generation.

In the interest of establishing greater coherence in Russian literary history, it is useful to note the striking contrasts between the Symbolists and the Futurists.[46] If the Symbolists, like their counterparts in the Bloomsbury Group, came from prominent families, the Futurists did not. They primarily came from families with agricultural or industrial interests in the provinces. The Symbolists were an openly, even defiantly, elitist group; the Futurists were such avowed individualists that they were neither elitist nor democratic in their social attitudes. Indeed, the Futurists were such avowed individualists that religion and myth, which were essential for the Symbolists, were basically irrelevant for the Futurists. The Futurists defiantly opposed their primitivism to the Symbolists' elegance.

Irina Azizyan explains this opposition in the following way:

> The nihilistic reaction of the avant-garde of any and all authorities is connected to a great degree with the task of shocking the bourgeois public has as its basis the rejection of the "elegance" of the poetry of the Symbolists and the Acmeists,

of the graphic art and painting o the World of Art Group as inadequate to the ferment of the kettle of Russian reality of the 1910s. [47]

While it is certainly true that the Futurists were reacting against the Symbolists, Azizyan's use of Stalinist words like "task" and "Russian reality" show that she is imposing a latter-day Soviet mentality on Futurism. The Futurists would have laughed at the thought they were performing tasks of any kind, and would not have known what to make of "Russian reality." I will have more to say about the Futurists' lack of social program below.

Just as the opposition of Aleksandr Blok and Andrey Bely proves useful in the study of Symbolism, so in the same way, the opposition of Benedikt Lifschitz and Vladimir Mayakovsky proves useful in the study of Futurism. Lifschitz was an articulate, productive writer in various genres. He was the only Futurist who wrote a most revealing essay about what the Futurists were doing, "The Emancipation of the Word," as well as an invaluable memoir, *The One-and-a-Half Eyed Archer*. He was also the only Futurist who was a Jew, which probably explains why he was also the only Futurist who was shot in the purges of the late thirties. By contrast, equally prominent Futurists, Vasily Kamensky and Aleksey Kruchonykh, who were not Jews, and who remained in the Soviet Union were not arrested, and lived into the sixties.

Lifschitz seems to have had a sunny disposition with numerous enthusiasms. Mayakovsky, on the other hand, was a deeply troubled man. His manic-depressive disorder was surely related to the early death of his father, and left him sullen and angry. (Significantly, although there are numerous photographs of him, none of them show him smiling.) His early work, "Vladimir Mayakovsky. A Tragedy," shows that he was as capable of self-absorption as any of the Symbolists. Because of the exertions of his lover and mentor Lilya Brik, he is the only Futurist whose statue stands in a major square in Moscow that is named in his honor. In a related manner, he is also the only Futurist who left a compromised moral legacy.

The manic phase of his manic-depressive disorder famously found poetic expression in rapturous verse about his two fixations. The first of these, of course, was Lilya Brik; the Vladimir Mayakovsky-Lilya Brik-Osip Brik *ménage á trois* seems to have been the last one that mattered for Russian literature. His imaginative poem to and about her, "About This," from 1923, may qualify as the most important Futurist work. In the next year, though, Lenin died, and in his "Vladimir Ilyich Lenin" Mayakovsky wrote the famous line that must be examined for its moral implications in the post-Soviet era: "Even now Lenin is more alive than all the living." It may now be impossible to reconstruct the mindset that produced that belief, and the ongoing re-evaluation of Mayakovsky's legacy is a challenging task.[48] A kind judgment about Mayakovsky may probably conclude that he was a prodigiously gifted poet with minimal self-awareness, and his suicide shows his inability to confront what he had said and done. (The fact that another major manic-depressive writer, Ernest Hemingway, also committed suicide reminds us that no simple interpretation of Mayakovsky's life and death has any persuasive power.)

There was one professional musician, Mikhail Matyushin (1861-1934), who belonged to the Futurist group. He wrote the music for the extraordinary Futurist opera *Victory Over the Sun*. Matyushin was over 20 years older than most of the Futurists, and served as a father figure for them. Matyushin was married to Yelena Guro, and their house on Sand Street in the outskirts of St. Petersburg served as the Futurist headquarters, very much as the Ivanov-Zinovyeva-Annibal apartment, the Tower, which was located across town in an upscale neighborhood on Tavrida Street, served as the Symbolist headquarters. In general, though, the Futurists had little interest in music. Like so many artists and intellectuals in early twentieth-century Europe, what they cared about, deeply and passionately, was painting, especially recent avant-garde painting.

The Futurists took a serious interest in painting. Even Matyushin, a violinist and composer, took drawing courses. Guro and Mayakovsky attended art school; Guro was a painter and Mayakovsky did work in various visual media, especially in the twenties. Burlyuk is better known as a painter than as a writer.

When understood in a general way, an analysis of the painting-literature connection yields significant insights into Futurism, and distinguishes it decisively from what other groups had done in the past. To be sure, in the previous generation, Mikhail Vrubel had been fascinated by Lermontov's poem "The Demon" and painted several versions of it. It is, however, one thing when a painter takes images from a literary work and puts them on the canvas. What the Futurists did was something quite different.

For a general understanding of Futurism as an esthetic movement, we may define it as the first movement that proposed to remake literature in the image of painting. The history of Futurism abounds in statement about this, such as this one by Nikolay Kulbin, a major arts entrepreneur at the time. He once proclaimed, "An artist of the word always has the ability to paint."[49] To understand the implications and limitations of this statement for the Futurist movement as a cultural phenomenon, we need an understanding of the differences between painting and literature.

In the opposition established in the eighteenth century by Gotthold Lessing, painting is a spatial art, while literature is a temporal art. We see the totality of a painting in an instant, although appreciation can, and often does, take longer. Literature, on the other hand, is a temporal art, like music. It takes time to read a work of literature, just as it takes time to listen to a piece of music. What the Futurists did was to take seriously—more seriously than anyone ever had—the attempt to make literature resemble painting, which was the attempt to transform a temporal art into a spatial art.

There is, of course, an inherent contradiction in such a project, and this contradiction explains a great deal about Futurism. Irina Sakhno, who has done important work on the Futurists' visual esthetics, uses the apt expression, "a simultaneity of expressions" to convey the painterly quality of the layout of a page of a Futurist work.[50] She also quotes Aleksey Kruchonykh, who wrote in a letter to Matyushin, "I am becoming more and more convinced that a letter is like a drawing-painting [*risunok-zhivopis'*]."[51]

The question of when the Age of the Isms ends is probably the most difficult one in any discussion of Russian literary history. It gives too much importance to the immediate effects of the revolution to say that the period ends in 1917. I therefore propose 1918, the year in which Lenin and the Bolsheviks shut down the Constituent Assembly, thereby precluding any possibility of representational democracy in the Soviet Union. Fatefully, 1918 was also the year Lenin moved the capitol to Moscow, thereby ending the 206-year hegemony of St. Petersburg/ Petrograd.

The End of the Age of Isms

In literature, 1918 matters because it was the year of the last great St. Petersburg poem by a Silver Age poet, Blok's "The Twelve." The staccato rhythms and snappy rhymes of this work show the direct effect of social chaos on literary style. I have explicated "The Twelve" in *Stalin's Soviet Monastery*,[52] but here I want to mention the often-misunderstood image of Christ, who leads a detachment of revolutionary guard/disciples as they patrol a snowy street (a poetic version of Pobedonostsev's "icy desert"?) of St. Petersburg (presumably Nevsky Prospect). Yet again Russians find themselves seeking direction in open spaces without any landmarks.

The people at the time who protested that Christ couldn't/wouldn't lead a detachment of revolutionary guards because the Bolsheviks were atheists missed the point that Blok's intuition grasped, namely that in Russia Christ primarily represented asceticism and self-denial, and that Lenin and the Bolsheviks would bring asceticism and self-denial out of the monastery to an unheard of degree. And then after Lenin died, Stalin would draw on his years in an Orthodox seminary to rule the Soviet Union as a sadistic elder of a monastery who imposed vows on poverty, chastity and obedience on hapless Soviet citizens.

After 1918, the deaths of Andreyev in 1919, of Gumilyov in 1920, of Blok in 1921, of Khlebnikov in 1922, and of Bryusov in 1925 seemed like aftershocks, and are comparable to the series of deaths that changed Russian culture in the 1880s. Since Blok was who he was, his death hit Russian writers very hard. They knew what they had lost, and that there was no one to replace him. Tsvetayeva wrote, "Blok's death was a thunder strike at the heart."[53] In his essay "The Fate of Blok," critic Boris Eichenbaum wrote in the same vein, "The death of Blok shook us all. And not at all because he won't write any more poetry—let us not act falsely over a fresh grave."[54] In this very emotional piece Eichenbaum goes on to say that:

> In Blok's death and in the hysterical cries of Andrey Bely is the fate of a whole generation, the date of all of symbolism, which is outliving itself amid the horrors of our iron age. And this fate is tragic because it is not a random one; it didn't descend from without, but was in preparation for a long time and moved forward from within.[55]

Like other thoughtful intellectuals of his time, Eichenbaum sensed that the death of Blok meant that end of an era; I would suggest, though, that Blok's death affected Eichenbaum and Tsvetayeva as it did because it was an additional confirmation of what they already knew but did not want to accept. As Eichenbaum says, Blok's career as a poet, and thus his era, ended in 1918. Andreyev and Blok as well as the Acmeists and the Futurists had been left behind in St. Petersburg/ Petrograd, which had formed their artistic sensibilities. By 1919 the city, covered with ice and inhabited by hungry people, had lost its status as a capital and thus its identity. It was a hive without a queen, to borrow an image from *War and Peace*.

The Age of Isms, cut short though it was by the turbulence that followed 1917, is marked by the split between the Acmeist Generation and the Futurist Generation. This split between two groups of contemporaries, most of whom were born in the 1880s, involves a fundamental difference in concepts of literature that is not addressed in the various manifestoes that were so much a part of the atmosphere of the time. Although Mandelstam, for example, wrote poems about architecture and art, he had no interest in practicing these arts, nor did his soul mate Anna Akhmatova. Although Akhmatova was capable of giving mesmerizing poetry readings, she and Mandelstam were introverts, preferring private space to public space. If the Acmeists were introverts who kept literature separate from the other arts, the Futurists were extroverts who delighted in public events. They proposed to bring about a *rapprochement* among the arts, specifically poetry, music, painting, and performance. This desire reached its apogee in the Futurist opera *Victory Over the Sun*, which remains innovative and startling over a century after its premiere in 1913. In this sense the Futurists practiced in public what the Symbolist Generation had done in private.

Notes

1 V. Ya. Linkov, *Istoriya russkoy literatury*, 25.

2 *Ibid.*

3 See yl.ru/article/347113/periodizatsiya-russkoy-literaturyi-xix-veka-istoriya-etapyi-razvitiya-i-interesnyie-faktyi.

4 Yury Tynyanov, "Literaturnyi fakt," in *Arkhaisty i novatory* (Leningrad: Priboy, 1929), 10.

5 *Ibid.*, 12.

6 Andrew Kahn, Mark Lipovetsky, Irina Reyfman, and Stephanie Sandler. *A History of Russian Literature* (Oxford: Oxford U. Press, 2018).

7 Yu. N. Tynyanov, *Literaturnaya evolyutsiya. Izbrannye trudy.*, Vl. Novinov, ed. (Moscow: AGRAF, 2002), 34.

8 See Robert Hughes, *The Shock of the New: The Hundred-Year History of Modern Art—Its Rise, Its Dazzling Achievements, Its Fall* (New York: Alfred E. Knopf, 1991).

9 See Astrid Erll, "Generations as Literary History; Three Constellations of Generationality, Genealogy, and Memory." *New Literary History*, Vol. 45, No. 3 (Summer, 2014), 385-409.

10 *Ibid.*, 388.

11 Julian Marías, *Generations. A Historical Method.* Harold C. Raley, trans. (University, AL: The U. of Alabama Press, 1970), 186.

12 *Ibid.*, 168.

13 *Ibid.*, 155.

14 It was the brilliant Boris Eichenbaum who first used the term *skaz* to define Leskov's use of vernacular Russian. See Igor Rudometkin, "Eykhenbaumovskaya kontseptsiya literaturnogo skaza." *Izvestiya BGPU*, No. 4 (265), 75-8.

15 Kahn, Lipovetsky, et al., *A History of Russian Literature*, 347.

16 Donald Rayfield, "The Golden Age of Russian Poetry," *Russia's Golden Age*, Rachel Stauffer, ed. (Amenia: Grey House Publishing, 2014), 33

17 *Ibid.*, 48.

18 See Vyacheslav Bondarenko, *Vyazemsky* (Moscow: Molodaya Gvardiya, 2004).

19 Laurie Manchester, *Holy Fathers, Secular Sons. Clergy, Intelligentsia, and the Modern Self in Revolutionary Russia* (DeKalb, IL: Northern Illinois U. Press, 2011), 40.

20 See *Stalin's Soviet Monastery*, 71-3.

21 N.G. Chernyshevsky, *Esteticheskiye otnosheniya iskusstva k deystvitel'nosti* (St. Petersburg, 1865), iii.

22 The subtitle *Stories about New People* shows the origin of the work in the anthologies of the 1840s. (Chernyshevsky had come to St. Petersburg to enter the university in 1846.)

23 See Dean Keith Simonton, "The Swan-Song Effect: last-works effects for 172 classical composers." *Journal of the Psychology of Aging* (March, 1989), 42-7.

24 Pierre Bourdieu, *The Rules of Art. Genesis and Structure of the Literary Field*. Susan Emanuel, trans. (Stanford: Stanford U. Press, 1995), 118.

25 There are four major precursor-ephebe pairings in the history of Russian prose, and taken together, they define a great deal of Russian literary history: Gogol-Dostoyevsky; Turgenev-Chekhov; Pushkin-Mandelstam; and Tolstoy-Solzhenitsyn. I will discuss the last two of these pairings in the Epilogue

26 I.S. Turgenev, *Polnoye sobraniye sochinenii i pisem v tridtsati tomakh* (Moscow: "Nauka," 1979), 203.

27 A.P. Chekhov, *Polnoye sobraniye sochinenii i pisem*, 7 (Moscow: "Nauka," 1985), 132.

28 On Morozov and Shchukin, see Natalia Semyonova, *Moskovskiye kollektsionery* (Moscow: Molodaya Gvardiya, 2010).

29 Osip Mandelstam, *Ob Iskusstve*, 252.

30 Aleksandr Blok, *Stikhotvoreniya i poemy*, 397.

31 Vera Shvarsalon, "Dnevnikovye zapisi," www.silverage.ru/shvarsalon.

32 Lyubov Blok, "I byli i nebylitsy o Bloke i o sebe," www.silverage.ru/blokobloke.

33 Zinaida Gippius and Dmitry Merezhkovsky, *Zhivye litsa. Vospominaniya* (Tbilisi, n.p., 1991), 1, 230-1.

34 On Vengerov and his Pushkin Seminar, see Dzh. Kertis. *Boris Eykhenbaum.Yego sem'ya, strana i russkaya literatura* (Sankt-Peterburg: Akademicheskii proyekt, 2004), 70-2.

35 See Lidiya Zinov'yeva-Annibal, *Tridtsat' tri uroda* (Moscow: Agraf, 1999).

36 On the Tsvetayeva-Parnok affair and Tsvetayeva's poems about it, see Lily Feiler, *Marina Tsvetayeva. The Double Beat of Heaven and Hell* (Durham and London: Duke U. Press, 1994), 66-77.

37 The affinities between the Bloomsbury Group and St. Petersburg esthetes appear in a strikingly similar situation that unfolded. In both London and St. Petersburg a straight woman fell in love with a gay man and experienced great distress as a result.

Margarita Sabashnikova fell in love with Mikhail Kuzmin, and Dora Carrington fell in love with Lytton Strachey. The hopelessness of the situation actually caused Carrington to commit suicide. Her story is told in the 1995 film *Carrington.*

38 See Nelson R. Orriger, "Redefining the Spanish Silver Age and '98 Within It," *Annales de la literatura española comtemporánea*, No. 1-2 (1998), 315-26.

39 I have taken most of the information in the following table from Aleksandra Chaban, "Lyubovnye treugol'niki Serebryanogo veka." See https://arzamas.acad emy/materials/796

40 Ye. R. Govsiyevich, *Serebryanyi vek glazami ochevidtsev* (Moscow: n.p., 2013), 56.

41 Catherine Evtuhov, "On Neo-Romanticism and Christianity: Some 'Spots of Time' in the Russian Silver Age." *Russian History,* Vol. 20, No. 1/4 (1993), 198.

42 See Emerson, *Cambridge Introduction to Russian Literature,* 16 ff.

43 See Magnus Lyundgren, "Blok and Bely," in *Poetry and Psychiatry. Essays on Early Twentieth Century Russian Symbolist Culture.* Charles Rougle, trans. (Boston: Academic Studies Press, 2014), 18-26.

44 See Curtis, *Stalin's Soviet Monastery, 95.*

45 For a reliable guide to the dizzying array of manifestoes, readings and exhibits of the avant-garde, see Andrey Krusanov, *Russkii avangard* (Moscow: NLO, 1996, 2003, 2010).

46 See also Irina Sakhno, "Simvolizm i avangard: Pereklichki i sopryazheniya," in *Otkryvaya sovremennost' zanovo* (Moscow: Rossiisky universitet druzhby narodov, 2011), 370-88.

47 I.A. Azizyan, "O dialoge iskusstv serebryanogo veka," o-dialoge-iskusstv-serebryanogo-veka.pdf, 128.

48 See A.M. Ushakov, *Tvorchestvo V.V. Mayakovskogo v nachale XXI veka: novye zadachi i puti issledovaniya* (Moscow: IMLI RAN, 2008).

49 Quoted in Vladimir Markov, *Russian Futurism. A History* (Berkeley and Los Angeles: U. of California Press, 1968), 3.

50 Irina Sakhno, "Bukvennaya grafika v russkom futurizme: strategii vizualizatsii," *Vestnik RGTU, Seriya "Filosofiya. Sotsiologiya, Iskusstvovedeniye.* 2016, No. 3, 58. URL: https://cyberleninka.ru/article/n/bukvennaya-grafika-v-russkom-futurizme-strategii-vizualizatsii (accessed: 22.08.2020). The Futurists' interpretation of letters in visual terms has suggestive analogies with Ezra Pound's interest in Chinese ideograms. See Aleksandr Genis, "Bez yazyka. Ezra Paund," *Inostrannaya literatura,* 1999 (9).

51 Quoted in *Ibid.*

52 See *ibid.,* 129-30.

53 Quoted in Marina Tsvetayeva, *Izbrannye proizvedeniya* (Moscow–Leningrad: Sovetskiy Pisatel', 1965), 736.

54 Boris Eichenbaum, *Literatura. Teoriya. Kritika. Polemika* (Leningrad: Priboy, 1927), 265.

55 *Ibid.*, 269.

Epilogue: The Heart of Russian Literature

The collapse of the Soviet Union in 1991 sent shock waves through all aspects of Russian society. We now know that a small group of tough, ambitious men sensed unprecedented opportunities to acquire wealth. They took advantage of the chance to create generational wealth by buying up economic institutions left vulnerable in the general confusion of runaway inflation and food shortages.

Inevitably, such a profound change affected literary scholars as much if not more than other Russians, and their reactions offer considerable interest as cultural history. A few remarks about these reactions may serve to introduce the questions that this essay asks as way of bringing the book to a coherent conclusion: What is the heart of Russian literature? What connects the writers who constitute the heart of Russian literature to other Russian writers?

The collapse of the Soviet Union affected literary critics more than other intellectuals such as, say, mathematicians, because critics had operated within strict, artificial limits set by government censorship. They had not been allowed to so much as mention some writers such as Solzhenitsyn and they could not acknowledge the greatness of other writers, such as Akhmatova and Mandelstam. In the new post-Soviet world in which they found themselves, however, the restrictions that had previously determined their professional behavior no longer existed. The searchings of critics in response to this new situation constitute part of Russian intellectual history in the early twenty-first century, and can thus be offered here as an introduction to the essay itself.

Post-Soviet Statements about Literature

To understand post-Soviet statements about literature, it is helpful to keep in mind the age-old distinction between the capitals, Moscow and St. Petersburg, on one hand and the provinces on the other. For an expression of what were surely wide-spread attitudes, let us begin far from the capitals, with their prestigious universities and institutes. Let us begin in provincial Samara.

A Samara professor of literature named Lev Fink (1918-98) greeted the collapse of the Soviet Union with particular enthusiasm. He had been arrested with so many others in 1937 and then rehabilitated—once again, with so many others—in 1955. What interests us here is the volume that he co-wrote with several other local intellectuals, *Literature and General Human Values* and published in 1995. In it he says:

> The recognition of the priority of general human values came in connection and in connection with that the priority of the esthetic analysis of a work has arrived to replace the sociology (or more narrowly the class) approach. We call general human values those values that have identical (or similar) significance in the most varied eras, in the most varied countries, in the most varied groups. Among the values man himself, his life, freedom, and happiness play the leading role.[1]

How satisfying it must have been for a former *zek* to write those words! Yet the years of intellectual isolation took their toll on Fink, as they did on so many other Russians. Fink does not ground his belief in values in spirituality or in his country's history, except in the broadest sense. Still, the abstractness of his comments helps to understand that Russian intellectuals were searching for new professional identities. Russians' search for values in a post-Soviet world is a subject for a major book and only a few comments about it can be made here.

In the past, Marxism-Leninism had purported to explain everything. Now, in the bewildering post-Soviet world, critics such as Fink lacked a general cultural framework for interpreting literature. The need to impose order on their untidy literature in the absence of a generally accepted set of ideas may explain why Russian critics use the eighteenth-century words "poetics" and "genre" much more frequently than their Western colleagues.

Russian scholars who wished to make sense of Russian literature in the aftermath of 1991 faced three daunting tasks. First, they wished to chronicle the work written in the past that could now be published. Second, they wished to acknowledge the new work written in the aftermath of 1991. Third, they wished to organize all this material in some coherent fashion. Hence, no one can dispute what Katherina Hodgson and Alexandra Smith say in their introduction to the important book *Twentieth-Century Russian Poetry: Reinventing the Canon*: "The process of reshaping the poetry canon is complex and multi-faceted."[2] The specific studies in this important volume make it clear just how stimulating and demanding this reshaping is.

However, Caryl Emerson's characterization of Russian literature as "self-reflexive" once again comes to mind while reading the authors' statement, "The emergence of so much 'new' material made it clear that the existing narrative was fragmented, disjointed, and filled with gaps caused by the deliberate suppression of information or by the straightforward lack of knowledge."[3] Overwhelmed by the issues in this existing narrative, the authors understandably had neither the energy nor the need to think about the fact that other critics and scholars were dealing with closely comparable issues.

It is most instructive to notice that in America, as in Russia, the issue of the canon has been hotly debated in the twenty-first century. The fact that American critics have felt the need to confront issues similar to those that Russian critics have confronted serves as a useful reminder that just because government control played an exceptional role in creating literary policies in Russia, that does not mean that commonalities did not exist between the decisions of government critics in Russia and the decisions of private critics in the West. In fact, such commonalities did exist, and thoughtful critics will want to keep them in mind. For decades a widespread and still unresolved debate has raged over the question of who belongs in the canon of a national literature. Who gets to decide? What criteria are appropriate?

As usual, Harold Bloom had controversial opinions on the subject, and expressed them in his 2014 volume, *The Western Canon: The Books and School of the Ages*.[4] Critics who championed the work of women and minorities have called for precisely what Hodgson and Smith call a "reshaping" of literary history.

In America, as in Russia, the controversies grew especially heated about the status and meaning of women writers. Michael Boyden has drawn attention to the ongoing controversies about Emily Dickinson. Feminist critics have said that anthologies edited by men "have systematically projected a false image of Dickinson."[5] They did so for reasons that differed from those of their Soviet contemporaries, but—feminist critics would argue—the results were similar. If the reshaping of Russian literary history has brought into new prominence the work of Yelena Schwartz, a member of the Leningrad underground of the 1960s, the reshaping of American literary history has brought into new prominence the work of African-American poet Gwendolyn Brooks.

Russian critics' need to make sense of literature in a holistic way produced a major conference in 2016, *Russian Literature of the Twentieth and Twenty-first Centuries as a Single Process*, which was held at Moscow State University. The proceedings of the conference show that Russian scholars are producing exciting scholarship.[6] However, while the old restrictions and limitations have fallen away, the absence of any generally accepted concepts of the relationship between literature and society produced curious effects. For example, Ivan Nichiporov wrote an essay that he called "Leniniana as Myth-Making: V. Mayakovsky and A. Voznesensky." On one hand, it is a clear sign that we are in a post-soviet era when a scholar can refer to poems about Lenin about myth-making. Unfortunately, however, Nichiporov does not mention the cult of Lenin as such; he seems not to have read Nina Tumarkina's exemplary book *Lenin Lives! The Lenin Cult in Soviet Russia*.[7] He has nothing to say about the origin or significance of the cult of Lenin. What he does do, and does with great skill, is to compare Mayakovsky's and Voznesensky's poems about Lenin purely as a matter of words on the page. He implies that Leniniana has no social implications—certainly not any that he cares to mention.[8]

One other essay in this exceptionally rich and diverse volume deserves a brief comment here. In an essay with a very traditional title, "Russian Literature as a Source of Values," Ye. N. Popova proudly proclaims, "Literary study does not know closed borders, as Russian literature has not known borders."[9] (This statement surely had particular resonance for people who had grown up with the celebration of Border Guard Day, May 28th, as a major holiday complete with fireworks and parades.) She says that Russians suffer from cognitive dissonance when they discuss their country, and that "The transformation of cognitive dissonance into catharsis is one of the high goals of Russian literature."[10] Her proposals for values to help with this transformation are as traditional as Fink's: the Golden Rule from Christianity and philosopher Immanuel Kant's belief in an internal law.[11]

No discussion of literature in post-Soviet Russia would be complete without some comments by the always perceptive and provocative Mikhail Epstein. In his essay "Communism and Postmodernism" he cites Jean Baudrillard, a key postmodernist philosopher on the disappearance of imitation; television shows, for example, do not imitate anything. They exist in and of themselves without reference to anything outside themselves. And, in his provocative way, Epstein goes on to say that the absence of imitation was a key factor of Soviet life as well. He writes, "One cannot say that such characteristically Soviet phrases as 'the kolkhoz' or 'the party nature of literature' or 'the unity of the party and the people' were distorting reality insofar as they did not distort reality but created it."[12] What Epstein is doing is something of major significance in the postmodern intellectual world; he is juxtaposing two seemingly different things—Communism and postmodernism—and finding similarities and therefore meaning in them. It is precisely juxtapositions, connections, of writers and of the eras that they represent, that create the heart of Russian literature.

Postmodernism and its juxtapositions have produced one major writer, Viktor Pelevin (b.1962). As his website indicates,[13] he has produced a dazzling variety of work—epigrams, short stories and novels. These often surrealistic works defy clear description and ready summary. It is indicative for the evolution of post-Soviet literature that for him the key juxtaposition is with America and specifically with American popular culture, which has had a huge if often unrecognized impact in Russia.

Two Case Studies in Literary Relationships

These comments and references make it clear that the basic concepts of literary history are in flux in America as well as in Russia, and that serious scholars are addressing the relevant issues in productive ways. The present chapter cannot address such global issues, and limits itself to two case studies. However, these case studies matter because they bring up the deeply problematic issue of the relationship between the nineteenth and the twentieth centuries. Soviet scholars necessarily gave a simple answer to the question of this relationship by making a sharp distinction between the era before 1917 and the era after 1917. Even though no one now takes the Soviet version of events seriously, the fact remains that huge changes did occur in Russia in 1917 and afterwards, and that these changes affected—sometimes drastically—writers and the work that they produced. How is one to make sense of these changes in a non-ideological way? This chapter has the modest goal of offering two case studies in how this might be done. However, these case studies have exceptional importance because they deal with the heart of Russian literature.

The heart of Russian literature consists of four writers who have essential importance for Russia, and for Russian literature. They are two novelists—Leo Tolstoy (1828-1910) and Aleksandr Solzhenitsyn (1918-2008) —and two poets—Aleksandr Pushkin (1799-1837) and Osip Mandelstam (1891-1938). One can speak of the heart of Russian literature in this way because the Russians themselves think of certain writers as essential, the way the heart is essential to the human body. No serious person would dispute the proposition that Pushkin and Tolstoy are essential not just for Russian literature, but also for the Russians' understanding of themselves. There is an enormous amount of literature, both scholarly writings and journalistic essays, that supports this proposition. Alhtough Russians like to argue, it is difficult to imagine that any serious Russian would argue with the proposition that Pushkin and Tolstoy are essential Russian writers.

There is something else about Pushkin and Tolstoy that deserves mention here. Pushkin experienced some anxiety of influence from Byron, as expressed in his 1832 poem "I'm not Byron; I'm someone else," and Tolstoy felt a twinge of anxiety about Anthony Trollope. Nevertheless, their genius, and their historical circumstances, enabled them to write with such confidence and authority that they seem to posterity—and especially to subsequent writers—free of anxiety. One can say of Pushkin and Tolstoy something like what Bloom says about Shakespeare: "Shakespeare belongs to the giant age before the flood, before the anxiety of influence became central to poetic consciousness."[14] For Russians, and especially for subsequent Russian writers, Pushkin and Tolstoy belong to the giant age before the flood, a fact that makes them both attractive and intimidating.

However, time does not stand still, and other Russian writers wrote masterpieces after Pushkin and Tolstoy died. If we understand the whole of Russian literature not as a static quasi-metaphysical entity but as a function of readers' perceptions, then in the spirit of Eliot's "Tradition and the Individual Talent" works that supersede those of Pushkin and Tolstoy change our perceptions of Pushkin and Tolstoy. This change occurs with particular importance when subsequent writers explicitly take on Pushkin and Tolstoy as precursors, as Mandelstam and Solzhenitsyn did. Because of what Mandelstam and Solzhenitsyn wrote, and the way they engage Pushkin and Tolstoy respectively, these four writers are inextricably linked. Because of these linkages, it is fair to say that Pushkin and Mandelstam combine with Tolstoy and Solzhenitsyn to form a whole that constitutes the heart of Russian literature. This heart pumps metaphorical life-giving blood into literary history by making the problematic, deeply meaningful connection between the nineteenth and twentieth centuries.

Nobody can hope to understand Russian literature (or Russia as a country for that matter) without knowing and understanding the work of these four writers. Moreover, knowing and understanding their work in isolation is not adequate. Intricate connections exist between these pairs of writers, and such connections constitute the essential subject matter of literary history. In Bloom's terms, Tolstoy was Solzhenitsyn's precursor, just as Pushkin was Mandelstam's precursor. As this epilogue will show, each twentieth-century writer refers to his nineteenth-century precursor by name and uses his precursor's work to inform his own work in sophisticated, complex ways.

In a previous essay, I mentioned Mikhail Epstein's observation, bolstered by a quotation from Mandelstam, that it is characteristic of Russian literature to develop in recurring patterns, and I have cited the arrival motif as an instance of such a recurring pattern. In the present context I can say that pairings of writers also form a recurring pattern. I know of no analogies in any major Western literature for the deep, richly productive affinities between nineteenth-century writers and twentieth-century writers that we find in Russian literature between Pushkin and Mandelstam, and between Tolstoy and Solzhenitsyn.

To begin the discussion in a very basic way, the dates of the writers' births and deaths show some of these affinities. Simply put, the novelists lived long lives, and the poets lived short lives. Both Pushkin, who died at the age of 38, and Mandelstam, who died at the age of 47, died deaths in which the government was indirectly implicated. Pushkin died in a duel that was in various convoluted ways related to court intrigue. Although Mandelstam did die in the gulag, he was not executed, and Stalin never issued orders for his execution.

Solzhenitsyn and Tolstoy

Solzhenitsyn had deep, pervasive, multi-faceted connections with Tolstoy. Even the basic facts of Solzhenitsyn's life bear a striking resemblance to Tolstoy's. Tolstoy died at 82, and Solzhenitsyn died at 80. Although the novelists lived into their eighties, they both had serious troubles with the government, which found them quite simply unacceptable members of society. Tolstoy was excommunicated by the Russian Orthodox Church in 1901, and, of course, Solzhenitsyn's decades-long martyrdom at the hands of the Soviet government included arrest, years in the gulag, and exile before he was finally exiled from the Soviet Union in 1974.

Both Solzhenitsyn and Tolstoy positioned themselves as righteous Jeremiahs, speaking out against the increasingly secular quality of their times, and especially against the secular nature of life in the West. Their public statements attracted widespread publicity and large numbers of admirers. In particular, Solzhenitsyn's denunciations of American secularism made him a hero to the religious right in America.[15] In his later years Solzhenitsyn even imitated Tolstoy's appearance, and sported the same flowing white beard that made Tolstoy so distinctive in his later years.

Both Solzhenitsyn and Tolstoy had a strong sense of who they were, and what they meant for Russia. This sense created a need to speak out, to assert themselves as individuals by asserting their authority on matters of public interest. In turn, this need created a tension that tended to interfere with the operation of the deepest levels of their creative forces. Thus, in "Twilight of All the Russias: *The Red Wheel* as Literary Historiography," his very informative introduction to Solzhenitsyn's magnum opus, Richard Tempest quotes the author to the effect that "People forgot God; that's why it all happened."[16] Here speaks public figure who understood the power of sound bites in the twenty-first century. He knew perfectly well that this line would play well with his conservative admirers. However, as Tempest quickly points out, Solzhenitsyn himself shows in exhaustive detail over thousands of pages in *The Red Wheel* that in the twentieth century, piety was not enough. Both Nicholas II and Aleksandr Samsonov, the general who committed suicide after the disastrous Battle of Tannenberg, were men of exemplary, not to say extreme, piety. What Solzhenitsyn does not want to acknowledge here—what he cannot bring himself to say—is that it was precisely their piety, their acquiescence to Orthodox fatalism, that rendered them incapable of taking forceful action in Russia's time of extreme peril. This is something that Solzhenitsyn—like many pious Russians—knew all too well but could not bring himself to admit. An appropriate conclusion about Solzhenitsyn's statement, and others like it, is that even a great man can give in to the temptations of the platform that his fame has created for him.

More generally, Solzhenitsyn could not doubt that his achievements gave him the moral authority to denounce Western decadence. He did so in public for the first time during his Harvard address in 1978, when he said, among other things, "Today, well-being in the life of Western society has begun to reveal its pernicious mask."[17] Solzhenitsyn could also not understand that he was articulating monastic values to a post-monastic society, and that the authority that he claimed for himself derived from the same historical sources as the authority that Lenin and Stalin claimed for themselves. Moreover, Lenin and Stalin would have agreed with Solzhenitsyn's assertion that material well-being has a "pernicious mask." They certainly had no interest in making well-being an important priority in Soviet life. For understandable historical and personal reasons, Solzhenitsyn believed in the unalterable opposition between himself and Soviet leaders when in fact he had more in common with them than he was able to admit. He was unable to understand that authoritarianism in defense of non-material values was still authoritarianism. Solzhenitsyn was an extraordinary man who lived an extraordinary life, and his moral dilemmas deserve a more detailed treatment than I can give them here.

The Significance of Geography and Relationships

To return to the quartet of writers, geography also has significance for them. While Pushkin was born in Moscow, and Tolstoy was born in the heart of Russian estate country, Mandelstam and Solzhenitsyn were born on the periphery of the Russian empire, as were various other major writers. Mandelstam was born in Warsaw (like Aleksandr Blok) and Solzhenitsyn was born in the south (like Anna Akhmatova), in Kislovodsk. Both were outsiders, and as a Jew, Mandelstam was doubly an outsider. Mandelstam and Solzhenitsyn thus participated in a major process in the cultural history of twentieth-century Russia, the movement of artists—both dissidents and those who served the government—from the periphery to the center.

In this epilogue, we wish to understand these four great writers not just for what they did and where they lived, but also for their interrelationships. In this respect, Csikszentmihalyi makes a relevant comment when examining the careers of several innovative individuals: "Creative individuals don't *have* careers; they *create* them."[18] (Csikszentmihalyi's emphasis) Like so many of his pithy comments, this comment helps to give coherence to the careers of the Russian classics. It is not enough to say that Pushkin was a great poet, and that Tolstoy was a great novelist. We also wish to specify what specific features of their careers make them so important for Russian culture as a whole. What careers did they invent, and how did they invent them?

Beginning with Pushkin, of course, we may say that among the many other things he did, Pushkin invented the career of the doomed, tragic poet who dies at an early age at the height of his powers, with untold masterpieces left to write. Pushkin began Russian writers' engagement with history in *Boris Godunov*, and with the effects of government power in allegorical works like *The Bronze Horseman* and *Feast During a Plague*.

For his part, Tolstoy was a great novelist who invented the career of the great writer who fearlessly spoke out on social issues, who took on the heavy mantle of the conscience of Russia. It is not the least of the paradoxes in Tolstoy's career that his neurotic narcissism enabled him to embody the spirit of Russia as no one had before, and as no one did again until Solzhenitsyn.

Solzhenitsyn and Mandelstam Came After Giants

Like Chekhov before them, Mandelstam and Solzhenitsyn had an intense awareness that they came after giants. And, again like Chekhov, their experiences of an impaired relationship with their fathers gave them a need to seek a precursor. Chekhov's father went bankrupt, and Mandelstam's father experienced severe financial difficulties; and Solzhenitsyn, the posthumous son, never had any kind of relationship with his father at all. What could be more natural, more understandable, than the need on the part of a talented young man than to compensate for the absence of a satisfactory relationship with his father than to seek out a connection with a father figure who just happened to be a great writer? But, of course, the problem, as Bloom was the first to point out, is that a beginning writer makes this connection with a literary father who had already written his masterpieces, whereas the ephebe has done nothing. It leaves the ephebe with a nagging question: "Is there anything left for me to say?"

We now understand that the legendary stature of Pushkin and Tolstoy brought out Mandelstam's and Solzhenitsyn's greatness. It challenged them to respond to their precursors' masterpieces with masterpieces of their own and thereby become precursors for subsequent writers. Thus does literary history perpetuate itself. Fortunately for literary history, the ephebe-precursor relationships that Bloom calls "revisionary ratios" help to clarify Mandelstam's relationship with Pushkin, and Solzhenitsyn's relationship with Tolstoy. Defining these ratios at the outset will set the stage for subsequent detailed discussions.

In his essay "Pushkin and Skryabin," first delivered as a speech, Mandelstam says something that gives us an essential clue about his deep connection to Pushkin: "I wish to speak of the death of Skryabin as the highest act of his creative work. It seems to me that one must not exclude the death of an artist from the chain of his creative accomplishments."[19] There is a subtext here, as there so often is in Mandelstam's statements, and it is the death of Pushkin. We now understand that Mandelstam's fixation on Pushkin's death during the Pushkin Centennial of 1937 was an intimation of his own death.[20] It is thus appropriate to conceptualize Mandelstam's relationship to Pushkin as what Bloom calls "apophrades, or the return of the dead." In apophrades, Bloom tells us, "The mighty dead return, but they return in our colors, and speaking in our voices, at least in part, at least in moments, moments that testify to their own persistence, and not their own."[21] For Mandelstam, Pushkin did indeed return to inform his work. Of course, much more can be said about the thematic complex Pushkin/death/Mandelstam, as a subsequent discussion will show.

Solzhenitsyn's complex, multi-leveled relationship with Tolstoy begins with a general fact about Russian literary history.[22] Russian writers who undertake to write a historical novel do so with the intense awareness of Tolstoy's famous bearded visage looming over their shoulders. In the essay "Why Are Russian Novels So Long?" I addressed some of the responses of Russian writers to Tolstoy's presence, but the topic clearly deserves a book-length treatment. What is at issue here is Solzhenitsyn's relationship to Tolstoy, which—like Pasternak's relationship to Dostoyevsky—can be characterized as what Bloom calls "tessera." As mentioned before, Bloom's definition of a tessera is that "Tessera…is the completion and antithesis…A poet antithetically 'completes' his precursor, by so reading the parent poem as to retain its terms but to mean them in another sense, as though the precursor had failed to go far enough."[23] History played into Solzhenitsyn's hands by giving him a war, World War I, that allowed him to retain the terms of the parent poem, *War and Peace*, but mean them in quite another sense indeed in *The Red Wheel*.

Earlier I mentioned the numerous connections between Solzhenitsyn and Tolstoy. These connections even extend to scholarship about them. In both cases scholars use the author, and the author's life and beliefs, as reference points that lead away from the work in question. They thereby deny the work its status as a coherent whole. This critical practice caused Tempest to make the following statement, with which I fully concur: "It is my belief that Solzhenitsyn is yet to be fully understood and appreciated as a teller of tales, an inspired intuiter of alternative realities, even a purveyor of pleasure for all those who love a good story."[24]

War and Peace and *The Red Wheel*

Tempest says that *War and Peace* serves as the "referent of referents" for *The Red Wheel*, but does not define this referential system.[25] We might begin such a discussion by asking the basic question: What are these works, anyhow? We know that Tolstoy vehemently denied that *War and* Peace was a novel; in the same spirit, Solzhenitsyn characterized *The Red Wheel* not as a novel, but as a "Narrative in Discrete Time Periods" (*Povestvovaniye v otmerennykh srokax).* Both works depict the flow of historical events with gaps between key episodes and are usefully described as historical narratives.

Much can be said about the relationship between *War and Peace* and *The Red Wheel*, as Yekaterina Tikhomirova has shown in her dissertation on the subject.[26] The following table sets the general terms for such a discussion.

War and Peace	*The Red Wheel*
Comedy	Tragedy
Victory	Defeat
Napoleon	Lenin
Kutuzov	Samsonov

In a general way, these oppositions seem straightforward enough. *War and Peace* is a comedy in the spirit of Shakespeare's *All's Well That Ends Well.* In it, Tolstoy resolves the initial unstable configuration of five major characters at the beginning into a stable arrangement of two happily married couples in the countryside at the end. (To be sure, he adumbrates the next threat to the social order in Pierre's involvement in a secret society and in the person of Nikolenka Bolkonsky, a future Decembrist.) In contrast, there are no happy marriages at the end of *The Red Wheel,* only the slow-paced, inexorable fragmentation of a once proud society. If in Tolstoy's work the social order and the threats to the social order are held in a delicate, uncertain balance, in Solzhenitsyn's work the threats to the social order fragment and devastate that order.

If Tolstoy shows us Napoleon, with his soft hands, as a *poseur* who is caught up in vast historical forces that he neither understand nor controls, Solzhenitsyn shows us Lenin as Napoleon's opposite. Solzhenitsyn's Lenin believes that he is the embodiment of historical forces, a man obsessed with achieving power at any cost. Unlike Tolstoy's Napoleon, Solzhenitsyn's Lenin can and does bring about historical change.

If Nicholas II and Lenin are the two diametrically opposed historical characters in *The Red Wheel*, then we can understand the relationship between them by saying that Nicholas' refusal/inability to take decisive action when decisive action was needed, created a power vacuum that Lenin rushed to fill. It is an essential feature of the Solzhenitsyn/Tolstoy relationship that Solzhenitsyn breaks decisively with Tolstoy's understanding of great historical events as vast tidal waves over which no one has control. In *The Red Wheel*, leaders do have control over events, and their decisions about whether or not to exercise that control have consequences—usually disastrous ones. Solzhenitsyn had no patience with Tolstoy's ideas about history as a series of vast tidal waves. Among other things, such a scheme has the effect of absolving historical figures of responsibility for their actions, and Solzhenitsyn wanted above all to hold Lenin responsible for his actions.

Although many pages in both *War and Peace* and *The Red Wheel* present discussions of war, their treatments of this all-important topic have systematic differences. If General Mikhail Kutuzov led the Russian troops to a victory at Borodino, General Aleksandr Samsonov led the Russian troops to the greatest defeat in military history, the battle of Tannenberg. It is Tolstoy's Kutuzov who declares, *"The battle of Borodino is a victory."* (7, 211) (Tolstoy's emphasis), and who has the same kind of quasi-mystical connection with the Russian people that Natasha shows in her dance at Uncle's house. Tolstoy asks a key question about Kutuzov and answers it in the following passage:

> But in what way could this old man then, alone, in opposition to the opinion of everybody, guess, guess so accurately the significance of the national meaning of the event, that not once did it betray him in all his activity?
> The source of this unusual force of insight into the meaning of occurring phenomena lay in that national feeling that he carried in himself in all its purity and force. (7, 212)

In *August 1914*, Solzhenitsyn plays up the contrast between the outcomes of Borodino and Tannenberg by giving Samsonov the same connection with the people.

> There moved in him that invisible, untouchable thing that was occurring in the forests, over a spread of 60 miles, and about which staff officers didn't rush to get through to him with their reports. (273)[27]

Whereas Kutuzov intuits victory, Samsonov intuits defeat. His intuition gives him such an acute understanding of the defeat that his only recourse is to commit suicide.

When *August 1914* first appeared, critics immediately noted the autobiographical implications of the name of Sanya Lazhenitsyn, the young man who is the first major character to appear in the novel. What they did not sufficiently appreciate at the time was the extraordinary scene, told in a flashback to 1909, in which young Lazhenitsyn goes to Yasnaya Polyana and talks to Tolstoy. In opening his work to Tolstoy, his awe-inspiring precursor, as a fictional character of his own making in this way, Solzhenitsyn may have created something unique in world literature. He created a scene in which a quasi-autobiographical character directly encounters and enters into dialog with the author's intimidating precursor. Tempest says of this scene, "In a certain sense we are dealing with Solzhenitsyn's literary encounter with Tolstoy."[28] Indeed we are, and it is therefore of paramount importance to make the general meaning of the scene more precise.

In this scene, once Lazhenitsyn gets up enough courage to enter the grounds of Yasnaya Polyana, there seems to be nobody around.

> And…Somebody appeared along the paths, and walked rather briskly. Sanya hid behind a thick linden tree, and looked out. And he saw—The Gray-Haired One, the Gray-Bearded One! In a long shirt with a belt. He was shorter than he expected, but so like his pictures that he felt like shaking his head to get rid of the mirage. (24)

It is indeed Tolstoy himself. Lazhenitsyn screws up his courage to the sticking point and asks him what the goal of life is, and Tolstoy predictably answers, "Serve the good. And through that create the Kingdom of Heaven on earth." (25) And then comes the crux of the matter. Here is the question that Lazhenitsyn really wants to ask Tolstoy. This is why he came to Yasnaya Polyana.

> "Lev Nikolayevich, are you sure that you're not exaggerating the power of love innate in man? Or, in any case, that remains in contemporary man? And what if love is not as strong, not as obligatory in everyone, does not rise above everything—that your doctrine will turn out to be….without…." He could not complete his thought. "Very-very premature?" (25-6)

Shocked by his own audacity, Lazhenitsyn then objects to Tolstoy's philosophy and says, "Evil doesn't want to know the truth." Tolstoy imperturbably replies, "Everybody is born with reason."(26) Here it is as though Solzhenitsyn is calling on Dostoyevsky to help him come to terms with Tolstoy. After all, dialogs about the nature of good and evil in the world immediately remind us of Dostoyevsky. In *The First Circle,* one of Solzhenitsyn's characters calls this "the little Karamazov question," about the presence of evil in the world.[29]

We recall here that Bloom says that, in a tessera relationship, the effect of the ephebe's work is to show that the precursor "failed to go far enough." Subsequent developments in *The Red Wheel* suggest that Tolstoy failed to go far enough in his understanding of human nature. Protected by his legendary status and his social position, Tolstoy never had to confront the presence of evil in the world, as Solzhenitsyn did, so it was easy for him to deny it.

Twentieth-century history makes such a powerful case for the presence of evil in the world that the topic deserves a brief digression here. No one can dispute Solzhenitsyn's statement in his Nobel Lecture, "The twentieth century has turned out to be more cruel than the previous ones."[30] If he had had the courage, Lazhenitsyn would have said to Tolstoy what Solzhenitsyn has said to the world, namely that the twentieth century abundantly demonstrates the presence of evil in the world. Moreover, it is important to understand that discussions of evil do not have to involve metaphysics. We know that because of the work of a Cambridge professor of developmental psychopathology, Simon Baron-Cohen, the author of the book *The Science of Evil*.[31] Baron-Cohen's studies have shown that what we call evil is at root a psychological problem, the inability to feel empathy. The great historic upheavals of the twentieth century brought to the fore large numbers of people—primarily men—who wielded power without the ability to feel empathy. There is of course more, much more, to this matter than these brief comments suggest, but Lazhenitsyn's conversation with Tolstoy raises an issue that the Russians still have been unable to address because they tend to veer off into metaphysics and abstractions when asked to discuss evil and violence.

To return to Lazhenitsyn, he is conflicted about evil and violence, which is what makes him interesting to Solzhenitsyn. Later, in 1914, as he is going off to war, Lazhenitsyn has another Dostoyevskian dialog about Tolstoy. This time it is with the philosopher Varsonofyev. When he tells Varsonofyev that he is a Tolstoyan and is going off to war, Varsonofyev expresses surprise. (368-9)

As part of his project of presenting the Russia that would be swept away after 1917, Solzhenitsyn introduces numerous characters and then places them into carefully detailed settings. In doing so, he takes character traits and story elements from Tolstoy, and then integrates them into his own vast narrative. After the first episode of the Lazhenitsyn story, he describes the wealthy Tomchak family in the south of Russia. Perhaps because this is his first transition from one story to another, he uses and revises the opening of *Anna Karenina* by telling us the stream of consciousness of the wife, Irina Tomchak. "Already at the first break from sleep, before remembering that you're young, and what a summer day it is, and how one can live happily, something cold and blunt comes in—the quarrel! She and her husband had been quarreling since yesterday." (28) However, no intermediary, like Anna Karenina, will arrive to make peace between the quarreling spouses. (In general, Solzhenitsyn also breaks with Russian tradition by not using the arrival motif to set the plot in motion.)

In addition to Anna Karenina, Tolstoy's other vivid female character is, of course, Natasha Rostova, who serves as the model for the impulsive, self-absorbed Ksenya Tomchak. (A useful book could be written about the adaptations of, and references to, Natasha in modern Russian literature, beginning with the Natasha in Chekhov's play "The Proposal.") She is waking up, too. Then Ksenya Tomchak's stream of consciousness follows, "No, nowhere are things as good as at home!—And the bed in such a pleasant, bluish room, still dark now, but the sun's rays are coming through the blinds. And such a carefree possibility of being lazy—for a day, a week, a month!" (35) The spontaneous immediacy of this carefree young girl reminds us of the young Natasha, and when we learn that she is a dancer, that establishes the connection. "And Ksenya herself in her Hungarian laces and little boots with spurs! Or in her ethereal veil-like dress with a little medallion, barefoot—she was all in flight." (40)

If Solzhenitsyn had simply been imitating Tolstoy or borrowing from him, he would have left the matter there. However, in keeping with other reversals in *The Red Wheel*, he reverses the character. If Natasha is the embodiment of the Russian spirit when she dances at Uncle's, Ksenya Tomchak has taken on big-city airs and is alienated from country life, i.e., Russian life. Naturally, she has a brother, and their attitudes are the opposites of those of the fervent patriots Natasha and Nikolay Rostov: "It united the sister and brother that only the two of them in the whole family had critical advanced views. The others were primitives, Pechenegs." (38).

Solzhenitsyn also adapts Andrey Bolkonsky from *War and Peace* for his own purposes. If Tolstoy's Andrey has the life-denying qualities of St. Petersburg, and is destined for death and transcendence, he undergoes a major transformation to appear in *The Red Wheel* as Georgy Vorotyntsev, who bears of the name of the saint who is a dragon-slayer.

In *War and Peace,* we read of Andrey that, "Of the activities that were presented to him, military service was the simplest and most familiar to him. In the office of duty general attached to Kutuzov's staff, he stubbornly and diligently occupied himself with affairs, amazing Kutuzov with his eagerness for work and his efficiency." (6, 41) Actually, we see very little of Andrey in his capacity as an ultra-efficient staff officer, but we see a great deal of Vorotyntsev as a competent, dedicated soldier.

Tolstoy is not really interested in details of soldiering, but Solzhenitsyn, who did fight in World War II, is. He tells us that just before the battle of Tannenberg, Vorotyntsev was the man of the hour: "At the commander-in-chief's map, Vorotyntsev took in this situation, this operation—as though he had not just arrived, but for all the three weeks he had been dealing with it—not for his whole life, his entire military career had been nothing but a preparation for this operation!" (99) Vorotyntsev is more than efficient, as Prince Andrey is when he serves on Kutuzov's staff; Vorotyntsev is inspired to make plans and act on them in *August 1914* and in subsequent volumes as well. He is as close as there is to a hero in *The Red Wheel*.

For all the references to Tolstoy and Tolstoyan elements in *The Red Wheel*, I have found only one direct borrowing, and it is an indicative one. Although Tolstoy and Solzhenitsyn were both patriots, they were also humane moralists, and they wished above all to avoid demonizing the soldiers who were Russia's opponents in war. They both understood the social and moral consequences of doing so.

Tolstoy shows the common humanity that the Russians and French share in an incident during the confusion of the Battle of Borodino, when Pierre runs into somebody.

> Pierre, instinctively shielding himself from the encounter, since they were running towards each other, without seeing, put out his hand and with one hand grabbed this man (it was a French soldier) by the shoulder and with the other grabbed his throat. The officer, letting go of his sword, grabbed Pierre by the collar.
>
> For several seconds they both, with wide eyes, looked at the faces that were foreign to each other, and they both did not understand what they had done and what they were to do. Each of them thought, "Am I taken prisoner, or is he taken prisoner by me?" (6, 268-9)

After a moment of indecision, Pierre and the French officer let go of each other and they run back to ther respective armies.

Solzhenitsyn took this incident and amplified it, while retaining its meaning. During the battle, Vorotyntsev and three other Russian soldiers ride their horses up a hill and suddenly come upon a group of German officers in a car. (The opposition of the Russians on horseback and the Germans in a car in this scene is an effective metonymical analogy for the technical superiority of the Germans over the Russians, which is a recurring theme in the battle sections.) It is the car of German general Hermann von Francois. The German general and Vorotyntsev introduce themselves. (The omnicompetent Vorotyntsev speaks German, of course). Vorotyntsev thinks, "Oh, So…The commander of the first German corps! He's almost in our hands, can we take him?"(335) Then comes a close paraphrase of the key passage about Pierre and the French soldier from *War and Peace*, and an amplification of it: "He's almost in our hands, but it's unknown who has taken who prisoner. But the main thing is that to shoot and cut is natural when you're not acquainted. But once you're acquainted you can't do it in a human way."(335) And indeed once they have made human contact, the Russians and the Germans cannot kill each other, so they go their separate ways, as Pierre and the French soldier do.

Although Bloom increases the drama of ephebe/precursor encounters by making them seem like fights to the (creative) death, it does not always happen like this. Perhaps such high drama occurs more frequently in poetry, which was always Bloom's great passion; in prose, however, there is room for a middle ground in which the ephebe can so thoroughly assimilate a technique from a precursor that no trace of the precursor is left. This is what Solzhenitsyn did when he learned from Tolstoy to make scenes vivid through the use of vivid details, as in Solzhenitsyn's sketch of Kislovodsk, his home town:

> Saratovkin's three-story house stood on the corner of Lermontov and Noble Streets. Little open trams going to Proval turned around there. Despite the war, even today, they were full of resort people. They crawled higher and higher to the foothill of Mashuk, by the expensive white dachas, villas, and pensions—in that direction toward the Aeolian Harp, toward the Lermontov grotto. And in the other direction, toward the bazaar, Lermontov Street dipped sharply; the roofs fell away into the greenery. (61)

Anything like a complete discussion of Solzhenitsyn's use of Tolstoy in the thousands of pages of *The Red Wheel* is not practical here, so this preceding passage must stand for many others.

Sanya Lazhenitsyn, in his conversation with the philosopher Varsonofyev, says that he is not a "pure Tolstoyan." Solzhenitsyn was not a pure Tolstoyan, either. If he had been, he would have given up his artistic integrity. To understand how Solzhenitsyn was not a pure Tolstoyan, we may recall Bloom's description of the tessera revisionary ratio between the ephebe and the precursor. We recall that Bloom says that the ephebe retains the terms of the parent poem (*War and Peace*, in this case) but means them in another sense, as though the precursor had failed to go far enough. Solzhenitsyn retained the terms of *War and Peace* by writing another vast historical novel, but showed that Tolstoy did not go far enough, and not just in his limited understanding of the extremes of human nature. What Tolstoy did not do, and indeed could not have done, and what Solzhenitsyn did do, was to assimilate the modernist culture of his time, of the twentieth century, by using imagery and devices that Tolstoy could not have imagined.

Evidence of this assimilation appears on the very first page of *August 1914.* In its verbal density and thematic gravitas, the first page of *August 1914* may be the most important single page in modern Russian prose. The first sentence of the novel is: "They left the Cossack village at daybreak on a transparent morning when, at first sunlight, the entire Mountain Range, bright white with blue ravines, stood accessibly close, visible in every gorge, so close that a man not accustomed to seeing it would think that he could reach it in two hours." (11) The characters in question are Isaaky (Sanya) and his brother Yevstrat (Yevstrashka) Lazhenitsyn, and they are among the last characters in Russian fiction to encounter the wide-open spaces traversed by Gogol's troika, metaphorically speaking. They are traveling in a *brichka,* a light Russian cart, and have set off to go to the university. They immediately remind us of Yegorushka in Chekhov's "The Steppe," who is also traveling in a *brichka,* and is also leaving home to get an education, which will inevitably alienate him from the village life that he is leaving behind. In fact, what we learn about Sanya and Yevestrashka's journey closely tracks Yegorushka's journey in "The Steppe."

The act of leaving home to get an education represents a microcosm of the social change that transformed twentieth-century Russia. To show just how widespread and significant this process was, it is worth noting that, although Solzhenitsyn could not have known it, this was the fateful journey that young Iosif Djugashvili (later known as Stalin) took with his mother Keke. In August 1894 the two of them left his native village of Gori, in Georgia, for the capital city, Tbilisi, to enter the Orthodox seminary there. The three years and nine months that young Djugashvili spent in the seminary changed his life, and later when as Joseph Stalin he became General Secretary of the Communist Party, the long-term effects of his seminary stay changed world history.[32]

When Solzhenitsyn wrote the first page of what would become *August 1914,* he himself was setting off on a literary journey much longer and much more fraught with danger than Lazhenitsyn's fictional one. According to a statement in Scammell's biography, Solzhenitsyn conceived of this vast project as early as 1937, when he was only nineteen years old.[33] He could not have imagined that he would eventually receive the Nobel Prize in literature, and also something more precious to him—ideal writing conditions in a pleasant house in Vermont that would allow him to write thousands of pages in peace and safety. But he knew that he was embarking on a huge task, and this may explain why he did something that Tolstoy never did in *War and Peace*. He chose the generalizing power of allegory at key moments—such as the first page of *August 1914*. He gives us a clue when he capitalizes "Mountain Range" (*Khrebet)* in the first sentence, and then continues with unmistakable religious vocabulary that includes a key Orthodox word not usually used in the West, "not made by human hands" (*nerukotvornyi)*:

> It rose so large in the world of petty human things, so not made by human hands, in the world of made things. For thousands of years, all the people who had ever lived could have brought here as much as they could carry and made heaping piles of everything that they had made and even conceived of—and they would not have made such a Mountain Range beyond thought. (11)

Clearly, this mountain range carries a heavy thematic load. The first thing we are told about it is that it is deceptive. Someone unaccustomed to seeing it would think that it is a two-hour ride away, but it is not. The historical allegory is clear. The sight of the mountain range is as deceptive as the belief in the revolution. Both the mountain range and the transformed Russia that the revolution promised seem close at hand, but they are not. For the Russians in *The Red Wheel*, this means that their belief that the revolution—any revolution—will immediately bring about the Kingdom of Heaven on earth, as Tolstoy puts it to Lazhenitsyn, is a chimera, a mireage. (We recall that when Lazhenitsyn first catches sight of Tolstoy, he thinks he has seen a mirage.) If ever there was a writer whose reputation made him seem like a mountain range, it was Tolstoy. There is an unmistakable quasi-metonymical relationship between Tolstoy and the Mountain Range. Lazhenitsyn is disappointed in Tolstoy's teachings, as Russians will be disappointed in the promises of the revolution.

More generally, though, the mountain range, which is described here as something beyond thought and beyond human endeavor, stands for the presence of the transcendent in the world. Ultimately, it attests to the vanity of human wishes. It is worth noting that such mountain imagery hardly ever appears in Orthodox symbolism, or in Russian literature for that matter. Solzhenitsyn's use of the mountain as an image of transcendence may attest to the influence of Buddhism, in which the sacred mountain is a key symbol, on his work. (Let us recall here the chapter "The Buddha's Smile" in *The First Circle*.)

Unlike Tolstoy, Solzhenitsyn had both a verbal and a visual imagination. In this he had an affinity with Dostoyevsky, who repeatedly referred to paintings in his work. However, Solzhenitsyn was a child of the twentieth century, and was deeply affected by film, the great art form of his time. More specifically, he was entranced by the work of his second precursor, Sergey Eisenstein, the greatest Russian filmmaker, and one of the greatest and most influential filmmakers of all time. His ephebe-precursor relationship with Eisenstein appears clearly in the montage scenes in *August 1914* and in subsequent volumes of *The Red Wheel*.

Solzhenitsyn and Eisenstein

Eisenstein was a deeply problematic—and therefore stimulating—precursor for Solzhenitsyn. If Tolstoy was a patriot, he was a patriot in his own idiosyncratic way. Eisenstein, however, eagerly put his genius at the service of the Soviet government and made what Solzhenitsyn could only have perceived as high-level propaganda for it. If there was ever an ephebe-precursor relationship that conforms to what Bloom calls "clinamen," in which "A poet swerves away from his precursor,"[34] it is the Solzenitsyn-Eisenstein relationship. Bloom observes, "The stronger the man, the larger his resentments, and the more brazen his *clinamen*."[35] As the scope of *The GULag Archipelago* attests, Solzhenitsyn had enormous resentments against the Soviet regime in general, and against Eisenstein in particular, although they do not appear directly in *August 1914*.

In his insightful book *The Machines of a Famous Time*, Ilya Kukulin associates Solzhenitsyn with the little-known writer Pavel Ulitin, and shows that between the two of them what he calls "hypermontage" passed from Eisenstein's films into what might be called the mainstream of the Soviet literary underground. Without referring to Bloom at all, Kukulin refers to Solzhenitsyn's "multi-year polemic with the films and esthetics of Sergey Eisenstein," and notes that the two artists concentrated on the same themes. These themes were Russian history, the meaning of the revolution, and the meaning of violence in the revolution.[36] He even invents a cumbersome but accurate term for them. He says that both Eisenstein and Solzhenitsyn created what he calls "Epic Polyphonic Agitational Art." To be sure, Solzhenitsyn was not alone in his ambiguous attitude toward Eisenstein. After 1991, various scholars began a re-evaluation of Eisenstein, and Eisenstein's collaboration with Stalin and Stalinism.[37]

Kukulin very appropriately takes Solzhenitsyn's unproduced 1959 film script *The Tanks Know the Truth* as emblematic of Solzhenitsyn's reaction against Eisenstein. The script, which shows an uprising mounted by zeks in a remote gulag camp, is written against Eisenstein's film *Strike*. In Eisenstein's film, the workers mount a strike, while in Solzhenitsyn's script, it is the prisoners (the zeks)

234 | *The Coherence of the Russian Classics*

who do (and the Soviet army uses tanks to suppress the strike, hence the title). One can thus say that, roughly speaking, *The Tanks Know the Truth* is to *Strike* as *August 1914* is to *War and Peace*. In particular, Kukulin points out that the ending of *The Tanks Know the Truth* precisely recreates the ending of *Strike*—for the opposite effect. The ending of *Strike* commemorates strikers in pre-revolutionary Russia, while the ending of *The Tanks Know the Truth* commemorates those who mounted uprisings in the gulag.

Clearly, *The Tanks Know the Truth* meant a lot to Solzhenitsyn, because he included what Kukulin calls a "remake" of it in chapter 26 of *October 1916*. This detailed screen segment, which is four pages long, and includes a "red wheel,"[38] features a workers' uprising that repels a tsarist cavalry detachment. The segment uses such Eisensteinian trademarks as a screen that changes size and numerous changes in camera angles. Kukulin also mentions a striking similarity between Solzhenitsyn and Eisenstein in the way they presented their texts. He says that Eisenstein's script for his film *Ivan the Terrible* consists of precisely the same unnumbered sequences of images that we find in the screen sequences of *The Red Wheel*.

The Red Wheel: The Meaning of the Title

A key question for all of *The Red Wheel* is this: What does the title mean? The most obvious thing to say is that it refers to the wheel on a train, and thus we wish to have a general understanding of the symbolic possibilities of railroads. It was obvious to everybody in the century between 1850 and 1950 that railroads were creating major social and economic changes, so it was natural for people to use them as metaphors. One might say that the very title *The Red Wheel* is over-determined, which is a scholarly way of saying that it has multiple sources. In cultural terms, most obviously, it is a train kills Anna Karenina. And, as Kukulin points out, Marx himself once said that "Revolutions are the locomotives of history." (One could consider that pithy remark as a summary of *The Red Wheel*!)

It is very likely that Soviet filmmakers in the twenties were familiar with that remark. In any case, several of them used phrases like "the wheel of history." As Kukulin points out, wheel imagery appears in Eisenstein's *October* (1927); Vsevolod Pudovkin's *The End of St. Petersburg* (1927): and Friedrich Ermler's *A Fragment of an Empire* (1929). Most satisfyingly, Kukulin mentions Gogol's troika in connection with all this wheel imagery, thus creating the kind of connection between the nineteenth and twentieth century that Mandelstam dreamed of.

However, Kukulin does not mention the first reference to a red wheel in *August 1914,* which occurs in chapter 22, and which has exceptional importance. Solzhenitsyn begins this chapter with a stream of consciousness, and it is not immediately apparent whose stream of consciousness it is. (It is worth noting that Solzhenitsyn, as part of his desire to give us a vivid sense of the inner life of a society that is about to be destroyed, uses stream of consciousness much more frequently than Tolstoy ever did.) As we read the passage, we gradually realize that we are inside the head of Vladimir Lenin. In this, the first time we meet Lenin in *August 1914,* Solzhenitsyn uses an expanded version of a metonymical situation to put him in a train station. As Lenin walks to his train, we read an isolated comment that simply conveys what he sees: "A large red wheel on the locomotive, about a head high." (193) Before anything else, before the cultural precedents for this image, and before any discussion of its meaning, we must note that what Solzhenitsyn says here is historically accurate. Early locomotives really did have middle wheels that were five or six feet tall, and some of them were painted red. Historians speculate that they were painted red to make it easier for inspectors to identify cracks or defects in the wheels.[39]

In important passages in *The Red Wheel*—and this is one of the most important—we, first of all, wish to ask whether Tolstoy has any relevance. The answer here is an emphatic "yes," because we can connect the red wheel to Anna Karenina's red purse. Both images relate to death, with an indicative difference. In *Anna Karenina*, Tolstoy tells personal stories. While his characters in various ways acknowledge social change, it rarely impinges directly on their lives. In *The Red Wheel,* however, social change is the story that Solzhenitsyn wants to tell. This interplay of similarities and differences is just what we would expect in the complicated ephebe-precursor relationship that existed between Tolstoy and Solzhenitsyn.

In his understated way, Tolstoy makes an isolated reference to Anna's purse, and lets it go at that. Solzhenitsyn, however, gives us an extended interior monologue that reveals Lenin's personality and how he thinks.

> No matter how careful, prudent, distrustful you are—the damned lulling quality of ordinary life, which is philistine by nature, has been lulling you for seven years in a row. And in the shadow of something large, without noticing, you lean against a massive iron support, like a wall—and it suddenly moves, and it turns out to be a large red wheel of a locomotive; a large open wrench turns it—and it crushes your back—and you go down! Under the wheel!! And, floundering with

your head at the tracks, you manage too late to figure out what some stupid new danger has crept in. (193-4)

Unlike the fearless, decisive Lenin of Soviet propaganda, this is an insecure, anxious (and historically believable) Lenin, whom Solzhenitsyn associates with Anna Karenina. He mistakenly believes that the metonymical red wheel is a firm wall, and will always support him. To his dismay, however, it turns out that it is not a wall at all; it does what wheels are supposed to do—it moves.

We are meant to understand the red wheel in relationship with the mountain range described in the first sentence of *August 1914*. The mountain range and the wheel are both deceptive in different ways—one moves and one does not. The mountain seems accessible, but it is not. The wheel seems stable, but it is not. Lenin has the well-founded anxiety that the wheel will crush him, as it crushed Anna Karenina. But the wheel is more than a wheel, just as Anna's purse is more than a purse. The wheel is a metonymical symbol for the historical process that, once set in motion, crushes everything in front of it. Lenin understands this, only fleetingly. He is too obsessive and too self-centered—ultimately too egotistical—to acknowledge that he cannot control events.

August 1914 contains both a metonymical red wheel and a metaphorical red wheel as well. Solzhenitsyn introduces the metaphorical red wheel in a screen sequence. (As elements set apart from the rest of the text, all his screen sequences are by definition metaphorical.) A key screen sequence begins, "The windmill is burning!" (241) (Solzhenitsyn gives intensity to the passage by using exclamation marks in a way that recalls Blok's practice in his poem "On Snipe Field," a kindred and equally intense work which is about another Russian defeat.) In all, the screen passage takes up 22 lines, and it concludes:

> And for some reason the blades—from the streams of hot air?—without falling off begin slowly,
> Slowly,
> Slowly to turn. Without any wind, what kind of miracle [is this]?
> The reddish-golden blades consisting of nothing but the ribs move in a strange rotation—
> Like
> Like a fiery wheel rolling along the air.
> And it falls apart.
> It falls apart into pieces,
> Into fiery shards. (242)

If Tolstoy used anticipatory microcosms to suggest his characters' innate personalities, Solzhenitsyn here shows his change of emphasis from individuals to the society as a whole. Unlike the inaccessible mountain, which stands apart from human striving, the windmill is constructed by human hands and is thus another version of the red train wheel that Lenin could not rely on; it is moved by the wind and consumed by fire, and is thus red, like the wheel. In "On Snipe Field," Blok wrote, "The sunset is covered in blood!" (*Zakat v krovi!*) The fiery windmill is the color of blood and represents the sunset, the utter collapse of Russian society. The fiery wheel in the sky is the first suggestion of the title of the series as a whole.

In the same passage with the wheel of the windmill is also a wheel from a medical cart that comes off, which is presented like this:

> It gets bigger and bigger!
> It fills the whole screen! It gets bigger and bigger!!
> THE WHEEL!—lit by the fire!
> Autonomous!
> Unstoppable!
> Crushing everything! (294)

This is Lenin's nightmare come true. The wheel crushes everything! But then in a manner consistent with the ambiguities of modern art, it changes. The camera that made it look huge also makes it look ordinary. It turns out that it is yet another variant of Gogol's troika, a medical cart. Here it takes on an allegorical meaning, suggesting that there will be no healing, no treatment that will cure Russia's ills.

The remaining question to be addressed is this: "What is the respective significance of metonymy and metaphor in *The Red Wheel*?" Generally speaking, Solzhenitsyn uses very little metonymy in character development, and, in this respect, he firmly rejects much of Tolstoy's legacy. Lenin's metonymical connection to the red wheel is the exception that proves the rule, because it gives the whole series its title.

Solzhenitsyn uses a great deal of metaphor, and very effectively, too, in the screen sequences, but hardly anywhere else. In the volumes that follow *August 1914*, there are long passages— hundreds of pages—in which Solzhenitsyn uses neither metaphor nor metonymy. One has the feeling that he felt such urgency to tell his long-suppressed story that he was willing to sacrifice imagery for detail, and that imagery would have impeded the all-important flow of the narrative. In its scope, if nothing else, *The Red Wheel* remains a unique work that dominates Russian literature in the late twentieth- and early twenty-first century.

Mandelstam and Tradition

If Solzhenitsyn relied on tradition less and less as he matured, Mandelstam is the consummate artist of tradition, the artist who intuitively understood that it was his cultural mission to keep tradition alive, and that he had to innovate in order to do it. It is therefore appropriate to discuss various topics relating to Mandelstam under the rubric of "Mandelstam And…" No version of this rubric tells us more about the social history of art in the Soviet period than "Mandelstam and Eisenstein."

In the history of Soviet culture, Eisenstein and Mandelstam form a complementary pair of artists, [40] because each man is generally considered to be the best in his field; they thus create a unique pairing. Socially, they have striking similarities that illustrate the variety of Jewish experience in the twentieth century. Both came from assimilated non-observant Jewish families on the periphery of the Russian empire (Riga and Warsaw). Both made their way from the provinces to St. Petersburg, where they began their careers, which developed in radically different ways.

Mandelstam and his wife Nadezhda lived in poverty and isolation for most of the post-1917 era. Although Eisenstein was presumably a latent homosexual, we have no evidence that he ever had an intimate relationship with anybody of any gender. It was as though he took a vow of poverty, chastity, and obedience in exchange for having a career in the world.

Mandelstam the introvert practiced his art very privately. We would have lost most of his work if his wife had not memorized his later poems and remembered them until such a time as it was (relatively) safe to write them down. In this respect the contrast between Mandelstam and Eisenstein could hardly be greater. Eisenstein the extrovert practiced the very public, very collaborative art of film-making. It is no small part of his genius that he was able to walk the extremely fine line between what he wanted to do (create great films) and what the Soviet authorities would let him do (create propaganda).

Mandelstam was an introvert with an auditory sensibility that made him intensely responsive to music. Eisenstein was an extrovert with a visual sensibility that made him intensely responsive to images. After 1917, Mandelstam did not, and could not, respond to the Soviet ambience that was oriented toward the external world. Eisenstein, on the other hand, came into his own in the 1920s, and made a series of films that manipulated images as no previous films ever had. Mandelstam was so otherworldly that he did not care about success. Eisenstein, however, enjoyed spectacular success that was constantly imperiled by incessant attacks, which so weakened his system that he died of a heart attack in 1948.

A more general sense of "Mandelstam And..." is that more than with Solzhenitsyn, or for that matter, more than with Mandelstam's poetic soul mate Anna Akhmatova, an in-depth understanding of his work must begin with a general concept of his genius. Thus, a key element of his work that makes sense of what otherwise seems puzzling or arbitrary is its dynamism. Mandelstam is rarely content to allow any name or image a fixed, autonomous existence in a semantic field. Any name or image implies, and, in fact, may be transformed or assimilated, into its opposite. To illustrate, consider the programmatic first line of his poem "Nature is also Rome and was reflected in it."[41] Here Mandelstam expresses his integrative sensibility by decisively breaking with the Romantic opposition of nature versus culture, by associating the two. More specifically, in the phrase "in the colonnade of the grove" from this poem, he may be reacting against Baudelaire's equally programmatic poem "Correspondences" in which the French poet uses the phrase "forests of symbols." Whereas Baudelaire implies that although nature speaks, it is nevertheless set apart from people, nothing is really set apart from anything else in Mandelstam. One can also cite an earlier poem that has relevance here, which is Fyodor Tyutchev's "Nature is not what you think it is" (1836). As Baudelaire would do later, Tyutchev asserts that nature is alive, but does not connect nature and culture, as Mandelstam does.

The concept of the connection between polar opposites helps us to return to Mandelstam's key 1915 essay "Pushkin and Skryabin". Mandelstam says in a previously cited passage, "I wish to speak of the death of Skryabin as the highest act of his creativity. It seems to me that one should not exclude the death of an artist from the chain of his creative accomplishments, but view it as a final conclusive word."[42] Thus, life in the form of creativity implies life, and life implies death. This is, of course, a deeply Christian belief, as Mandelstam acknowledges, "From this final Christian point of view the death of Skryabin was amazing."[43] But for Mandelstam, the esthete, only one death mattered, a death that implies poetic life, and that was the death of Pushkin. "Pushkin was buried late at night. He was buried secretly. Marble St. Isaac's Cathedral—a magnificent sarcophagus—did not receive the sunny body of the poet."[44] But for Mandelstam, death implies life, and for his career what this means is that the Christian dialectic of death and resurrection appears in a secular estheticized form as the death of Pushkin and the resurrection of Pushkin in Mandelstam's poetry, which gave it new life. The Mandelstam-Pushkin relationship is the most intense and the most productive ephebe-precursor relationship in all of modern literature.

Fortunately, Irina Surat's magisterial book *Mandelstam and Pushkin* sets forth in exhaustive detail what one would like to know about the connections between Pushkin's life and work and those of Mandelstam. In particular, in what she calls the "Pushkinian paradigm" for Mandelstam, she discusses the affinities between the death of Christ and the death of Pushkin, in which the "black sun" is a unifying image.[45] She also identifies a key, little-known moment in 1921. On February 14 of that year, the 84th anniversary of Pushkin's death, Mandelstam arranged for a funeral mass to be held in the majestic St. Isaac's Cathedral, the former official church of the Romanov family. Mandelstam distributed candles to the other poets from the House of Men of Letters.[46] Surat sums up the importance of this event in the following way: "Having entered into this state after death [*poslesmertiye*], Mandelstam simultaneously entered into his own state of death as well, set out on his own direct and conscious path to his own demise."[47] Her analysis here is consistent with my interpretation of Mandelstam's recitation of his poem "We live not feeling the country beneath us"[48] to a group of people when he knew it was likely that one or more of them would inform on him. This reading led directly to his arrest and to his death in the gulag in 1938.

In *Stalin's Soviet Monastery*, I have interpreted this sequence of events as an elaborate Russian equivalent of a phenomenon known in American slang as "suicide by cop." In suicide by cop, people deliberately act in a threatening way toward police officers and force them to shoot them.[49] In choosing a death in which the government was implicated but not directly guilty (Stalin never gave orders to have Mandelstam shot), Mandelstam was following Pushkin's death, and committing "the highest act of his creativity," as he put it in his essay "Pushkin and Skryabin." (This phrase has a relevant, disturbing analogy with the phrase "the highest measure," which was the Stalinist euphemism for execution.)

It will never be possible to understand in any satisfactory way the depths of Mandelstam's psyche in the late 1930s. We can only make more or less well-informed guesses. If he consciously, unconsciously, or otherwise, brought about, or was complicit in, his arrest and death, then he was in some sense imitating Pushkin. In the Russian context, he was a passion-sufferer, a *strastoterpets*, in the long-standing, well-known tradition that associated the acceptance of suffering with sanctity. Claire Cavanaugh refers to such an interpretation as "the Christological reading of the poet's life and art."[50]

Surat mentions two poems by Mandelstam that state, or imply, crucifixion. The first one begins, oddly, "Do not attempt foreign adverbs, but try to forget them." The powerful concluding couplet formulates the fate of a creative person in the age of Stalinism in this way: "In punishment for your pride, incorrigible sound-lover/You will receive a vinegar sponge for your treasonous lips." [51] The idea that the very act of creativity is an act of pride, which is to be punished by literal or metaphorical crucifixion, and thereby transformed into humility, has deep roots in both Russian monastic culture and in secular culture as well. In literature it is implied in the confrontation between Chichikov and Nozdryov in *Dead Souls,* in which Nozdryov says "You lie" to whatever Chichikov says. In *Crime and Punishment,* the old pawnbroker whom Raskolnikov kills is a passion-sufferer, as he himself becomes a passion-sufferer when he accepts his punishment for the murder. And, of course, the intuitive Mandelstam understood the dynamic in which Stalin drew on his seminary training to justify finding and punishing pride wherever he imagined it might lurk.

Surat also finds the theme of crucifixion in one of Mandelstam's last poems, "Like the martyr of chiaroscuro, Rembrandt,/I've gone off deeply into a mute time." [52] Here, however, the evidence is not so clear. To be sure, the poet asks for forgiveness, but punishment is neither stated nor implied.

This discussion of the Mandelstam-Pushkin connection provides a useful context for interpreting a key Mandelstam poem written in 1920 that begins, "Let's get together again in St. Petersburg, /As though we had buried the sun in it." [53] At the time, the city formerly known as St. Peterburg was named Petrograd, so the "get together" cannot occur in a real place. No, the return is a return to a metaphorical place, to the place where "we buried the sun," meaning Pushkin.

This poem has two related meanings, neither of which excludes the other, as it often happens in Mandelstam's work. First of all, returning to the traumatic scene where "we buried the sun" suggests what Freud called "neurotic repetition." Freud's essay "Beyond the Pleasure Principle," was written in 1920 and thus just at the same time as Mandelstam's poem. In the essay, Freud observed a child engaged in repeated actions and concluded that "In the play of children we seem to arrive at the conclusion that the child repeats even the unpleasant experience because through his own activity he gains a more thorough mastery than was possible by the more passive experience." [54] Since the child plays the game over and over again, "We at once see that the *repetition-compulsion* must be absorbed by the repressed element in the unconscious." [55] (Freud's emphasis)

Since the death of Pushkin was a cultural wound that would not heal, it would not remain repressed for long. Sensitive intellectuals such as Mandelstam returned to it again and again. This is a poignant and very Russian version of repetition-compulsion. A mild version of it continues even today, when Russians gather on Pushkin's birthday every year to lay flowers at the base of the Pushkin statue in Moscow and recite his poems. Given the importance of passion-suffering in Mandelstam's life and work, it is significant that Pushkin Square (where the statue now stands) was formerly called Passion Square, because it was the site of the Convent of the Passion. The transformation of Passion Square into Pushkin Square surely did not go unnoticed by Mandelstam.

Mircea Eliade articulates another possible interpretation of recurrence that has relevance to Mandelstam's return to the place where we buried the sun. He writes in his book *The Myth of the Eternal Return:* "To assure the quality and the enduringness of a construction, there is a repetition of a divine act of perfect construction: the Creation of the worlds and of man."[56] Such a repetition of a divine act, Eliade says, occurs *in illo tempore,* or what is called *vo vremya ono* in Russian. That is to say, it occurs in mythical time, which exists apart from linear, historical time. And, of course, Mandelstam thought and created *in illo tempore,* which is why he could deny the importance of linear time and write, "No, I have never been anyone's contemporary."[57] For Mandelstam, isolated time periods—profane time as opposed to sacred time, in mythological terms—literally had no meaning. What mattered to him was making connections—above all, connections between the present and some version of the past that he could convert into sacred time.

If "we" buried the sun, i.e., Pushkin, i.e., poetry, then we may be at least complicit in the death. To be complicit in the death of the father is to be complicit in the act of patricide, the act that every ephebe must commit in order to individuate and become a mature poet. This is why Mandelstam writes that only after we have buried the sun, "And the blessed, meaningless word/We will pronounce for the first time."[58] The death of the precursor releases the creativity of the ephebe. Mandelstam is using *slovo,* meaning word, here in the usual way in Russia, where it carries a heavy semantic weight. *Slovo* can mean "doctrine," but here it also serves as shorthand for "creativity." For Mandelstam, creativity relied on what Bakhtin called the "dialogical word." It is in this sense that he uses it in this key sentence in his essay, "The Word and Culture": "All other distinctions and oppositions grow pale before the division now of people into friends and enemies of the word."[59]

Life and Death in Mandelstam's Poetry

Surat appropriately associates Mandelstam's poem "Let's get together again in St. Petersburg" with a poem written the next year (in 1922) "Concert at a Train Station," which goes back to Mandelstam's memories of the concerts at the Pavlovsk train station where his mother took him as a child. As Mandelstam usually does, however, he dematerializes this specific place, which is not the source of the music. Rather, it comes from Greek myth: "The train station trembles from the singing of the Aonides."[59] However, the poem is not about music, but the death of music. As Surat says, the poem "sounds like a farewell to the very spirit of music, as a requiem for poetry and poets." [60]

But in Mandelstam's ubiquitous cultural dialectic, death implies life, and Mandelstam finds life in the death of civilization in his major poem "The Man Who Found a Horseshoe." This poem has exceptional affinities with T.S. Eliot's *The Wasteland,* which was written a year earlier, in 1922. Eliot responded to the devastation caused by World War I very much as Mandelstam responded in the same way to the devastation caused by the Bolshevik revolution. If Mandelstam's man found a horseshoe, a fragment from a time when men in chariots roamed the earth, Eliot writes, "These fragments I have shored against my ruins."[61] Near the beginning of *The Wasteland* there is a phrase "A heap of broken images," a phrase that Mandelstam would have appreciated.[62]

Although a detailed comparison of "The Man Who Found a Horseshoe" and *The Wasteland* would be a most rewarding exercise, it would be out of place here, so it must suffice to say that both Eliot and Mandelstam found striking ways to assert their main theme, the unity of past and present, against abundant evidence to the contrary. Very much in the spirit of Mandelstam, Eliot wrote, "The nymphs are departed./Sweet Thames, run softly, till I end my song."[63]

Like Pushkin, Mandelstam cannot forget Peter the Great, and begins "The Man Who Found a Horseshoe" with a reference to him. His transformative imagination works its magic on a forest, and he says in the poem's second line, "Here is a ship forest, a mast forest."[64] Like most external objects in Mandelstam's poetry, the forest is not a stable construct; it exists in and of itself in one time period, and also simultaneously in another time period as a group of masts for Peter the Great's ships.

About halfway through the poem, Mandelstam gives us a metonymical image for the way a traditionalist artist creates: "The man who found a horseshoe/Blows the dust from it/And rubs it with wool until it gleams."[65] More commonly, though, the connection between the past and the present is preserved—a frequent word in the poem—as an action. Making a sound is an essential creative act, so "The sound still resounds, although the cause of the sound has disappeared."[66] And "Human lips, which no longer have anything to say/Preserve the form of the last spoken word."[67]

Preservation and continuity are keys to interpreting Mandelstam's poetry, and also to interpreting his larger cultural significance. The years leading up to the revolution in 1917 were years of intense cultural ferment in Russia, [68] and some of the major works of this period were filled with gloom and death. Death appears with dramatic force in two major Russian performance pieces. In the Stravinsky-Nijinsky-Roerich ballet known in English as *The Rite of Spring* (the Russian name is *The Holy Spring*), the dancer known as The Chosen One dances herself to death. The extraordinary importance of the ballet, which shocked its Parisian audience at the now famous premiere in May 1913, suggests a more general meaning for this act, namely that it represents the death of the feminine archetype in Russia. The Soviet regime did everything it could to repress such archetypal feminine traits as compassion.

It has rarely happened in cultural history that two contemporary literary movements in the same country showed such diametrically opposed styles as Acmeism and Futurism. The rowdy, provocative Futurists might seem to have little in common with the sedate, reserved Acmeists. Nevertheless, the Malevich-Matyushin-Kruchonykh opera *Victory over the Sun*, also from the last year of peace in Russia (which was1913) strikingly anticipates not just Mandelstam's theme of death as exemplified in the death of Pushkin, but specifically the death of the sun. To be sure, *Victory over the Sun* does not associate the death of the sun with the death of Pushkin, as Mandelstam does. Still, it is hard to believe that he did not hear about its much-desired *success de scandale*. Whether or not it influenced Mandelstam is not as important as its significance for the theme of death, and specifically the theme of cultural death that Mandelstam later developed in the 1920s.

However, as we know, any given imagistic entity in Mandelstam implies its opposite. As opposed to the image of death, there is also the image of life, and for Mandelstam, life means the body. "A body is given to me/What am I to do with it?"[69] Mandelstam asks in a 1909 poem in the poem collection *Stone*. Note that only a poet in a monastic culture would even pose this question. We cannot imagine that a French or Italian poet would ever ask this question, for example. I interpret the changes that the Soviet government imposed on Russia after 1917 as decorporealization, a way of bringing monastic culture out into the world and imposing it on hapless Soviet citizens.[70] Mandelstam's response in the 1920s to decorporealization, which appeared in the cults of Lenin and Stalin, as well as in many other ways in Soviet life, was to make frequent reference to his body parts. This topic deserves further investigation as a part of his poetic language in general. Here are some salient examples:

> "Take for joy out of my palms"[71]
> "Because I could not restrain your hands"[72]
> "A chill tickles the back of my head" and "Apparently the movement of these Lips/Does not pass in vain."[74]
> "Who kisses time in the martyred back of the head"[73]

It is appropriate here to go from the literary history of literature to the social history of literature, in which Mandelstam's role has not been adequately addressed. Because Surat was concerned only with the relationships between texts, she did not consider the key role of ethnicity, for example. Mandelstam says in "Slate Ode" that "I am a double-dealer, with a double soul."[74] He did have a double soul—a Russian soul and a Jewish soul. As a Jew, he was very much more of an outsider seeking a place in Russian literature than Chekhov had been in the previous generation. Thus, Mandelstam's Jewish heritage, about which he had ambiguous feelings, gives multiple meanings to his deep-rooted connection with Pushkin. Pushkin was the obvious choice for a poet's precursor, to be sure. But he was also a Christian precursor who as a father figure could potentially legitimize a Jewish outsider. When defined in this way, the Mandelstam-Pushkin dynamic raises the question of whether Mandelstam as a Jew was alone in his fixation of on Pushkin, or whether there were any other Jewish intellectuals who created for themselves a deep identification with Pushkin as a subconscious way of legitimizing their membership in the family of Russian letters. It enriches our understanding of Mandelstam's significance for Russian culture to know that he formed part of a larger pattern. Among other things, a discussion of this topic contributes to the project, so near to Mandelstam's heart, of connecting pre-1917 Russia with post-1917 Russia.

Jewish Intellectuals and Pushkin

In early twentieth-century St. Petersburg, other Jewish intellectuals in addition to Mandelstam had a serious engagement with Pushkin. One such intellectual was Mikhail Gershenson (1869-1925), a professional man of letters and friend of the Symbolist poets. Gershenson's major book was entitled *The Wisdom of Pushkin*

(1919). In fact, Pushkin was so important to Gershenson that Brian Horowitz's book was entitled *The Myth of Pushkin in Russia's Silver Age. M.O. Gershenzon, Pushkinist.*[75] In an article, Horowitz wrote that Gershenson wanted to become a true participant in Russian culture, [76] and that becoming a Pushkin scholar was one way to do that. Although Gershenzson was a scholar and Mandelstam was a poet, the affinities between them are unmistakable.

However, the Jewish Pushkin scholar who had the greatest impact on Russian letters in the broad sense was surely the formidable Semyon Vengerov (1855-1920), who taught for many years at St. Petersburg University. Like Gershenzon, Professor Vengerov loved Russian literature, and published widely about it, but he is best remembered as the organizer of the Pushkin Seminar that met for 14 years. According to Surat, Mandelstam did sit in on the seminar from time to time during his university years.[77] (He could hardly have resisted, after all.)

In addition to Mandelstam, the list of participants with Jewish names in Vengerov's Pushkin seminar includes Sergey Bernstein, Aleksandr Blumenthal, Pyotr Guber, Esther Rosenberg, Nikolay Rosenberg, Lazar Rosenthal, Nikolay Rosenthal, and Leyba Feldman. However, the three Jewish participants who went on to have the most important and consequential careers did not have obviously Jewish names: Viktor Zhirmunsky, an exceptionally prolific scholar; Aleksandr Dolinin, a Dostoyevsky expert, and Yury Tynyanov, a theoretician and novelist.

Tynyanov, Mandelstam, and Pushkin

Tynyanov's double career as a scholar and novelist gives him exceptional importance for modern Russian literature. Moreover, he is unique in that he seems to have experienced no harassment from Soviet authorities, although he certainly knew people who did. Beginning in 1919, he published important scholarly works on Russian literature, which established his solid reputation, and then wrote historical novels about the Pushkin era, which were not censored or denounced in the official press. These works include *Kyukhlya* (1925), about Pushkin's eccentric friend Wilhelm Kűchelbecker, *The Death of Vazir-Mukhtara* (1928) about the death of Aleksandr Griboyedov, and his magnum opus *Pushkin*, part of which was published in 1936, and which remained unfinished at his untimely death in 1943.

Tynyanov and Mandelstam have a remarkable array of affinities, and not just because they were close friends. They were both brilliant Jewish Pushkinists who belonged to the same generation, and yet they had diametrically opposed careers.

The opposition between them continues even in their deaths. Although both died at a relatively early age, Mandelstam died in the gulag, and Tynyanov died in the Kremlin hospital reserved for the Soviet elite.

The abundant, glowing accounts of Tynyanov as a friend and teacher that are collected in the volume *Yu. Tynyanov, Portraits and Meetings* tell us very little about his personal life. However, as we know, Tynyanov (1895-1943) was born in Rezhita, a *shtetl* near Vitebsk, into a prosperous family. Like so many other Jewish intellectuals at the time, he had a successful career, but his education, first at the *Gymnasium* in Pskov, and then at St. Petersburg University, and the transformation that it required, must have cost him considerable effort. I have found one reference to his inner life that is in a letter that he wrote to Viktor Shklovsky on November 23, 1928 from Berlin, where he had gone for treatments for multiple sclerosis. He told Shklovsky that his doctors agree that "The cause of my disease is psychic upheavals, my constitution, and Russian tobacco."[78] If we want to connect the young Yura Tynyanov growing up in Rezhita with the universally admired scholar in Petrograd/Leningrad in the 1920s, we can do so only tentatively.[79] His experience of "psychic upheavals" probably included both the stresses of individuation and the stresses caused to others by Soviet censorship.

Fortunately, Mikhail Epstein has provided a possible way to understand Tynyanov, even without specific knowledge of his upheavals. In Epstein's essay cited in a previous essay, "The Hasid and the Talmudist. A Comparative Essay on Pasternak and Mandelstam,"[80] he suggests that what might be called cultural transmission helps us understand the distinctive features of the work of Mandelstam and Pasternak, who unconsciously inherited aspects of Jewish spiritual tradition. Epstein's opposition of the Hasid and Talmudist helps us understand, not only the relationship between Pasternak and Mandelstam, but also the relationship between Tynyanov and Mandelstam. Their sensibilities were formed in the same urban environment, pre-revolutionary St. Petersburg. The contrasts in the way they used Pushkin in their work is most instructive.

Tynyanov and Mandelstam knew each other when they were students before the revolution. In one of Mandelstam's last surviving letters written to Tynyanov, dated January 31, 1937, he states his case for his own historical importance:

> It has now been a quarter of a century that I, mixing what is important with trifles, have been sailing towards Russian poetry; but soon my verses will merge with it and be dissolved in it, having changed something in its structure and composition.[81]

In this extraordinary sentence, the doomed Mandelstam imagines that he is Odysseus, coming home at last, but in the dialectic of his imagery, he is coming home to a port that his work has changed. In the spirit of Eliot's guiding principle in "Tradition and the Individual Talent," he asserts that he has not just made a contribution to Russian poetry, as the cliché has it, but he asserts that he has fundamentally changed Russian poetry.

To understand how Tynyanov the novelist dealt with Mandelstam the poet, it is helpful to keep in mind that in the chaos of the post–revolutionary years, people were thrown together in desperate conditions. When some of those people were writers, the result was a series of books that contained thinly disguised portraits of other writers. Thus, Olga Forsh's *The Crazy Ship* (written in 1930) portrayed the writers and intellectuals who took refuge in the House of the Arts in Petrograd. Similarly, Veniamin Kaverin portrayed Viktor Shklovsky's forceful personality in his novel *The Troublemaker* (written in 1928). It is in this context that we can best understand Tynyanov's portrayal of Mandelstam in his novel *The Death of Vazir-Mukhtara*. Rimma Moshinskaya has noted that the novel includes a stand-in for Mandelstam, a character named Osip Senkovsky, who was born in Poland and does not suffer fools gladly. Moshinskaya notes that Tynyanov even pokes good-natured fun at Mandelstam's clothing.[82] It is startling, then, to realize that for all their biographical similarities and personal connections, Mandelstam and Tynyanov treat Pushkin very differently in their work. As Surat showed, Mandelstam associated Pushkin with death, with the black sun that "we" have buried, and that therefore gives life to poetry.

Nothing remotely like this metaphoric gravitas is in Tynyanov's novel *Pushkin*, and the difference can be explained by saying that Hasidic tradition informed Tynyanov's consciousness as Talmudic tradition informed Mandelstam's. To be sure, Tynyanov does not write of sparks and the ecstatic experience of nature, as Pasternak does. What he does do is to situate Pushkin in a detailed physical environment, and his model for doing so is *War and Peace*. After all, Pushkin, born in 1799, was a contemporary of the fictional Natasha Rostova born in 1793. The opening chapters of *Pushkin* read very much like the first Moscow chapters of *War and Peace*, but without the metonymical connections.

Unlike Tolstoy, Tynyanov is interested in the older generation and its habits and activities. He adopts a gossipy tone in presenting Pushkin's father Sergey Lvovich and his mother:

> Sergey Lvovich had married two and a half years ago. His wife [Nadezhda Osipovna] was an unusual being. The Petersburg Guard officers called her

"the beautiful Creole" and "the gorgeous African," and her servants, whom she annoyed with her caprices, called her an Arab behind her back.

She was the granddaughter of an Arab, a general-en-chef, formerly the friend and gentleman in waiting to Peter the Great, the famous Abram Petrovich. Her evil father had abandoned her and her mother at a very early age, and she had grown up as an orphan.[83]

Tynyanov also tells us that:

In the depths of her soul, she considered her home and in general the basic place of her life the city of Lipetsk, not far from which was her father's estate, in which she had lived as a grand lady. The city was clean; the main streets were planted with oaks and lime trees. There were lots of pears and cherries. The girls wore sleeveless outfits and embroidered tops. And the lime trees were blooming at the time; a thick pleasant aroma came from them.[84]

Here Tynyanov anticipates what Solzhenitsyn will do in *The Red Wheel*. Since he could reasonably assume that his readers would be familiar with the general features of Pushkin's life, he was free to concentrate on details. Here and elsewhere, he brings the past alive by establishing the physical features of a place. I cite these two passages to make the point that Tynyanov establishes the personalities and natural settings of early nineteenth-century Russia because they serve as a backdrop for what really matters—poetry. If the interpretation of Tynyanov as an urbanite, a secularized Hasid, is allowed, then we can say that he never glorified nature, as Pasternak did. Unlike a traditional Hasid who believed that nature represents emanations from God, Tynyanov presents poetry as a manifestation of the essential creative act. The word *stikhi* (verses) occurs no less than 188 times in *Pushkin*. That word occurs modestly enough for the first time in an improvisation by the character Neyelov. Then, Tynyanov establishes Pushkin's lineage by referring to the humorous verses by his uncle Vasily Lvovich. Other characters such as Derzhavin and Karamzin also write, and recite, poetry.

Although Tynyanov and Mandelstam do form polar opposites in most ways, one Mandelstamesque moment occurs in *Pushkin*. The scene occurs between young Sasha Pushkin and his French tutor Montfort:

Once he was telling the boy about all the great duels during the reigns of two tsars. Standing in front of him at a distance of three paces, he showed him how to defend himself. They did not have swords, but Montfort got so worked up that he shouted to Aleksandr, "You are killed!"[85]

In the spirit of Mandelstam's way of bringing together the past and the future, this scene is intended to give the reader a *frisson* of anticipatory dread.

When Tynyanov presents the awakening of young Sasha Pushkin's creativity, he is thinking of Mandelstam, the poet he knew best. Nadezhda Mandelstam tells us that her husband created, not by writing things down, but through a method that we would now call channeling. And we read of the budding poet that:

> Aleksandr often wandered around the rooms without hearing or noticing anything, gnawing his fingernails…Someone else's, false, dubious verses tormented him; without noticing he would write them down without changing anything… These verses were not quite his own and not quite someone else's.[86]

Tynyanov delivers his hero to the *lycée* that will change his life and give him life-long friends at the beginning of Part Two of the novel. And as the young Pushkin matures, he sounds more and more like Mandelstam: "He did not recite [his verses] to anybody. It seemed like it was difficult for him to acknowledge his verses, *as though they were a crime.*"[87] (My emphasis)

Tynyanov takes us through the experiences of Pushkin and his friends at the *lycée*, through the turmoil of the War of 1812, and ends with Pushkin in exile. Then it is as though the association of Pushkin in exile with Mandelstam in exile was so emotionally charged that Mandelstam takes over. Tynyanov's poet in exile is not a young genius whose triumphs of *Yevgeny Onegin* and *Boris Godunov* lie ahead of him. Rather, he is an outcast, doomed and rejected. In 1943, the year of his own death, it is not clear what Tynyanov knew about Mandelstam's situation, and whether he knew that Mandelstam had died. But he surely guessed that nothing good was going to happen to him. The final lines of Tynyanov's *Pushkin* are: "And here he wrote an elegy about the impossible love that the times had refused him. *Like someone cursed, not daring to name his name, he sailed on,* full of strength, filled with the recollection of everything that was forbidden to him, that could not come to pass."[88] Of course, Tynyanov knew perfectly well that the historical Pushkin never sailed anywhere. I suspect that what we have here is Tynyanov's memory of Mandelstam's letter from 1937 in which he associated himself with Odysseus sailing toward his home in Russian poetry, the only real home he ever had.

Notes

1   *Literatura i obshchechelovecheskiye tsennosti*, L. A. Fink et al, eds. (Samara: Samarskii universitet, 1996), 3.

2   Katherina and Hodgson and Alexandra Smith, "Twentieth-Century Russian Poetry and the Post-Soviet Reader: Reinventing the Canon," *Twentieth-Century Russian Poetry: Reinventing the Canon* (n.p.: Open Book Publishers, 2017), 1.

3   *Ibid.*, 5.

4   Harold Bloom, *The Western Canon: the Books and School of the Ages* (New York: Houghton Mifflin, 2014).

5   Michael Boyden, *Predicting the Past. The Paradoxes of American Literary History* (Leuven: Leuven U. Press, 2021), 127.

6   Indeed, Russians are writing so much interesting work, both fiction and non-fiction, that no one can read or properly evaluate it. See the list of the 100 best books published in Russia in the twenty-first century, https://polka.academy/materials/748.

7   Nina Tumarkin, *Lenin Lives! The Lenin Cult in Soviet Russia* (Cambridge, MA: Harvard U. Press, 1997).

8   I. B. Nichiporov, "Leniniana kak mifotvorchestvo: V. Mayakovsky i A. Voznesensky," *Russkaya literatura XX-XXI vekov kak yedinyi protsess (Problemy Teorii i metodologii izucheniya)* (Moscow: Max Press, 2016), 24-27.

9   Ye. N. Popova, "Russkaya literatura kak istochnik tsennostey," in *ibid.*, 57.

10 *Ibid.*, 60.

11 *Ibid.*

12 Mikhail Epshteyn, "Kommunizm i postmodernizm," https://www.emory.edu/INTELNET/pm_kommunizm.html.

13 See http://pelevin.nov.ru

14 Bloom, *The Anxiety of Influence*, 11.

15 See the essays collected in *Solzhenitsyn and American Culture. The Russian Soul in the West*, David P. Deavel and Jessica Hooten Wilson, eds. (Notre Dame: Notre Dame U. Press, 2020).

16 Quoted in Richard Tempest, "Twilight of All the Russias: *The Red Wheel* as Literary Historiography." *Russian Literature*, Vols. 100-102 (2018), 13.

17 See https://thesaker.is/alexander-solzhenitsyns-harvard-address/.

18 Csikszentmihalyi, *Creativity*, 197.

19 Mandel'shtam, *Ob iskusstve*, 194.

20 See *Stalin's Soviet Monastery*, 93 ff.

21 Bloom, *The Anxiety of Influence*, 141.

22 Although in this essay I discuss Solzhenitsyn's relationship to Tolstoy as a fiction writer, biographical similarities also exist between the two writers. Like Tolstoy, Solzhenitsyn believed that his credemtials as a writer gave him the necessary expertise to offer proposals for social reform. See, for example, Aleksandr Solzhenitsyn,

Rebuilding Russia: Reflections and Tentative Proposals (New York: Farrar Straus and Giroux, 1991).

23 *Ibid.,* 14.

24 Richard Tempest, *Overwriting Chaos. Aleksandr Solzhenitsyn's Fictive Worlds* (Brookline: Academic Studies Press, 2019), xviii.

25 Tempest, "Twilight of All the Russias," 24.

26 Yekaterina Tikhmirova, *"Krasnoye koleso" A. I. Solzhenintsyna i traditsii romana-epopei v russkoy literature XX-XX vv* (Kostroma, 2010).

27 Page numbers after quotations from *August 1914* refer to the following edition: Aleksandr Solzhenitsyn, *Sobraniye sochinenii v tridtsati tomakh*, VII. *Krasnoye koleso. Povestvovaniye v otmerennykh srokakh. Uzel I. Avgust chetyrnadtsatogo, I* (Moscow, Vremya, 2017).

28 Richard Tempest, 'Tolstoy i Solzhenitsyn: Vstrecha v Yasnoy Polyane," *Mezhdu dvumya yubileyami* (Moscow: "Russkii Put', 2005), 398.

29 On Solzhenitsyn's use of Dostoyevsky, see "Dostoyevsky," in James M. Curtis, *Solzhenitsyn's Traditional Imagination* (Athens: U. of Georgia Press, 1984), 91-127.

30 See Aleksandr Solzhenitsyn, "Nobelevskaya lektsiya," http://rushist.com/index.php/rus-literature/5611-solzhenitsyn-nobelevskaya-lektsiya-chitat-onlajn.

31 Simon Baron-Cohen, *The Science of Evil. On Empathy and the Origins of Cruelty* (New York: Basic Books, 2012).

32 See Curtis, *Stalin's Soviet Monastery,* 65ff.

33 See Michael Scammell, *Solzhenitsyn. A Biography,* 730.

34 Bloom, *the Anxiety of Influence*, 14.

35 *Ibid.* 43.

36 Ilya Kukulin, *Mashiny zashumevshego vremeni* (Moscow: NLO, 2015), 299.

37 For a thoughtful discussion of this topic that surveys both English and Russian publications, see Yuliya Vasilyeva, "Eyzenshteyn: politicheskiye i estheticheskiye vektory tvorchestva. Vzglyad iz XXI veka," *Kinovedcheskiye zapiski*, 92/93 (2007), 5-31.

38 Aleksandr Solzhenitsyn, *Oktyabr' Shestnadtsatogo* (Paris: YMCA-Press, 1984), 433.

39 See*, J.T.* Shackleton, ed., *History of Railways* (Secaucus: Chartwell Books, 1976), 55. This page features an illustration of a red locomotive with a red middle wheel that would be head-high for an average adult.

40 Eisenstein belongs in a pairing with another artist, Vladimir Mayakovsky. Both of them devoted themselves and their talent to promoting the cause of the Soviet Union, and therefore in the post-Soviet period their work requires a searching re-evaluation. Cultural historians will want to sort out what is purely propagandistic in the work of Eisenstein and Mayakovsky from what has lasting value, with the understanding that this may be not always be possible.

41 Mandelstam, *Stikhotvoreniya*, 77.

42 Mandelstam, *Ob iskusstve*, 194.

43 *Ibid.*

44 *Ibid.*, 195.

45 Irina Surat, *Mandel'shtam i Pushkin* (Moscow: IMLI RAN, 2009), 20ff.

46 See *ibid.*, 34.

47 *Ibid.*, 39.

48 See Mandelstam, *Stikhotvoreniya*, 255.

49 See Curtis, *Stalin's Soviet Monastery*, 95.

50 Claire Cavanaugh, *Osip Mandelstam and the Modernist Creation of Tradition* (Princeton: Princeton U. Press, 1995), 282.

51 Mandelstam, *Stikhotvoreniya*, 253.

52 *Ibid.*, 323.

53 *Ibid.*, 141.

54 Sigmund Freud, *The Major Works of Sigmund Freud* (Chicago: Encyclopedia Britannica, 1952), 651.

55 *Ibid.*, 644.

56 Mircea Eliade, *The Myth of the Eternal Return*, 20.

57 Mandelstam, *Stikhotvoreniya*, 180.

58 *Ibid.*, 141.

59 Mandelstam, *Stikhotvoreniya, 151.*

60 Surat, *Mandel'shtam i. Pushkin*, 36.

61 T.S. Eliot, *The Complete Poems and Plays 1909-1950* (New York: Harcourt Brace and World, Inc., n.d.), 50.

62 *Ibid.*, 38.

63 *Ibid.*, 42.

64 Mandelstam, *Stikhotvoreniya*, 165.

65 *Ibid., 169.*

66 *Ibid.*, 168.

67 *Ibid.*, 169.

68 See the chapter "Searching for *Stikhiinost'* and Anticipating Doom: Some Continuities in Modern Russian Culture," in *Stalin's Soviet Monastery*, 51-64.

69 Mandelstam, *Stikhotvoreniya*, 34.

70 See Curtis, *Stalin's Soviet Monastery*, 133 ff.

71 *Ibid.*, 140.

72 *Ibid.*, 143.

73 *Ibid.*, 176.

74 *Ibid.*, 173.

75 See Brian Horowitz, *The Myth of Pushkin in Russia's Silver Age. M.O. Gerzhenzon, Pushkinist* (Evanston: Northwestern U. Press, 1996).

76 Brian Horowitz, "Jewish Identity and Russian Culture: The Case of M.O. Gershenzon, *Nationalities Papers*, Vol. 25, No. 4 (1997), 701.

77 Surat, *Mandel'shtam i Pushkin*, 7.

78 *Ibid.*, 24.

79 We recall that in a key programmatic statement about literary evolution, Tynyanov said that there is no continuation of a straight line, but a pushing away. It is not unreasonable to read this statement both as a principle of literary history and also as autobiographical statement. The fictional example of young Sanya Lazhenitsyn who leaves home at the beginning of *August 1914* to pursue his education invites comparison with the historical example of young Yura Tynyanov.

80 Mikhail Epstein, "Khasid i Talmudist: Sravnitel'nyi opyt o Pasternake and Mandel'shtame," *Zvezda*, 2000, No. 6, 82-96.

81 See https://rvb.ru/20vek/mandelstam/01text/vol_4/01letters/4_215.htm.

82 See Rimma Moshinskaya, "Mandel'shtamovskiye podteksty romana Yu. N. Tynyanova, "Smert' Vazir-Mukhtara," https://www.sunround.com/club/22/146_m osh.htm.

83 Yu. N. Tynyanov, *Pushkin* (Moscow: Khudozhestvennaya literatura, 1987), 12.

84 *Ibid.,* 27.

85 *Ibid.,* 121.

86 *Ibid.,* 241.

87 *Ibid.,* 341.

88 *Ibid.,* 532.

Conclusion

These discussions have shown the inadequacy of merely saying that Russia is different and leaving it at that. Russia and Russian culture have an interplay of similarities and differences with the West. The same general principles of creativity, of the effects of the family environment (parental loss and birth order, for example) both apply as well in Russia as in the West. With regard to culture, however, and above all, to Tolstoy and Dostoyevsky, we can identify genuine differences between Russian culture and Western culture. Different social structures and religious practices created different literary structures. The great Western novelists of the nineteenth century (Melville, Dickens, Eliot, Flaubert, Stendhal) did not create anything like the coherent, interrelated literary structures as Tolstoy and Dostoyevsky did. None of them created an overarching metonymical network of associations such as the one that we find in *War and Peace*, and none of them created polyphonic novels in which the characters have shared existences, as the characters in *Crime and Punishment* do. Any general understanding of the Western novel in the nineteenth century includes the awareness that the Protestant Reformation, the French Revolution, and the Industrial Revolution combined to create systemic secularizing and fragmenting effects. Great writers in the West were sensitive to these effects and incorporated them into their works. Without these secularizing and fragmenting effects, the great Russian novelists wrote works that are characterized by greater coherence in a variety of ways. This coherence is carried over from individual works to the relationships between writers, poets and novelists, which also have greater coherence in Russia than in the West.

The absence of robust, socially condoned individualism in Russia creates a significant difference between literary history in Russia and literary history in the West, which is the presence of crucial, era-defining precursor-ephebe relationships in Russia. As a solitary act done in private, writing promoted Western writers' already strong sense of individualism. Russian writers, on the other hand, had a strong sense of their connection with their country and the way their predecessors had presented it. As a result, four major precursor-ephebe relationships have defined much of Russian literary history: Gogol-Dostoyevsky, Turgenev-Chekhov, Pushkin-Mandelstam, and Tolstoy-Solzhenitsyn.

These relationships do not merely mark defining moments in the careers of great writers; they also mark transitions from one era to the next. Thus, the Gogol-Dostoyevsky relationship marks the transition from the 1840s to the 1860s; the Turgenev-Chekhov relationship marks the transition from the 1860s to the 1890s; the Pushkin-Mandelstam relationship marks the transition from the pre-revolutionary era to the post-revolutionary era; and the Tolstoy-Solzhenitsyn relationship marks the general transition from the nineteenth century to the twentieth century. It is fair to say, then, that the Russian classics exhibit both exceptional internal coherence (Tolstoy's use of metonymy, Dostoyevsky's use of metaphor) and external coherence in era-defining ephebe-precursor relationships.

Bibliography

Akhmatova, Anna. *Polnoye sobraniye poezii i prozy v odnom tome*. Moscow: Alfa-Kniga, 2009.

Altschuler, Mark. "Transition to the Modern Era, 1790-1820," in *The Cambridge History of Russian Literature*. Cambridge: Cambridge U. Press, 1989, 92-136.

Anderson, Roger B. "Raskol'nikov and the Myth Experience," *ASEEJ*, Vol. 20, No. 1 (Spring, 1975), 1-17.

Ayer, A. J. *Language, Truth and Logic*. New York: Dover Publications, 1952.

Azizyan, I.A. "O dialoge iskusstv serebryanogo veka," o-dialoge-iskusstv-serebryanogo-veka.pdf.

Bakhtin, Mikhail. *Problemy poetiki Dostoyevskogo*, 3rd ed. Moscow: Khudozhestvennaya literatura, 1967.

Bartalanffy, Ludwig von. *General Systsem Theory: Foundations, Development, Applications*. New York: George Braziller, 2015.

Berman, Anna A. "Lateral Plots: Brothers and the Nineteenth-Century Russian Novel," *The Slavic and East European Journal*, Vol. 61, No. 1 (Spring, 2017), 2-28.

Belknap, Robert. *The Structure of "The Brothers Karamazov."* The Hague: Mouton, 1967.

Bliss, William D. "Birth Order of Creative Writers," *The Journal of Individual Psychology*, Vol. 26 (1970), 200-2.

Blok, Aleksandr. *Stikhotvoreniya i poemy*. Moscow: EKSMO, 2009.

Blok, Lyubov. "I byli i nebylitsy o Bloke i o sebe," www.silverage.ru/blokobloke.

Bloom, Harold. *The Anatomy of Influence. Literature as a Way of Life*. New Haven and London: Yale U. Press, 2011.

____. *A Map of Misreading*. New York: Oxford U. Press, 1975.

Bondarenko, Vyacheslav.*Vyazemsky*. Moscow: Molodaya Gvardiya, 2004.

Boris Pasternak. Yekaterinburg: U-Faktoriya, 2003

Bourdieu, Pierre. *The Rules of Art. Genesis and Structure of the Literary Field*. Susan Emanuel, trans. Stanford: Stanford U. Press, 1995

Brown, Deming. *Soviet Attitudes toward American Writing*. Princeton: Princeton U. Press, 1962.

Browning, Gary L. *A "Labyrinth of Linkages" in Tolstoy's "Anna Karenina."* Brookline: Academic Studies Press, 2010.

Buber, Martin. *Tales of the Hasidim*. New York: Schocken Books, 1975.

Cavanaugh, Claire. *Osip Mandelstam and the Modernist Creation of Tradition*. Princeton: Princeton U. Press, 1995.

Carr, Virginia Spencer, *Dos Passos. A Life*. Garden City: Doubleday and Company, 1984.

Chaban, Aleksandra. "Lyubovnye treugol'niki Serebryanogo veka." See https://arzamas.academy/materials/796

Chekhov, A.P. *Polnoye sobraniye sochinenii i pisem*, 7. Moscow: "Nauka," 1985.

Cherniavsky, Michael, *Tsar and People. Studies in Russian Myths*. New Haven and London: Yale U. Press, 1961.

Chernyshevsky, N.G. *Esteticheskiye otnosheniya iskusstva k desystvitel'nosti*. St. Petersburg, 1865.

Chukovsky, Korney. *Dnevnik 1930-1969*. M. 'Sovremennyi pisatel', 1994.

Csikszentmihalyi, Mihaly. *Creativity. Flow and the Psychology of Discovery and Invention*. New York: HarperCollins, 1996.

____ and L.S. Csikszentmihalyi "Family Influences on the Development of Giftedness," *The Origins and Development of High Ability*. Chichester: John Wiley and Sons, 1997, 200-16.

____ and O. Beattie, "Life Themes: A Theoretical and Empirical Exploration of Their Origins and Effects," *The Journal of Humanistic Psychology*, Vol. 19 (1979), 45-63.

Curtis, Jim. "Anticipations of 'War and Peace' in Tolstoy's Early Short Stories," *The Ulbandus Review*, Vol. 2, No. 2, 1982, 52-78.

____. "Ephebes and Precursors in Chekhov's The Seagull,'" *Slavic Review*, Vol. 44, No. 3 (Fall, 1985), 423-38

____. "Spatial Form as the Intrinsic Genre of Dostoevsky's Novels." *Modern Fiction Studies*, Vol. 18, No. 2 (Summer, 1972), 135-54.

____ *Stalin's Soviet Monastery. A New Interpretation of Russian Politics*. New York: Peter Lang, 2020.

Diagnostic and Statistical Manual of Mental Disorders, 5th ed. Washington and London: American Psychiatric Publishers, 2013.

Dos Passos, John. *Three Soldiers*. New York: The Modern Library, 2002.

____. *The Big Money* New York: The New American Library, 1963.

Dos Passos. A Collection of Critical Essays. Andrew Hacker, ed. Englewood Cliffs: Prentice-Hall, 1974.

Eichenbaum, Boris. *Literatura. Teoriya. Kritika. Polemika.* Leningrad: Priboy, 1927.

Eisenstadt, J. Marvin. "Parental Loss and Genius," *American Psychologist*, March, 1978, 211-23.

Eliade, Mircea. *The Myth of the Eternal Return*. New York: Bollingen Foundation, 1954.

Eliot, T. S. *The Complete Poems and Plays 1909-1950*. New York: Harcourt Brace and World, Inc., n.d.

____. *The Sacred Wood and Major Early Essays*. Mineola: Dover Publications, Inc., 1998.

Epshteyn, Mikhail. *Ironiya ideala. Paradoksy russkoy literatury.* Moscow: NLO, 2015.

_____. "Khasid i talmudist. Sravnitel'nyi opyt o Pasternake i Mandel'shtame," *Zvezda*, Vol. 4, 2000, 82-98.

Erll, Astrd. "Generations as Literary History: Three Constellations of Generationality, Genealogy, and Memory," *New Literary History*, Vol. 45, No. 3 (Summer, 2014), 385-409.

Evtuhov, Catherine. "On Neo-Romanticism and Christianity: Some 'Spots of Time' in the Russian Silver Age," *Russian History,* Vol. 20, No. 1/4 (1993), 197-212.

Fadeyev, Aleksandr. *Molodaya Gvardiya.* N.p.: Izdatel'stvo TsK BLKSM "Molodaya Gvardiya" 1971.

Fanger, Donald. *Dostoevsky and Romantic Realism: A Study of Dostoevsky in Relation to Balzac, Dickens and Gogol.* Cambridge, MA: Harvard U. Press, 1965.

Feiler, Lily. *Marina Tsvetayeva. The Double Beat of Heaven and Hell.* Durham and London: Duke U. Press, 1994.

Fonvizin, Denis. *Nedorosl'.* Leningrad, 1952.

Freud, Sigmund. *The Major Works of Sigmund Freud.* Chicago: Encyclopedia Britannica, 1952.

Friedman, S.S. "World Modernism, World Literature, and Comparativity," in *The Oxford Handbook of Global Modernisms*, Mark Wollaeger with Matt Eatough, eds. New York: Oxford U. Press, 2012, 499-525.

Frye, Northrop. *The Critical Path and Other Writings on Critical Theory, 1963-1975,* Jean O'Grady and Eva Kushner, eds. Toronto: U. of Toronto Press, 2009.

_____. *The Great Code: The Bible and Literature.* New York: Harcourt Brace Jovanovich, 1982.

Gasparov, Mikkhail. *O stikhakh.* Moscow: FTM, 2017.

Gladwell, Malcolm. *Blink. The Power of Thinking Without Thinking.* Boston: Little Brown and Company, 2005.

Gippius, Zinaida, and Merezhkovsky, Dmitry. *Zhivye litsa. Vospominaniya.* Tbilisi, n.p., 1991.

Gill, Richard. "The Bridges of St. Petersburg: A Motif in *Crime and Punishment.*" *Dostoevsky Studies,* Vol. 3 (1982), 145-55.

Glebkin, Vladimir. "Cultural-historical Psychology and the Cognitive View of Metonymy and Metaphor," *Review of Cognitive Linguistics*, Vol. 12, No. 2 (2014), 288-303.

Gogol, N.G. *Sobraniye khudozhestvennykh proizvedenii v pyati tomakh,* 2nd ed. Moscow, 1960.

Govsiyevich, Ye. R. *Serebryanyi vek glazamie ochevidtsev.* Moscow: n.p., 2013.

Grossman, Vasily. *Zhizn' i sud'ba.* Kishinyov: Literatura Artistike, 1989.

Heldt, Barbara. *Terrible Perfection. Women and Russian Literature.* Bloomington and Indianapolis: Indiana U. Press, 1987.

Helfant, Ian. *The High Stakes of Identity. Gambling in the Life and Literature of Nineteenth-Century Russia.* Evanston: Northwestern U. Press, 2002.

_____. "His to Stake, Hers to Lose: Women and the Male Gambling Culture of Nineteenth-Century Russia." *The Russian Review,* Vol. 62, No. 2 (April, 2003), 223-42.

Horowitz, Brian. "Jewish Identity and Russian Culture: The Case of M.O. Gershenzon, *Nationalities Papers*, Vol. 25, No. 4, 1997.

_____. *The Myth of Pushkin in Russia's Silver Age. M.O. Gerzhenzon, Pushkinist.* Evanston: Northwestern U. Press, 1996.

Ilizarov, Boris. *Iosif Stalin.* Moscow: AST, 2015.

Jackson, Robert Louis, *Close Encounters*. Brookline: Academic Studies Press, 2019.

Jakobson, Roman. "Two Aspects of Language and Two Aspects of Aphasic Disturbances," *Selected Writings II*. The Hague-Paris: Mouton, 1971, 239-60.

Jones, James. *From Here to Eternity*. New York: Charles Scribner's Sons, 1951.

Karlinsky, Simon, *The Sexual Labyrinth of Nikolay Gogol*. Chicago: U. of Chicago Press, 1992.

Kaufman, Scott Barry, and Gregoire, Carolyn, *Wired to Create: Unraveling the Mysteries of the Creative Mind*. New York: TarcherPerigee, 2015.

Kertis, Dzh. *Boris Ejkhenbaum: Yego sem'ya, strana i russkaya literatura*. St. Petersburg: Akademicheskii proyekt, 2004.

Kolchin, Peter. *A Sphinx on the American Land: The Nineteenth-Century South in Comparative Perspective*. Baton Rouge: LSU Press, 2003.

Krusanov, Andrey. *Russkii avangard*. Moscow: NLO, 1996, 2003, 2010.

Kukulin, Ilya. *Mashiny zashumevshego vremeni*. Moscow: NLO, 2015.

Lehrman, Edgar. *A Guide to the Russian Texts of Tolstoy's 'War and Peace'*. Ann Arbor: Ardis., 1980.

Leman, Kevin. *The New Birth Order Book. Why You Are the Way You Are*. Grand Rapids: Fleming R. Revell, 1998.

Levi-Strauss. Claude. *Structural Anthropology*. New York: Basic Books, 1974.

Lindstrom, Thais S. *A Concise History of Russian Literature*. Volume I. *From the Beginnings to Chekhov*. New York: NYU Press, 1966.

Linkov, V.Ya. *Istoriya russkoy literatury (Vtoraya polovina XIX veka)*. Moscow: Izdatel'stvo moskovskogo universiteta, 2010.

Ljundrgren, Magnus "Blok and Bely," in *Poetry and Psychiatry. Essays on Early Twentieth Century Russian Symbolist Culture*. Charles Rougle, trans. Boston: Academic Studies Press, 2014, 18-26.

Lodge, David. *The Modes of Modern Writing*. Ithaca: Cornell U. Press, 1977.

Manchester, Laurie. *Holy Fathers, Secular Sons. Clergy, Intelligentsia, and the Modern Self in Revolutionary Russia*. DeKalb: Northern Illinois U. Press, 2011.

Mandel'shtam, Osip. *Ob iskusstve*. Moscow: Iskusstvo, 1995.

____. *Stikhotvoreniya*. Moscow: Eksmo, 2006.

Marías, Julian. *Generations. A Historical Method*. Harold C. Raley, trans. University, AL: The U. of Alabama Press, 1970.

Markov, Vladimir. *Russian Futurism. A History*. Berkeley and Los Angeles: U. of California Press, 1968.

Maroshi, V.V. "Troyka kak simvol istoricheskogo puti Rossii v russkoy literature XX veka," *Philology and Culture*, No. 2 (40), 2015, 204-8.

Men and Violence. Columbus: Ohio State U. Press, 1998.

Metaphor and Metonymy in Comparison and Contrast. René Dirven and Rolf Pörings, eds. Berlin and New York: Mouton de Gruyter, 2002.

Merezhkovsky, Dmitry. *L. Tolstoy i Dostoyevsky*. Moscow: Nauka, 2000.

Mersereau, John, Jr., "The Nineteenth Century: Romanticism, 1820-40," in *The Cambridge History of Russian Literature*. Cambridge: Cambridge U. Press, 1989, 136-88.

Morson, Gary Saul. *Hidden in Plain View: Narrative and Creative Potentials in "War and Peace"*. Stanford: Stanford U. Press, 1987.

_____. "Crimes Against Culture," *New Criterion*, May 1, 2017, 18.

Moshinskaya, Rimma. "Mandel'shtamovskiye podteksty romana Yu. N. Tynyanova, "Smert' Vazir-Mukhtara," https://www.sunround.com/club/22/146_mosh.htm.

Nagina, K.A. "Raspadayushchysya dom: sud'ba Anny Kareninoy," *Vestnik udmurskogo universiteta*, Vyp. 4 (2016), 32-47.

Naumann, Marina Turkevich, "Raskol'nikov's Shadow: Porforij Petrovich, " *SEEJ*, Vol. 16, No. 1 (Spring, 1979), 42-54.

Orriger, Nelson R. "Redefining the Spanish Silver Age and '98 Within It," *Annales de la literatura española comtemporánea*, No. 1-2 (1998), 315-26.

Ostrovsky, Nikolay. *Kak zakalalyas' stal*. Moscow: Pravda, 1982.

Pasternak, Boris. *Doktor Zhivago*. Moscow: AST, 2010.

Perlina, Nina. *Varieties of Poetic Utterances: The Poetics of Quotation in "The Brothers Karamazov."* Lanham: University of Press of America, 1985.

Powelstock, David. *Becoming Mikhail Lermontov. The Ironies of Romantic Individualism in Nicholas I's Russia*. Evanston: Northwestern U. Press, 2011

Pushkin, A.S. *Mednyi vsadnik*. Leningrad: Nauka, 1978.

Rancour-Laferriere, Daniel. *Tolstoy on the Couch. Misogyny, Masochism, and the Absent Mother*. Houndmill: Macmillan, 1998.

_____. *The Slave Soul of Russia. Moral Masochism and the Soul of Suffering*. New York: NYU Press, 1996.

Rayfield, Donald, "The Golden Age of Russian Poetry," *Russia's Golden Age*, Rachel Stauffer, Ed. Amernia: Grey House Publishing, 2014, 33-50.

Reifman, Irina. *Ritualizirovannaya agressiya. Duel' v russkoy kul'ture i literature*. Moscow: NLO, 2002.

Rudometkin, Igor, "Eykhenbaumovskaya kontseptsiya literaturnogo skaza," *Izvestiya BGPU*, No. 4 (265), 75.

Ryrie, Alec. *Protestantism. The Faith That Made the Modern World*. New York: Viking, 2017.

Sakhno, Irina. "Bukvennaya grafika v russkom futurizme: strategii visualizatsii," *Vestnik RGTU, Seriya Filosofiya. Sotsiologiya, Iskusstvovedeniye*. 2016, No. 3, 58. https://cyberleninka.ru/article/n/bukvennaya-grafika-v-russkom-futurizme-strategii-vizualizatsii

_____."Simvolizm i avangard: Pereklichki i sopryazheniya," in *Otkryvaya sovremennost' zanovo*. Moscow: Rossijskij universitet druzhby narodov, 2011, 370-88.

Saunders, George. *A Swim in a Pond in the Rain. In Which Four Russians Give a Master Class on Writing, Reading, and Life*. New York: Random House, 2022, 2021.

Shackleton, J.T. ed. *History of Railways*. Secaucus: Chartwell Books, 1976.

Shestov, Lev. *Dostoevsky, Tolstoy, and Nietzsche*. Athens: Ohio U. Press, 1969.

Shklovsky, Viktor. *Eizenshteyn*. Moscow: Iskusstvo, 1973.

_____. "Gorod moyey yunosti," in *Vospominaniya o Yu. Tynyanove. Portrety i vstrechi* Moscow: Sovetskii pisatel', 1983, 4-37.

_____. *Mater'yal i stil' v romane L'va Tolstogo, "Voyna i mir"*. Moscow: Federatsiya, 1929.

_____. *O teorii prozy*, 2nd ed. Moscow: Federatsiya, 1929.

Shvarsalon, Vera. "Dnevnikovye zapisi," www.silverage.ru/sharsalon.

Simonov, Konstantin. *Zhivye i mertvye*. Moscow: Eksmo, 2013.

Simyonova, Natal'ya. *Moskovskiye kollektsionery*. Moscow: Molodaya Gvardiya, 2010.

Simonton, Dean Keith. *Genius, Creativity and Leadership. Historiometric Inquiries*. Cambridge and London: Harvard U. Press, 1984.

_____. *Greatness. Who Makes History and Why*. London: The Guilford Press, 1994.

_____. "The Swan-Song Effect: Last-Works Effects for 172 Classical Composers." *Journal of the Psychology of Aging*, March, 1989, 42-7.

Skabichevsky, A. M. *Pushkin. Yego zizn' i lteraturnaya deyatel'nost'*. St. Petersburg, 1891.

_____ *M. Yu. Lermontov. Yego zhizn' i lteraturnaya deyatel'nost'* Noginsk: "Osteon-Press, 2015.

Solzhenitsyn. A Biography by Michael Scammell. New York and London: W. W. Norton, 1984.

Solzhenitsyn, Aleksandr. *Oktyabr' Shestnadtsatogo*. Paris: YMCA-Press, 1984.

_____. *Sobraniye sochinenii*, VII, *Krasnoye koleso. Povestvovaniye v otmerennykh srokakh. Uzel I. Avgust chetynadtsatogo*, I. Moscow: Vremya, 2017.

Steiner, George. *Tolstoy and Dostoyevsky. An Essay in the Old Criticism*. New York: Dutton, 1971.

Struve, Gleb. "*Monologue interieure:* The Origins of the Formula and the First Statement of the Possibilities," *PMLA*, 69 (1954), 1101-11.

Irina Surat, *Mandel'shtam i Pushkin*. Moscow: IMLI RAN, 2009,

Surette, Leon. "Metaphor and Metonymy: Jakobson Reconsidered," *University of Toronto Quarterly*, Vol. 56, no. 4 (Summer, 1987): 551.

Tempest, Richard. *Overwriting Chaos: Aleksandr Solzhenitsyn's Fictive World*. Brookline: Academic Studies Press, 2019.

_____. "Tostoy i Solzhenitsyn: vstrechi v Yasnoy Polyane," *Mezhdu dvumya yubileyami*. Moscow: "Russkii put'," 2005, 393-408.

Tolstoy, L.N. *Sobraniye sochinenii v dvadtsati tomakh*. Moscow: Gosizdat, 1960.

Tomlins, T.B. *The English Middle-Class Novel*. New York: Harper and Row, 1976.

Trilling, Lionel. *The Liberal Imagination*. New York: The Viking Press, 1950.

Tsvetayeva, Marina. *Izbrannye proizvedeniya*. Moscow and Leningrad: Sovetskiy Pisatel', 1965.

Turgenev, I.S. *Polnoye sobraniye sochinenii i pisem v tridtsati tomakh*. Moscow: "Nauka," 1979.

Tynyanov, Yury. *Arkhaisty i novatory* Leningrad: Priboy, 1927.

_____. *Dostoyevskii i Gogol' (K teorii parodii)*. Petrograd: "Opoyaz", 1921.

_____. *Pushkin*. Moscow: Khudozhestvennaya literatura, 1987.

Vasilyeva, Yuliya. "Eyzenshteyn: politicheskiye i esteticheskiye vektory tvorchestva. Vzglyad iz XXI veka," *Kinovedcheskiye zapiski*, Vol. 92/93 (2007), 5-30.

Volkov, Solomon. *The Magic Chorus. A History of Russian Culture from Tolstoy to Solzhenitsyn*. New York: Alfred A. Knopf, 2008.

Watt, Ian. *The Rise of the Novel*. Berkeley: U. of California Press, 2001.

The Wiley-Blackwell Handbook of Disordered Gambling. Hoboken: Wiley, 2014.

Yegorov, B. F. *Ot Khomyakova do Lotmana*. Moscow: Yurayt, 2018.

Zinov'yeva-Annibal, Lidiya. *Tridtsat' tri uroda*. Moscow: Agraf, 1999.

Zubaryova, Vera. *Chekhov w XXI veke. Pozitsionnyi stil' i komedii novogo tipa*. Idylwild: Charles Schlacks, Jr., 2015.

Index

www.ingramcontent.com/pod-product-compliance
Lightning Source LLC
Chambersburg PA
CBHW071546110726
47908CB00007B/2014